W9-BMS-572

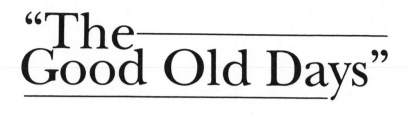

"The Good Old Days"

"The Good Old Days"

The Holocaust as Seen by Its Perpetrators and Bystanders

Edited by

Ernst Klee
Willi Dressen
Volker Riess

Foreword by Hugh Trevor-Roper

Translated by Deborah Burnstone

KONECKY&KONECKY

Konecky & Konecky
72 Ayers Point Rd.
Old Saybrook, CT 06475

Visit our web site: koneckyandkonecky.com

This edition published by special arrangement with The Free Press, an imprint of
Simon & Schuster, Inc.

ISBN: 1-56852-133-2

Contents

Part Two
'Delivered and Killed'
The Extermination Centres

Foreword
by Lord Dacre of Glanton

This is a horrible book to read, and yet one that should be read – not in order to revive old enmities (after all, it has been compiled by Germans and published in Germany), but in order that we do not forget the most sombre lesson of the Second World War: the fragility of civilization, and the ease and speed with which, in certain circumstances, barbarism can break through that thin crust and even, if backed by power and sanctified by doctrine, be accepted as the norm.

Such reminders are sometimes necessary. With the passage of time and the change of generations, we tend to forget or attenuate the horrors of war and, in retrospect, to 'relativize' them: that is, to place them in the long context of history and conclude that they were not unique, and therefore less inexcusable than was thought at the time. Hitler's war aims, we then find, were not so different from those of his predecessors in 1914, who also sought to create, by conquest, a German empire in Europe. The crimes and brutalities of his war had precedents in other wars made by other nations. But when all this has been said, there still remains one feature of the Second World War which cannot be thus 'relativized', which has no parallel in history, at least since the Dark Ages. I refer, of course, to the 'Final Solution', the attempted physical extermination, on merely racial grounds, of a whole people: the Jews.

There are indeed some writers who seek to minimize even that episode: to reduce its compass, to deny its deliberate purpose, to present it as a mere incident of the struggle. In order to do this, they challenge statistics, which indeed are uncertain; exploit the admitted gaps or inconsistencies of detail in the evidence; seek to discredit the witnesses, who, they say, being few and often Jewish, naturally exaggerate their sufferings in order to create a new myth. Wars, they remind us, have often generated 'atrocity stories' which historians have afterwards found to be grossly exaggerated, if not invented. Such are the arguments of some of those who today describe themselves as 'historical revisionists'.

History is always liable to revision and there are indeed some unresolved problems of the 'Final Solution'. Whether it was systematically planned from the beginning or acquired its momentum from events is a legitimate question. That anti-Semitism was not peculiar to Germany or to Nazism but was endemic in eastern Europe is undeniable. There are some genuine uncertainties about the exact structure and working of the gas-chambers and the number of their victims. However, these reasons for questioning the evidence where it is weak are not reasons for rejecting it where it is firm: they are reasons for looking it in the face.

The particular significance of this book is that in it the facts are recorded not by Jewish survivors but by German witnesses: men who, by chance, or in the course of duty, or out of curiosity, observed the events as they occurred and made a record, sometimes a photographic record, of them. Such records were strictly forbidden at the time – the SS did not want any evidence of its work to survive – and one witness at least, SS-Untersturmführer Max Täubner, got into serious trouble for taking photographs. The SS court, whose judgement is printed here, ruled that whereas his torture and murder of Jews, being inspired by genuine ideological hatred, was not to be censured, for 'the Jews have to be exterminated, and none that were killed is any great loss', nevertheless, his action in taking 'tasteless and shameless photographs', and having them developed by a commercial chemist in Germany, and showing them to his family and friends, was a serious offence: such photographs, in the wrong hands, could pose 'the gravest risks to the security of the Reich'. This book shows that the order forbidding photography was frequently repeated, but also that it was frequently disobeyed. The photographs themselves are the evidence. The verbal and written records come from various sources: post-war interrogations, contemporary official documents, but also – and psychologically perhaps the most revealing – private diaries and letters in which SS men describe, for their wives, children and mistresses, their exploits in the *Judenaktionen*. 'I am unmoved. No pity!' Felix Landau, in the Ukraine, tells his dearest Trudi, back in Radom, as he describes, in horrible detail, his methods with *diese Arschlöcher*, 'these arse-holes', the Jews. 'This is a war of annihilation, a war against the Jews,' SS-Obersturmführer Kretschmer writes to his dearest Soska; but now, he adds proudly, 'here in Russia, wherever the German soldier is, no Jew remains'.

The 'Final Solution' was carried out in overlapping stages of progressive rationalization. At first, the victims were rounded up by mobile Einsatzkommandos and killed mainly by shooting; later they were transported to fixed concentration camps, to be worked to death and gassed. The Einsatzkommandos were organized in four Einsatzgruppen (see page 282) and operated closely behind the advancing German armies, but under distinct SS command. The army commanders had no jurisdiction over them, and were happy to leave such dirty work to them. The SS, in their turn, were happy to pass much of it on to the natives, under their direction. This occurred especially in the Baltic states, where the natives sought revenge against the 'Jewish Bolshevism' from which the German armies had liberated them. Later, when the fixed extermination camps had been completed, the Jews of all occupied Europe were brought to them in the trains organized by Adolf Eichmann. But the change from mobile to fixed killing centres, from shooting to gas, was not sudden or complete: shooting continued to the end, whereas the gas-chambers were destroyed when the prospect of a German retreat threatened to reveal their existence to the enemy.

The most horrible photographs, and some of the most horrible narratives, in this book record the earlier stages in this process, for the first massacres, especially those in the Baltic states, were carried out in public. In Kaunas, Lithuania, where Einsatzkommando 3 operated, the Jews were clubbed to death with crowbars, before cheering crowds, mothers holding up their children to see the fun, and German soldiers clustered round like spectators at a football match. At the end, while the streets ran with blood, the chief murderer stood on the pile of corpses as a triumphant hero and played the Lithuanian national anthem on an accordion. By such indirect methods, repeated in other towns, the commander of the Einsatzkommando was able to report that the Jewish problem in his area had been solved: 'In Lithuania there are now no Jews.' In Russia, where the Jews often joined the partisans, the Einsatzkommandos had to act more openly; but they were equally effective, and could rely on the Ukrainians to do their bit, as in the terrible massacre of 33,000 Jews by Einsatzkommando 4a, in the gorge of Babi Yar, near Kiev. In Byelaya Tserkov, when even hardened SS men could not be trusted to shoot the orphaned children of murdered Jews, whose crying disturbed the sleep of German soldiers ('They are young men,' their commander explained, 'and they have small children as well'), the Ukrainian militia obligingly did the job.

How did the ordinary Germans look upon these grisly killings which they carried out or watched? At first there was some apprehension: if the war should be lost, it was said, surely there would be a heavy price to pay. But that stage soon passed: the war was not going to be lost – indeed, it seemed, it had already been won. Individually, some men were disgusted or ashamed, or suffered psychological stress. The strain on the nerves of the killers, it was said, was unimaginable and led to terrible nightmares; so many of them took to drink, and some even went mad and shot all around them, indiscriminately. Even Standartenführer Paul Blobel, who had carried out the Babi Yar massacre, went off his head for a time; but he soon recovered and went on with the work. There were nervous breakdowns and some suicides. Some men simply could not face the strain and refused to play their part. These were weeded out and posted elsewhere. They might be abused by their officers as cowards, but no one was punished for such refusal, so the excuse of duress – 'we would have been shot if we had refused' – so often invoked after 1945 was invalid. In fact there was no need of compulsion, for volunteers were always available to replace the defectors, who were anyway very few: most men accepted their orders automatically and soon got used to the work. Some were positively addicted to it and 'could not have enough of it'. There were also special inducements: extra rations of schnapps, cigarettes and sausage as reward for a hard day's butchery. That was for SS men only, as others complained. But some of the others needed no inducement. Ordinary soldiers of the Wehrmacht who came to watch would sometimes ask to join in, borrowing guns to share the sport and shooting Jewish children as they ran, 'like hares'.

At a higher level there were indeed occasional objections, but they were merely political or tactical: questions of priority, pragmatists versus doctrinaires, military or economic needs versus ideology. The ideologists generally won. The army commanders, after the initial protest of General Blaskowitz in Poland (which did him no good), accepted the facts and cooperated. Within the Party there was one interesting case of dissent. Wilhelm Kube, Gauleiter of White Russia, insisted that he was as 'hard' as anyone: had he not liquidated all the Jews in his Gau? But he believed that there were Jews and Jews, and that German Jews, having imbibed something of German culture, were a cut above East European Jews and should not be indiscriminately exterminated with them. What a torrent of denunciation this heresy would bring on him from the former theology student and commander of Einsatzkommando 2, now head of the SS in White

Russia, Obersturmbannführer Dr Eduard Strauch! The Gauleiter should be sacked at once, demanded Strauch, and he listed his various enormities: he had thanked a Jew who, at great personal risk, had rescued his official car from a blazing garage; he had mentioned Jews in the same sentence as German officials, which had caused 'boundless disgust' among the latter; and some of his associates were very unsuitable – city commissioner Janetzke, for instance, whose wife, at a drunken party, had ripped the clothes off a male guest and blackened 'some parts of his body with shoe-polish'. How could the SS 'daily and hourly perform their hard duty' if such things went on? Luckily this problem was solved when the Gauleiter was murdered by a White Russian housemaid, so the German Jews lost their protector and racialist orthodoxy was kept pure and undefiled in White Russia.

Were there no other objections? Certainly none springing from human sympathy – except, of course, for the murderers. Theirs, it was regularly said (and especially by themselves), was a 'hard and thankless task': never a day's rest – 'today gypsies, tomorrow partisans, Jews and suchlike riff-raff'; but 'faith in the Führer fills us and gives us strength' for it. Humanity, in the vocabulary of the SS, meant lightening that thankless task, both physically and morally: physically, by protecting the killers from the nasty accidents which could happen to them at work (such as being spattered by the brains of victims shot at point-blank range); morally by saving them from corrupt or weakening thoughts, such as equating their high calling with murder or seeing Jews as fellow human beings. One means of achieving these results was to devolve all the nastiest and most degrading jobs on to 'inferior' races 'in order to preserve the psychic balance of our own people'. That meant using Poles, Balts, Ukrainians, and of course Jews, who were going to be killed anyway. Another was to discover 'a better method of killing'. 'Better' meant tidier, cheaper, quicker, applicable to ever greater numbers, and, above all, less distressing to the executioners. The answer found was gas.

The shift from shooting to gas leads us into the very centre of Hitler's personal policy, 'The Führer's Chancellery', where a special department known as T4 had organized the 'Euthanasia Programme', the killing by gas, at installations in Germany, of the insane and incurably ill. That programme had been wound up after two years, in 1941: the secret had leaked out and there had been an outcry; but the expertise thus acquired was not to be wasted. It was now to be used outside Germany, on other victims. The method adopted was, first, by mobile gas-vans, then by fixed gas-chambers in a remote part of the 'General Government' of Poland.

The gas-vans were the invention of Dr August Becker, who had been gas-officer of T4, and were thought at first to be very handy. The Jews were pushed into the van; the driver started up the engine; as he drove, the poisonous fumes were discharged into the van; and when he reached his destination, which was the burial dump, all the Jews were already dead. Dr Becker was very pleased with his device: his vans, he claimed, had dispatched 97,000 Jews in six months without a hitch. But others found inconveniences in it. The screams of the slowly suffocated Jews in the closed van behind him disconcerted the driver, and those who had to unload the bodies, with distorted faces and covered with excrement, complained that it was 'no pretty business'. So the method was abandoned. The fixed gas-chambers, on the other hand, were a dreadful success. They too were the work of T4 experts – the first commandants of the extermination camps of Belzec and Treblinka, and several of their staff, were old boys of T4 – and they avoided all the disadvantages of older systems. They were more rational, more economic, less public – no survivors' stories (because there were no survivors), no horrible photographs to endanger the security of the Reich – and also less harrowing, or degrading, to the Herrenmenschen, who could parade with their riding-whips (a coveted status symbol) and leave the nastiest jobs to the Affenmenschen, 'the ape-men', the expendable Jews.

They were also positively useful: useful to the industrialists who could exploit the labour of those on the waiting-list for death, useful to the SS doctors, who could experiment on such vile bodies, alive or dead. Dr Benno Müller-Hill, in his terrible book, *Murderous Science,** has documented their story: how they too, members of a life-saving profession, were quietly absorbed into a life-destroying system and saw no evil in sustaining it and profiting by it. Here we have a macabre addition to that story in the diary of Untersturmführer Dr Johannes Paul Kremer, who, in the autumn of 1942, took a spell of duty at Auschwitz. It was, he said, a dreadful place, *anus mundi*, 'the arse-hole of the world', as he had been warned, but it had its compensations: a regular supply of *lebendfrisches Material*, human organs fresh from the body, for his experiments on the physical process of starvation; and such delicious menus at the SS officers' mess – roast hare and dumplings, half a chicken with potatoes and red cabbage,

*Tödliche Wissenschaft (Hamburg, Rowohlt-Verlag, 1984). English translation by George R. Fraser, Murderous Science (Oxford, 1988).

Bulgarian red wine and Croatian plum-brandy, 'wonderful vanilla ice-cream', and, on a special occasion ('a real feast' for the visiting head of the whole concentration-camp system, Obergruppenführer Oswald Pohl) 'baked pike, as much as you wanted, real ground coffee, excellent beer and open sandwiches'. This last meal must have been particularly refreshing for the doctor, who had just attended his sixth and seventh 'special actions' (in plain language, mass executions of Jews).

So, by 1942, the teething troubles are over. The problems have been solved; everything is running smoothly. Everyone knows the facts, but society has adjusted itself to them and learned to live with them: not, of course, to speak of them, or even publicly to show knowledge of them, but to recognize them as the necessary and by now natural condition of life in the new age of victorious Nazism. At the end of the story, instead of grisly photographs of pogroms and massacres, of naked Jews lined up for slaughter at the edge of the graves they have dug for themselves, or heaped corpses lying in city streets or desolate ravines, we see jolly groups of SS officials, men and women, with beer-mugs and wine bottles at their lips, and smiling colleagues in uniform, complacently fingering their riding-whips or playing with their dogs, in the routine and camaraderie of camp life in Auschwitz or Treblinka, Belzec or Sobibor. 'Schöne Zeiten' (Those were the Days) was the heading of a page in the commemorative album of the terrible Kurt Franz, who had graduated from T4 in the Führer's Chancellery to be the last commandant of Treblinka. Hence the title of this book: a record, and grim lesson, of the easy atrophy of the human conscience; a reminder how narrowly, and at what a cost, respect for humanity, thus lost, was restored.

Preface from the German Edition

Under the provocative title *'Those were the Days'* – taken from the private photo album of a concentration-camp commandant – the editors have gathered together a collection of powerful documents. They include contemporary texts (diaries, letters and reports) and the minutes of interrogations in which the murderers, accomplices and onlookers give an unembellished account to their interrogators of how the mass murder of the Jews was organized and carried out to the bitter end.

The book also contains a large number of photographs which speak for themselves. These pictures do not portray fanatics foaming at the mouth as they commit murder, nor do they show beasts who arouse our disgust, but perpetrators (spurred on by spectators) performing their 'work' and who afterwards, exhausted but satisfied, enjoyed a few beers in their free time. The pictures show people whose appearance does not betray that they were active participants in the mechanics of murder, or ready and willing operators.

The confidential and, indeed, sometimes private nature of the material shows with stark clarity how firmly the National Socialist 'Weltanschauung' was rooted in the German popular consciousness, part of the thinking of the time, and regarded as quite natural by all sections of the population.

Horrifying and instructive, this book carries a bitter message. It will not allow us to forget that there have been times in Germany when Jewish citizens could be beaten to death with iron bars in the street in broad daylight without anyone intervening to protect them.

Ernst Klee, born 1942, studied theology and education. Taught handicapped children at the Volkshochschule in Frankfurt (1973–82) and the Freihochschule in Wiesbaden. Also worked on the weekly, *Die Zeit*. His television film *Verspottet* (Mocked) won the Adolf Grimme

Prize (1981) and was acclaimed by the German Academy of Performing Arts in Frankfurt.

Author of *Der Zappler* (The Fidget) (1974), *Behinderten-Report* (Report on the Handicapped) (1974, published, as were the following, by S. Fischer Verlag), *Behinderten-Report II* (Report on the Handicapped II) (1976), *Psychiatrie-Report* (Psychiatry Report) (1978), *Behindert. Über die Enteignung von Körper und Bewusstein. Ein kritisches Handbuch* (Handicapped. On the Dispossession of Body and Consciousness. A Critical Handbook) (1980).

'Euthanasie' im NS-Staat. Die 'Vernichtung lebensunwerten Lebens' ('Euthanasia' in the Nazi State. The 'Liquidation of Valueless Life') (vol. 4326); *Dokumente zur 'Euthanasie'* (Documents on 'Euthanasia') (vol. 4327); *Wat sie taten – Was sie wurden. Ärzte, Juristen und andere Beteiligte am Kranken und Judenmord* (What They Did – What They Became. Doctors, Lawyers and Others Who Participated in the Murder of the Sick and the Jews) (vol. 4364).

Willi Dressen, born 1935, studied law in Cologne and Bonn. Lawyer. Employed at the Zentralstelle der Landesjustizverwaltungen zur Aufklärung nationalsozialistischer Verbrechen (Central Bureau for the Judicial Authorities of the German Länder for the Investigation of National Socialist Crimes) from 1967. From 1985 onwards, deputy director. Contributor to *Das grosse Lexikon des Dritten Reiches* (Chr, Zentner/Fr. Bedürftig, 1985), *Encyclopaedia Judaica* (1986/7) and numerous articles in learned journals.

Volker Riess, born 1957, studied history, and German language and literature. A historian, he is currently working on a doctoral dissertation.

Introduction

'Those were the Days' ('Schöne Zeiten') was a caption in the photograph album belonging to the last commandant of Treblinka (see page 226). Underneath the heading were pictures of the extermination camp where at least 700,000 people were sent to the gas-chambers.

A professor of medicine was ordered to visit Auschwitz during the university vacation. He was appalled by what he saw. None the less, in his diary he extols the excellent food ('first-rate vanilla ice cream'). The following entry recurs again and again: 'Extracted and examined fresh live liver, spleen and pancreas material.' This doctor, who did not lose his appetite in Auschwitz, was researching the effect of hunger on the human organism.

A policeman on the subject of his colleagues who participated in the massacres of the Jews said: 'They had a ball! . . . and they wanted money and gold. Don't let's kid ourselves, there was always something up for grabs during the Jewish actions.' Pity was reserved for one's own kind. When 33,771 Jews were shot dead in the space of two days at Babi Yar, one of the marksmen remarked: 'It's almost impossible to imagine what nerves of steel it took . . .'

What kind of men were these who accepted murder as their daily work? They were perfectly ordinary people, with one difference: they could act as members of the 'master race'. They decided whether a person lived or died, they had power. Hitherto undreamt-of chances for promotion revealed themselves. There were pay bonuses, extra leave and privileges such as alcohol and cigarettes. And at all times a sense of power, for the state was happy to remove all sense of personal responsibility from them.

Of course, there were isolated protests from the Wehrmacht, the armed forces. The Oberbefehlshaber Ost – commander of the eastern territories – deplored the free rein given to pathological and bestial instincts. Executioners suffered breakdowns, a number committed suicide (in some units gas-vans were used for the executions in order to spare the executioners, a method which further increased the torment of the victims). There were even members of the SS and police who refused to carry out orders to murder. Despite all the propaganda, they did not see Jews as vermin but as fellow human beings, and could not shoot defenceless, innocent people. As a result they were branded cowards or weaklings and on Himmler's orders were transferred to other units or replaced. Contrary to the myth nobody was shot or sent to a concentration camp for refusing to murder Jews.

The public mass executions were in many ways a festival. In Kovno (Lithuania) locals – among them mothers with their children – applauded as each Jew was beaten to death in front of them. Cheers and laughter rang out. German soldiers stood by and took photographs. The military authorities were aware of this but did not intervene. German soldiers were sometimes prepared to travel long distances in order to obtain the best places at the bloody 'shooting festivals'. This can only be described as 'execution tourism'. This book documents how mass murder was carried out in full public view over a long period of time.

On 20 January 1942 representatives from the various ministries, SS and police departments met in a villa by the Grosser Wannsee in Berlin. The subject under discussion was the 'Final Solution of the Jewish Question'. The purpose of the 'Wannsee conference' was to inform each of the government departments of the decisions already taken and to organize the continuation of mass murder on a still greater scale: for mass murder had already been going on for a long time. The Einsatzgruppen (special groups) and Einsatzkommandos (special squads) of the Sicherheitspolizei and the SD (security service) were devastating Jewish populations in the occupied territories. By the middle of October 1941 tens of thousands of Jews from metropolitan Germany, the Reichsgebiet, had been deported to Polish ghettos. Many of the Jews who travelled from the Reich to Kovno, Riga and Minsk, cities in the USSR, were shot immediately upon arrival. In Chełmno the gas-vans in which people choked to death in agony were already in operation. In the concentration camp of Auschwitz Zyklon B had already been in use for quite some time.

In the General-Gouvernement of Poland Himmler had entrusted the 'final solution' to the SS and police chief of Lublin district, SS-Brigadeführer Odilo Globocnik. The operation was later given the code-name 'Operation Reinhard', no doubt in commemoration of the head of the state security bureau (Reichssicherheitshauptamt), Reinhard Heydrich, who was assassinated in June 1942. The total annihilation of the Jews was, however, not possible by means of the usual methods of mass shootings or gassings in vans. And so Himmler availed himself of a slightly modified murder technique that had been applied in 1940–41 for the 'euthanasia' operation, the mass murder of the mentally ill, handicapped and other 'burdensome life forms'. Whereas previously the sick had been murdered in gas installations at Grafeneck, Brandenburg, Bernburg, Hadamar, Sonnenstein and Hartheim with carbon dioxide (bottled at the IG Farben plant), the exhaust fumes from diesel engines were now used.

Three extermination camps were built: Belzec (near Lvov), Sobibor (near the town of Włodawa) and Treblinka (near the village of Małkinia). Mass gassing began in March 1942 at Belzec and in May and July of the same year at Sobibor and Treblinka respectively. Key staff positions were filled with former 'euthanasia' assistants. In Belzec murder operations terminated in December 1942 and in Treblinka and Sobibor in the autumn of 1943 following uprisings by the 'worker Jews' in August and October there. Participants in 'Operation Reinhard' were subsequently ordered to the Adriatic coast where they helped deport Jews from that area to Auschwitz. At the time Auschwitz was a massive murder centre.

Not everybody who is given a say in this book is a 'perpetrator' in the strictly judicial sense of the word. Many were only small cogs in the overall murder machinery, for example people who assisted in transporting the victims or cordoning off the execution areas. Many, both those who gave and took orders, could point to the fact they were acquitted by the courts through lack of evidence. Think of the army chaplains who looked on while children died in the Byelaya-Tserkov region of the Ukraine and merely compiled reports 'so that no more would be said about the situation'. Two of them became suffragan bishops after the war. No public prosecutor would have laid charges against these chaplains for failing to denounce the inhumanity publicly. To say nothing of those who gawped at the murder of the Jews out of curiosity or watched stunned. But they were all, like it or not, accessories.

The texts included in this book were not edited for style. Obvious mistakes have been corrected and abbreviations have been explained to improve comprehension. Most of the perpetrators attempt to deny their part in the murders or to play down the facts. But even behind their excuses and cover-up attempts the gruesome truth remains unbearably plain. For many the years under National Socialism were indeed '*Schöne Zeiten*', even in the extermination camps.

Part One

'Acts of Violence . . . Carried Out Quite Openly'

The Murder of Jews in the Daily Life of the Einsatzgruppen

'The brutalization . . . of precious German manpower'

The occupation of Poland

Was Du für Volk und Heimat tust,

Ist immer recht getan!

A deed done for the People and the Homeland is a deed well done!

1. Notes of Eastern Territories Commander, Johannes Blaskowitz

Eastern Territories Commander   HQ Schloss Spala, 6.2.1940

1. Military/political situation:

In the industrial area of Kamienna for the first time the existence of a rebel and sabotage organization with wide ramifications has been confirmed. Leaders of the organization are members of the former Polish army. The material that was discovered during numerous arrests is currently being examined. The Staatspolizei are refraining from making further arrests in order not to jeopardize plans to eliminate the organization as a whole.

In connection with this matter, there is a danger emerging which demands a general comment on our treatment of the Polish population.

It is wholly misguided to slaughter some 10,000 Jews and Poles as is happening at the moment. Such methods will eradicate neither Polish nationalism nor the Jews from the mass of the population. On the contrary, the way in which the slaughter is being carried out is extremely damaging, complicates the problems and makes them a great deal more dangerous than they would be if dealt with by a well-considered and decisive policy. The effects are:

(a) It is hard to imagine there can be more effective material in the entire world than that which is being delivered into the hands of enemy propaganda. The foreign broadcasts have hitherto covered only a tiny fraction of what has actually occurred. We have to face the fact that outcry from overseas is continuously on the increase causing very great political damage, particularly since the atrocities did indeed take place and cannot be disproved in any way.

(b) The acts of violence carried out in public against Jews are arousing in religious Poles not only the deepest disgust but also a great sense of pity for the Jewish population, while formerly the Poles' attitude towards the Jews was fairly hostile. Very soon we will reach a point where our arch enemies in the Eastern Territories [Ostraum] – the Pole and the Jew with the backing of the Catholic Church – will be united in their hatred against their German torturers.

4

(c) The effects on the role of the Wehrmacht need hardly be mentioned. It is forced to watch these crimes without being able to do anything. It has irreparably lost a considerable amount of respect especially among the Polish population.

(d) The worst damage, however, affecting Germans, which has developed as a result of the current circumstances, is the tremendous brutalization and moral depravity which is spreading rapidly among precious German manpower like an epidemic.

If high-ranking SS and police officials demand and openly praise acts of violence and brutality, before long people who commit acts of violence will predominate alone. It is surprising how quickly such people join forces with those of weak character in order, as is currently happening in Poland, to give rein to their bestial and pathological instincts. It would still just be possible to keep them in check. They clearly feel they are being given official authorization and that they are thus justified to commit any kind of cruel act.

The only way to ward off this epidemic is to make those that are guilty and their followers answerable to the military authorities and to justice as quickly as possible. . . .

2. 'Bloody Wednesday' in Olkusz/Ilkenau

Market square of the Polish border town of Olkusz, called Ilkenau by the occupation forces. In 1940 some 7,000 Poles and 6,000 Jews were living there. On 16 July 1940 the German gendarme Ernest Kaddatz was shot by an unknown assailant. In reprisal twenty Jews were publicly executed

On Wednesday, 31 July 1940, Olkusz was surrounded by German police and army units. The Jewish inhabitants were taken from their homes and brought to assembly points

The Jews are made to lie on the ground. This happens in three places: on the 'Czarna Gora' green, at the old electricity plant and in the market-place. The Jews have to lie face down on the ground for hours. They are beaten with rifle butts and trampled on with boots. For this reason the day comes to be known as 'Bloody Wednesday'. Electrical assembler Tadeusz Lupa cannot stand the torture, attempts escape and is shot. According to their statements the locals and the German administrative officials and police officers did not see anything. Only the photos exist.

Olkusz Jews were transported to Auschwitz in 1942

3. 'Foreign Service'

Excerpts from the diary of a cycle battalion
Foreign service of the unit, Field Post No. 44762 D, for the
period 9.6.1941 to . . .

In accordance with R.F.S.S. and Chief of the German Police's order in
R.M.d.I. [Reichsministerium des Innern – Ministry of the Interior] Supreme
Command I.0(3)1 No. 56/41, our former training battalion, the Vienna-
Kagran, was redeployed as Police Battalion 322 and from 16.4.1941 was put
at the personal disposal for a special Einsatz of the R.F.S.S. and the Chief of
the German Police. Police Battalion 322 became a Cycle Battalion.

Following a waiting period of more than seven weeks, on 9.6.1941 on the
orders of the Reichsführer the battalion was dispatched to Warsaw to be
absorbed into Police Regiment Mitte.

3.6.1941
23.00 hours
Departure of the Vorkommando [advance party]:

Zugmachtmeister	Hametner	Wachtmeister	Schmidt
Wachtmeister	Menzel	"	Conrads
"	Pietschmann		

under command of Oberleutnant d. Sch. Kohlsaal.

7.6.1941
10.00
Formal discharge of the Battalion by the Inspector of the Vienna Ordnungs-
Polizei, Generalmajor Dr Retzlaff.

In a short address the inspector referred to the importance of the Einsatz
that lay ahead and urged everybody to fulfil his duty in enemy territory.
After an oath of allegiance and a 'Sieg Heil' to the Führer the inspector
finished with the singing of 'Deutschland' and the Horst Wessel song.
12.30
Communal lunch in the officers' mess together with the commander of the
Sch. Pol. Vienna, Oberst der Sch. Polmeier. Afterwards communal gathering
and formal discharge by Commander of Sch. Polmeier, Vienna.

8.6.1941
15.00   Loading of the Coy cycles at Vienna-Floritzdorf loading station.
15.30   Loading of lorries.

9.6.1941
5.00   Company reported to the Coy Commander (short address).

6.15   Address of Battn Commander, Major der Sch. Nagel, at barracks parade area.

Short departure address and a threefold 'Sieg Heil' to the Führer.

6.30   Departure to music to Stadlau railway station.

'Alte Kameraden' [Old comrades].

7.55   Departure from Stadlau to music: 'Muss i denn, muss i denn, zum Städtelein hinaus' [Must I, must I leave this little town?].

Wm. d. Sch. Matzoll had to stay behind due to illness.

Went through Prerou (Protektorat), Heidebreck (Oberschl.), Tschentsochau (Gov.) to Warsaw in magnificent sunshine. (Fast train)

Transport Officer, Oberleutnant d. Sch. Rasche

10.6.41

6.55   Arrival Warsaw West Station, 1 hour earlier than timetabled.

9.00   After instructions by advance party office personnel travels to allocated accommodation.

Advance party had done good work. All rooms decorated with flowers.

9.00   Arrival of goods transport at Warsaw West Station.

13.45   Arrival of Coy at accommodation.

28.6.1941

9.00   Battn and Regt units inspected by General von Schenkendorff and Höherer SS und Polizei Führer von dem Bach.

The general praised the battalion with the following words: 'The battalion's smart appearance, attitude and level of training is outstanding!'

He expressed his conviction that the battalion in this condition would fulfil the duties assigned to it.

Afterwards march past of the units to regimental music.

Subsequent to this the general paid his respects to the unit commander and exchanged a few words with him.

10.06   General von Schenkendorff accompanied by Höherer SS und Polizei Führer von dem Bach and Regimental Commander Oberstleutnant der Schutzpolizei Montua inspected the quarters and the vehicles outside.

30.6.1941

18.00   Battalion inspection by Battalion Commander, Major der Schutzpolizei Nagel.

Punishment of 2 members of 2nd Coy and 2 members of the N. platoon with 3 weeks' high-security detention.

The Battalion commander addressed the battalion with serious and reproving words about the punishment.

He demanded discipline, an unquestioning and obedient sense of duty and unswerving loyalty from each man.

Then he addressed sharp words to those who believed that they could incite the troops to disobedience, complaining and dissatisfaction and added that he would not tolerate such soldiers' council behaviour in his battalion.

He shouted to those men who complained about the rations, 'You have no reason whatsoever to grouse about the rations. The rationing is adequate. Think of your comrades who have recently achieved such superb success at the front against the Red Army.'

10.7.41

General Daluege inspected the prison camp accompanied by General-leutnant Riege and Höherer SS und Polizei Führer von dem Bach.

Russian officers and soldiers were presented to the gentlemen. The general inspected the Ukrainians very carefully and ordered that the best of them should be selected to form a Ukrainian company.

13.00   Special unit reports for duty in Bialystock to guard a war hospital and a captured-material store: strength 1/12. Coy takes over guard of the prison camp: strength 1/30.

2.00   5 Jews were shot by our guards while attempting to escape from the prison camp.

11.7.41

Marksmen 3, 4 and 5 from the h.m.g. [heavy-machine-gun] platoon were supplied with Russian rifles. Test shots with Russ. l.m.g. [light-machine-gun].

Jewish quarter in Bialystock burning.

12.7.41

During the night arrival of 11,000 prisoners.

Zugwachtmeister Hanzelner orders 10-man watch reinforcement to guard the prisoners. Number of prisoners in camp: 25,000.

Wachtmeister d. Sch. Schwertfeger and Zander detailed as regiment lorry drivers.

Water supply causing severe difficulties.

Prisoners break out into the street.

Fire brigade called in with tanks to bring water.

21.00

Informal get-together outside the quarters with two barrels of beer.

13.7.41

6.00   Oblt. d. Sch. Rasche, Zgw. Cimbal and Wm. Didrowski went to East Prussia on official business. (Allenstein)

9.00   Parade of the company commander, Oblt. d. Sch. Riebel. (Special jurisdiction, procedure against the Jews.)

No appropriation of booty material.

During the night 19 Jews shot attempting to escape.

14.7.41

During the night 40 Jews shot attempting to escape.

9.8.41

0.00   Start of evacuation action against Jews in Bialowi(e)za. All male Jews aged 16 to 45 were arrested and brought to the assembly camp. All remaining Jews of both sexes were evacuated by lorry to Kobryn. The Jews had to leave behind everything in their homes apart from some hand-luggage. Confiscated articles of value were collected in Bialowieza Hunting Lodge and handed over to the Ortskommandantur. The homes of the evacuated Jews were locked or boarded up.

10.8.41

7.00   Liquidation of Jews housed in the Bialowieza prison assembly camp. 77 male Jews aged 16 to 45 shot.
5 Jewish tailors, 4 Jewish cobblers and 1 Jewish watchmaker were not shot since their labour was urgently required by the company.

11.8.41

In Olschowka SS base a Jewish prisoner and 2 young White Russian peasants shot for looting.

12.8.41

Morning exercise training. Afternoon overhaul of weapons and cycles.

14.8.41

4.00   Jewish action in Narewka-Mala. 259 women and 162 children transferred by lorry to Kobryn.
    282 Jews were shot.
    During the action one Pole was shot for looting.
18.00   Hauptmann d. Sch. Podlesch arrived in Bialowieza and informed the company that it would soon be relieved by Battalion 323.

31.8.41

15.00   Jewish action in the city of Minsk ghetto.
    9th Coy manned the outer cordon while 7th Coy, N.S.K.K. Coy and the SD carried out search. All Jews aged between 15 and 60 were apprehended. In addition all Jewesses who were not wearing the prescribed yellow star on their clothing. A total of 916[?] Jews of both sexes were apprehended and taken to the police prison.

1.9.41

5.30   Execution of Jews apprehended yesterday some 10 km east of Minsk, north of the Minsk–Smolensk–Moscow highway. Three Execution Kommandos were deployed. The Kommando from 9th Coy shot a total of 330 Jews (of whom 40 were Jewesses).

'Foreign Service'

Auswärtiger Einsatz

Der Einheit
Feldpost Nr. 44762 D
in der Zeit vom 9. 6. 1941
bis

Laut Erlaß des R. F. ₷₷ und Chef der Deutschen Polizei im R. M. d. J. O. Kdo. I. O (3) 1 Nr. 56/41 wurde unser ehemaliges A. Btl. Wien-Kagran in Pol. Btl. 322 umgegliedert und stand ab 16. 4. 1941 für einen besonderen Einsatz dem R. F. ₷₷ u. Ch. d. D. Pol. zur persönlichen Verfügung. Pol. Btl. 322 wurde Radfahr-Btl.

Nach einer Wartezeit von mehrals 7 Wochen wurde das Btl. lt. Erlaß des Reichs-

Führers am 9. 6. 1941 nach Warschau in Marsch
gesetzt, um dort in den Verband des

Pol. Rgt. „Mitte"

aufgenommen zu werden.

———————— ∞ ————————

3. 6. 1941
23⁰⁰

Abfahrt des Vorkommandos:
Zugwachtm. Hametner,
Wachtm.   Menzel
   "   Pietschmann
   "   Schmidt
   "   Conrads
Unter Führung von:
Oblt. d. Sch. Kohlsaat.

7. 6. 1941
10⁰⁰

Verabschiedung des Btl.
durch den Inspekteur der
Ordnungs-Polizei-Wien
Generalmajor Dr. Retzlaff.

In einer kurzen Ansprache
wies der Inspekteur auf die
Bedeutung des bevorstehenden
Einsatzes hin und ermahnte
alle, gerade in Feindes Land seine
Pflicht zu erfüllen.

Mit einem Treuschwur

und Sieg Heil auf den Führer
schloß der Inspekteur sein Ansprache
die mit dem Singen des „Deutschland-
und Horst Wessel Liedes' ausklang.
12³⁰
 Gemeinsames Mittagessen
im Offizierskasino im Beisein
des Kommandeurs d. Sch. Pol. Wien,
Oberst der Sch. Polmeier.
Anschließend gemeinsames Bei-
sammensein und Verabschiedung
durch den Kommandeur d. Sch.
Polmeier Wien.

8. 6. 1941
15⁰⁰ Verladen der Komp.
Fahrräder auf dem Verlade-
bahnhof Wien-Floritzdorf.
15³⁰ Verladen der Kraftfahrzeuge.

9. 6. 1941
5⁰⁰ Meldung der Kompanie
an den Komp. Chef (Kurze Ansprache)
6¹⁵ Ansprache des Btl.
Kommandeurs Major d. Sch.
Nagel, auf dem Antreteplatz im
Barackenlager.
 Kurze Abschiedsworte
und ein dreifaches Sieg Heil
auf den Führer.
6³⁰ Abmarsch mit Musik

zum Stadlauer Bahnhof
„Alte Kameraden;"

7.⁵⁵ Abfahrt Bahnhof Stadlau
unter den Klängen der Musik
„Muß i denn, muß i denn, zum städtelein
hinaus."

Wm. d. Sch. Matzoll muß
infolge Krankheit zurückbleiben.

Bei herlichem Sonnenschein
ging die Fahrt über Prerau (Protektorat)
Heidebreck (Oberschl.) Tschentsochau
(Gov.) nach Warschau. (D Zug Wagen)

Transportoffizier,
Oblt. d. Sch. Rasche

10.6.41

6.⁵⁵ Ankunft Westbahnhof
Warschau. 1 Stunde früher als Fahr-
planmäßig vorgesehen war

9.⁰⁰ Nach Anweisung des Vor-
kommandos fährt das Geschäftsz.
Personal zur zugewiesenen
Unterkunft.

Das Vorkommando hatte
gut gearbeitet. Sämtliche Stuben
mit Blumen geschmückt.

9.⁰⁰ Ankunft des Gütertrans-
portes Westbhf. Warschau.

13.⁴⁵ Eintreffen der Komp.
vor der Unterkunft.

15

28. 6. 1941

9⁰⁰ Besichtigung des Btl. und der Rgt. Einheiten durch den General von Schenkendorff und höheren ϟϟ und Polizeiführer von dem Bach.

Der General lobte mit den Worten: "Das frische Aussehen, Richtung und Vordermann des Btl. sind hervorragend." das Btl.

Er gab der Überzeugung Ausdruck, daß das Btl. in dieser Verfassung die ihm gestellten Aufgaben voll erfüllen würde!

Anschließend Vorbeimarsch der Einheiten unter den Klängen der Rgt. Musik.

Im Anschluß daran begrüßte der General die Einheits- führer und wechselte mit ihnen einige Worte.

10⁰⁵ General von Schenkendorff besichtigt in Begleitung des höheren ϟϟ und Pol. Führers von dem Bach und Rgt. Kdr., Oberstltn. d. Sch. Montua, die Unter- kunft und die vor der Unterkunft aufgestellten Fahrzeuge.

8

30. 6. 1941.

18⁰⁰ Appel des Btl. durch den
Btl. Kdr. Major d. Sch. Nagel.

Bestrafung von 2 ange-
hörigen der 2. Komp. und 2 ange-
hörigen des N. Zuges mit 3 Wochen
geschärftem Arrest.

Der Btl. Kdr. sprach bezgl.
der Bestrafungen ernste und
mahnende Worte an das Btl.
Er verlangte von jedem einzelnen
Manneszucht, unbedingten Gehorsam,
Pflichtbewußtsein u. unerschütterliche
Treue.

Dann wand er sich mit scharfen
Worten an diejenigen, die glaubten
mismachen, meckern u. Unzufrieden-
heit in die Truppe bringen zu können.
Solche Soldatentatsmanieren dulde er
nicht in seinem Btl.

Denjenigen, die über die
Verpflegung meckerten rief er zu.
Sie haben gar keinen Grund über
die Verpflegung zu meckern.
Die Verpflegung ist ausreichend.
Denken Sie an Ihre Kameraden
die in diesen Tagen so gewaltige
Erfolge in vorderster Front gegen
die rote Armee errungen haben.

10. 7. 41

General Daluege besichtigt in Begleitung des Generalleutnant Riege und des höheren SS u. pol. Führer, von dem Bach das Gefangenenlager.

Russische Offiziere und Soldaten werden den Herren vorgestellt. Ganz besonders sah sich der General die Ukrainer u. ordnete an, daß die besten von Ihnen herausgezogen werden sollen, um sie zu Ukrainer Komp. zusammen zu stellen.

13.00 Gestellung einer Sonderwache in Bialystock zur Bewachung eines Kriegslazaret u. eines Beutelagers Stärke 1/12 die Komp. übernimmt Bewachung des Gefangenenlagers Stärke 1/30 200

5 Juden werden durch unsere Postierungen bei dem Fluchtversuch aus dem Gefangenen Lager erschossen.

11. 7. 41

Schützen 3, 4 u. 5 des 9. M.J. Zuges werden mit russischen

Gewehren ausgerüstet. Probe-
schiessen mit russ. k. M. G.

　　Judenviertel in Bialystock
brennt.

__12. 7. 41__

　　Während der Nacht
Eintreffen von 11.000 Gefangenen

　　Zgw Kanzelner fordert
für die Gefangenenwache
10 Mann Verstärkung an.
Zahl der Gefangenen im
Lager 25.000

　　Wm. d. Sch. Schwertfeger
und Zander als Kraftfahrer
zum Regt. abgeordnet.

　　Wasserversorgung bereitet
große Schwierigkeiten.

　　Gefangene brechen zur
Straße durch.

　　Feuerwehr wird mit Tank-
wagen zum Herbeischaffen
von Wasser herangezogen.

__21⁰⁰__

　　Gemütliches Beisammen-
sein vor der Unterkunft im
Freien. Ausschank von
2 Fässer Bier.

__13. 7. 41__

6⁰⁰ Oblt. d. Sch. Rasche, Zgw.

Cimbal und Wm. Piotrowski
dienstlich nach Ostpreußen.
(Allenstein)

9⁰⁰ Appell des Kompaniechefs.
Obll. d. Sch. Riebel.(Sondergerichts-
barkeit, Verhalten gegen Juden)

Keine Aneignung von
Beutestücken.

Während der Nacht
19 Juden bei Fluchtversuch
erschossen.

14.7 41
Während der Nacht
40 Juden bei Fluchtversuch
erschossen.

9. 8. 41
6⁰⁰ Beginn der Evaku-
ierungsaktion gegen Juden
in Bialowiża. Sämtliche Juden
männlichen Geschlecht im Alter
von 16 bis 45 Jahren wurden
festgenommen und im Ge-
fangenensammellager untergebracht. Alle übrigen Juden
beiderlei Geschlecht, wurden
mittels Lkw. nach Kobryn
evakuiert. Die Juden mußten
außer etwas Handgepäck alles
in ihren Wohnungen zurück-
lassen. Die sichergestellten Wert-

8

gegenstände wurden im Jagd-
schloß Bialowieza gesammelt
der Ortskommandantur übergeben.
Die Wohnungen der evakuierten
Juden wurden abgeschlossen
bezw. vernagelt.

10. 8. 41

7ᵉ Liquidierung der im
Gefangenensammellager Bialowieza untergebrachten Juden.

Es wurden 77 Juden
männlichen Geschlechts im Alter
von 16 bis 45 Jahren erschossen.

5 jüdische Schneider,
4 jüdische Schuster und 1 jüdischer Uhrmacher wurden nicht
erschossen, da sie als Arbeits-
kräfte für die Komp. dringend
gebraucht wurden.

11. 8. 41

Im SS Stützpunkt
Ochowka wurden wegen Plünderung ein jüdischer Gefangener und
2 weißrussische Bauernsöhne
erschossen.

12. 8. 41

Vormittags Exerzieraus-
bildung. Nachmittags Instandsetzen
der Waffen und Fahrräder.

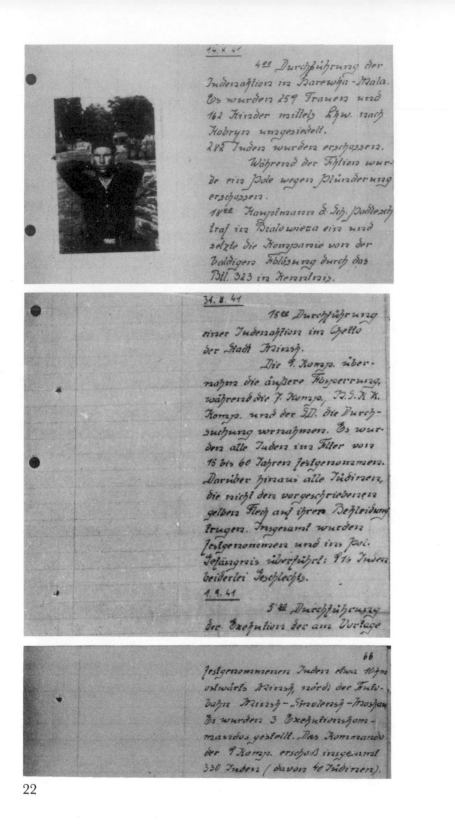

14.X.41

4te Durchführung der
Judenaktion in Harewka-Mala.
Es wurden 259 Frauen und
162 Kinder mittels Lkw. nach
Kobryn umgesiedelt.
288 Juden wurden erschossen.
    Während der Aktion wur-
de ein Pole wegen Plünderung
erschossen.
18te Hauptmann d. Sch. Podlesch
traf in Bialowieza ein und
setzte die Kompanie von der
baldigen Ablösung durch das
Btl. 323 in Kenntnis.

31.X.41
    15te Durchführung
einer Judenaktion im Ghetto
der Stadt Minsk.
    Die 9. Komp. über-
nahm die äußere Absperrung,
während die 7. Komp., R.S.K.K.
Komp. und der SD. die Durch-
suchung vornahmen. Es wurden alle Juden im Alter von
15 bis 60 Jahren festgenommen.
Darüber hinaus alle Jüdinnen,
die nicht den vorgeschriebenen
gelben Fleck auf ihrer Bekleidung
trugen. Insgesamt wurden
festgenommen und in das poln.
Gefängnis überführt: 916 Juden
beiderlei Geschlecht.

1.9.41
    5te Durchführung
der Exekution der am Vortage

66
festgenommenen Juden etwa 10 km
ostwärts Minsk, nörd. der Auto-
bahn Minsk-Smolensk-Moskau.
Es wurden 3 Exekutionskom-
mandos gestellt. Das Kommando
der 9. Komp. erschoß insgesamt
330 Juden (davon 40 Jüdinnen).

22

'Each time a victim was beaten to death they started to clap'

Pogroms in Kaunas and elsewhere in Lithuania

The 'Death-dealer of Kaunas'

1. 'Initially difficult to set a pogrom in motion'

Report by Stahlecker, head of Einsatzgruppe A

In accordance with orders Einsatzgruppe A marched into the assembly area on 23 June 1941, the second day of the eastern campaign, after the transfer of serviceable vehicles. Army Group North together with 16th and 18th Armies and Tank Group 4 had started the advance the previous day. It was now a matter of priority to establish swift contact with the leaders of the armies as well as the commanders of the rear army area. I am able to say that from the outset cooperation with the Wehrmacht was generally good, and in certain cases, as for example with Tank Group 4 under the command of General Höppner, extremely close, one might even say warm. Misunderstandings which arose in the first days with individual commands were in the main ironed out through personal discussions. . . .

Similarly, within a few hours of our entering the city, local anti-Semitic elements were induced to engage in pogroms against the Jews, despite the extremely difficult conditions. In accordance with orders the security police were bent on solving the Jewish question with extreme firmness using all the ways and means at its disposal. It was thought a good idea for the security police not to be seen to be involved, at least not immediately, in these unusually tough measures, which were also bound to attract attention in German circles. The impression had to be created that the local population itself had taken the first steps of its own accord as a natural reaction to decades of oppression by the Jews and the more recent terror exerted by the Communists.

In view of the fact that operations to extend the field of action were under way and the security police had their hands full, every attempt was made from the outset to ensure that reliable elements in the local population participated in the fight against the pests in their country, that is, the Jews and the Communists. Precautions, which will be described in more detail below, had to be taken when directing the first spontaneous self-cleansing actions that reliable people were engaged in the mopping-up work who could act as a permanent source of assistance to the security police. In order to do this the

Kaunas: Jews are herded through the streets by Lithuanian criminals

differing conditions in each part of the Einsatz territory had to be taken into account.

In Lithuania at the beginning of the eastern campaign national

Kaunas: Jews are publicly beaten to death by Lithuanians. German
soldiers look on and take photographs

activist forces had banded together into so-called partisan units in
order to engage actively in the struggle against Bolshevism. According
to their own accounts they lost 4,000 of their number.

In Kaunas four fairly large groups of partisans had formed with
whom the advance party had immediately established contact. These
groups had not been organized under one coherent leadership.
Instead, each group tried to gain superiority over the others and to
enter into closer association with the Wehrmacht so that they would
be included in a military operation against the Soviet army and as a
result the dominant group would be able to capitalize on the changes
in the government of Lithuania and thus be able to form a new
[Lithuanian] army. Whilst for political reasons military deployment
of the partisans could not be considered, within a short time a 300-
strong auxiliary group fit for action was formed from the reliable
members of the undisciplined partisan groups under the leadership of
the Lithuanian journalist Klimatis. This group, as it proved itself
satisfactory, was deployed not only in Kaunas itself but also in
numerous parts of Lithuania where it performed its duties, in particu-

lar preparation of and participation in the execution of large liquidation actions, under the constant supervision of the Einsatzkommando with no significant problems. . . .

In view of the fact that the population of the Baltic countries had suffered tremendously during their incorporation into the USSR under the leadership of the Bolsheviks and Jews, it could be assumed that after their liberation from this foreign domination they themselves would largely render harmless their enemies left behind in the country after the withdrawal of the Red Army. The task of the security police was to set these purges in motion and put them on to the right track so as to ensure that the liquidation goals that had been set might be achieved in the shortest possible time. It was equally essential to create an established and provable fact for the future that the liberated population had taken the hardest measures against their Bolshevik and Jewish adversaries of their own accord without directions from German authorities being discernible.

In Lithuania this goal was achieved for the first time in Kaunas through the deployment of partisans. It was initially surprisingly difficult to set a fairly large-scale pogrom in motion there. The leader of the above-mentioned partisan group, Klimatis, who was the first to be recruited, succeeded in starting a pogrom on the basis of instructions he had been given by the small advance party that had been deployed in Kovno without any German orders or incitement being discernible. During the first pogrom, in the night of 25/26 June, more then 1,500 Jews were eliminated by the Lithuanian partisans, several synagogues were set on fire or destroyed by other methods and a Jewish quarter of about sixty houses was burnt down. On following nights 2,300 Jews were rendered harmless in the same way. In other parts of Lithuania there were similar actions following the example of Kaunas, albeit on a smaller scale, but which included Communists that had remained in the area.

The Wehrmacht units were briefed and showed full understanding for the action. As a result, the cleaning-up operations went off very smoothly. From the outset it was clear that the possibility of carrying out pogroms only presented itself during the first days of the occupation. . . .

2. 'Cheers and laughter'

Mass murder in Kovno

Report of an *Oberst*:*

Before the start of the Russian campaign, between 21 June and 1 July 1941, the staff of Army Group North under the command of Field Marshal Ritter von Leeb was based at 'Waldfrieden', a health resort some 10 km from Insterburg.

As Adjutant (11a) to this staff I received orders to travel to 16th Army HQ, which was stationed in Kovno, and arrange quarters for the staff of the army group liaising with them. I arrived on the morning of 27 June. While I was travelling through the town I went past a petrol station that was surrounded by a dense crowd of people. There was a large number of women in the crowd and they had lifted up their children or stood them on chairs or boxes so that they could see better. At first I thought this must be a victory celebration or some type of sporting event because of the cheering, clapping and laughter that kept breaking out. However, when I inquired what was happening I was told that the 'Death-dealer of Kovno' was at work and that this was where collaborators and traitors were finally meted out their rightful punishment! When I stepped closer, however, I became witness to probably the most frightful event that I had seen during the course of two world wars.

On the concrete forecourt of the petrol station a blond man of medium height, aged about twenty-five, stood leaning on a wooden club, resting. The club was as thick as his arm and came up to his chest. At his feet lay about fifteen to twenty dead or dying people. Water flowed continuously from a hose washing blood away into the drainage gully. Just a few steps behind this man some twenty men, guarded by armed civilians, stood waiting for their cruel execution in silent submission. In response to a cursory wave the next man stepped forward silently and was then beaten to death with the wooden club in the most bestial manner, each blow accompanied by enthusiastic shouts from the audience.

*See table of ranks, page 280.

28

At the staff office I subsequently learned that other people already knew about these mass executions, and that they had naturally aroused in them the same feelings of horror and outrage as they had in me. It was, however, explained to me that they were apparently a *spontaneous action* on the part of the Lithuanian population in retaliation against the collaborators and traitors of the recently ended Russian occupation. Consequently these cruel excesses had to be viewed as purely internal conflicts which the Lithuanian state itself had to deal with, that is, without the intervention of the German army. Orders to this effect had been received 'from above'. I was also told that the public executions had already been forbidden and it was hoped that this prohibition order would be sufficient to restore calm and order.

That same evening (27 June) I was the guest of the army staff. During dinner a staff officer came up to the Commander-in-Chief (Generaloberst Busch) and informed him that the mass murders had started again in the town. General Busch replied that this was an internal dispute; he was at that moment powerless to take action against it and had been forbidden to do so. He hoped, however, to receive new instructions from above before long. The entire night volleys of rifle and machine-gun fire could be heard, which indicated that further shootings were taking place outside the town, probably in the old fortress.

The following day I did not see any more executions of the type I had witnessed the previous day in the streets. Instead, however, long columns consisting of some forty to fifty men, women and children, who had been driven out of their homes, were herded through the streets by armed civilians. A woman ran out of one of these columns and threw herself down in front of me and on bended knees begged with outstretched hands for help and mercy before she was roughly pushed back into line. I was told that these people were being taken to the city prison. I assume, however, that the route they were taking led directly to their place of execution.

When I left the staff headquarters the general instructed me to inform Army Group of the situation in Kovno. I remember with what outrage and concern my report was received by Army Group, but here too they believed they could still hope that indeed these were purely internal matters. I also learnt here that the military had been forbidden by the higher authorities to take any steps whatsoever. This was exclusively the job of the SD.

By the time the staff of Army Group arrived in Kovno on 1 July the

Kaunas: mass murder, watched by German soldiers and tolerated by the army staff

town itself had become calmer. However, civilians were being rounded up and led away on a daily basis. The squads of guards now wore a kind of militia uniform of German origin. Amongst these men there were also members of the SD who had, as I subsequently learned, started their activities in Kovno on 24 June.

Report of a photographer:

At the beginning of the Russian campaign on the morning of 22 June 1941 I was transferred with my unit to Gumbinnen. We remained there until the following Tuesday, 24 June 1941. On that Tuesday I was ordered to transfer from Gumbinnen to Kovno with an advance party. I arrived there with the head of an army unit on Wednesday morning (25 June 1941). My assignment was to find quarters for the group following us. My job was made substantially easier because we had already pinpointed a number of blocks of houses for our unit on an aerial photograph of Kovno that had been taken beforehand.

There were no more significant clashes in the city. Close to my quarters I noticed a crowd of people in the forecourt of a petrol station which was surrounded by a wall on three sides. The way to the road was completely blocked by a wall of people. I was confronted by the following scene: in the left corner of the yard there was a group of men aged between thirty and fifty. There must have been forty to fifty of them. They were herded together and kept under guard by some civilians. The civilians were armed with rifles and wore armbands, as can be seen in the pictures I took. A young man – he must have been a Lithuanian – . . . with rolled-up sleeves was armed with an iron crowbar. He dragged out one man at a time from the group and struck him with the crowbar with one or more blows on the back of his head. Within three-quarters of an hour he had beaten to death the entire group of forty-five to fifty people in this way. I took a series of photographs of the victims. . . .

After the entire group been beaten to death, the young man put the crowbar to one side, fetched an accordion and went and stood on the mountain of corpses and played the Lithuanian national anthem. I recognized the tune and was informed by bystanders that this was the national anthem. The behaviour of the civilians present (women and children) was unbelievable. After each man had been killed they began to clap and when the national anthem started up they joined in singing and clapping. In the front row there were women with small children in their arms who stayed there right until the end of the whole proceedings. I found out from some people who knew German what was happening here. They explained to me that the parents of the young man who had killed the other people had been taken from their beds two days earlier and immediately shot, because they were suspected of being nationalists, and this was the young man's revenge. Not far away there was a large number of dead people who according to the civilians had been killed by the withdrawing Commissars and Communists.

While I was talking to the civilians an SS officer came up to me and tried to confiscate my camera. I was able to refuse since in the first place the camera was not mine but had been allocated to me for my work, and second I had a special pass from 16th Army High Command, which gave me authorization to take photographs everywhere. I explained to the officer that he could only obtain the camera if he went through Generalfeldmarschall Busch, whereupon I was able to go on my way unhindered.

Report of a lance-corporal in 562nd Bakers' Company:

In the summer of 1941 I was a lance-corporal in 562nd Bakers' Company, field post number 07048, which was detailed to 16th Army. Shortly before the hostilities began against Russia we were in Rastenburg, which was where we were when the Russian campaign started on Sunday, 22 June 1941. On 23 June 1941 we crossed the German–Russian border at Wirballen. We arrived in Kovno in the late afternoon of the same day, where we were allocated quarters at a Russian barracks the name of which I do not know. On our way through the city of Kovno before we had reached our quarters, I saw a crowd of people gathered in a square somewhere in the centre of the town. I stopped my vehicle to find out what was going on. I had to climb on to my vehicle to be able to see as my view was blocked by a wall as well as the large number of people standing round. From where I was standing I saw Lithuanian civilians beating a number of civilians with different types of weapon until they showed no more sign of life. Not knowing why these people were being beaten to death in such a cruel manner, I asked a medical-corps sergeant standing next to me whom I did not know personally. He told me that the people being beaten to death were all Jews who had been apprehended by Lithuanians in the city and had been brought to this square. The killings were carried out by recently released Lithuanian convicts. Why these Jews were being beaten to death I did not find out. At that time I had not formulated my own thoughts about the persecution of the Jews because I had not yet heard anything about it. The bystanders were almost exclusively German soldiers, who were observing the cruel incident out of curiosity.

When I reached the square where the Jews were being beaten there must have been about fifteen dead or seriously injured people lying there on the ground. About five Lithuanian ex-convicts were just in the process of beating some more Jews. As far as I could make out, the convicts were wearing white shirts and dark trousers or dark-coloured training suits. As I was an amateur photographer I took two photographs of this unbelievable incident from where I was standing on top of my vehicle. As I had finished the film I took it out of the camera in order to put in a new one. Just then I was confronted by an officer of the Wehrmacht, a paymaster I think, who told me that it was not permitted to take photographs of such events. I had to give him my particulars and the name of my unit and he confiscated the camera. I was only able to save the pictures because I had already taken the film out of the camera. In the pictures you can clearly see five Lithuanian convicts with clubs and cudgels in their hands hitting the Jews, who are lying on the ground. There are also some members of the Lithuanian 'Freikorps' wearing armbands on their left arms. These 'Freikorps' people rushed back to the square with more Jews who were likewise beaten to death by the convicts. The Jews that were lying on the ground did not all die straight away. After they had been led into the square they were hit on the head or in the face indiscriminately and immediately fell stunned to the ground. Then they were beaten by the convicts until they no longer showed any sign of life. Then yet more Jews were led to the square and they too were beaten in the same way. I stayed in total some ten minutes at the scene of this cruel event and then left and continued my journey. While I stayed in the square I witnessed the beating to death of some ten to fifteen Jews. . . .

Before they were beaten to death, the Jews prayed and murmured to themselves. Some of them also said prayers to themselves as they lay badly wounded on the ground.

Report of a sergeant-major from 562nd Bakers' Company:

In 1941 at the beginning of the Russian campaign I was a Hauptfeld-webel (sergeant-major) in 562nd Bakers' Company, which was under the command of 16th Army. In the spring of 1941 we were transferred from France to East Prussia. Shortly before the beginning of hostilities we were in Rastenburg. If I remember correctly, we crossed the border at Stallupönen on 23 or 24 June 1941 and then travelled in the direction of Kovno (Kaunas). I no longer remember today the exact date we moved into Kovno, but I think we arrived two or three days after the town had been taken. To my knowledge, the whole unit entered Kovno together; a special advance party was not necessary. We were quartered in an old Russian barracks and immediately started to make bread for the troops. I think it must have been one day after we had arrived in Kovno that I was informed by a driver in my unit that Jews were being beaten to death in a nearby square. Upon hearing this I went to the said square. As I recall, other mem-bers of our unit also went there or went there together with me. The square was about twenty metres in area and cobbled. One side of the square abutted the road, two sides were lined with houses and the back gave on to open ground, perhaps a park.

In the square I saw civilians, some in shirtsleeves, others wearing other types of clothing, beating other civilians to death with iron bars. I was not able to tell whether the victims were Jews. Someone, however, remarked at the time that these were the Jews who had swindled the Lithuanians before the Germans had arrived. I heard from some soldiers standing near by, whom I questioned, that the victims were being beaten to satisfy a personal desire for vengeance. When I reached the square, there were about fifteen to twenty bodies lying there. These were then cleared away by the Lithuanians and the pools of blood were washed away with water from a hose. Upon asking where the bodies were being taken to, I learned that they were being taken to the cemetery. I saw the Lithuanians take hold of the bodies by their hands and legs and drag them away. Afterwards another group of offenders was herded and pushed on to the square and without further ado simply beaten to death by the civilians armed with iron bars. I watched as a group of offenders were beaten to death and then had to look away because I could not watch any longer. These actions seemed extremely cruel and brutal. A great many Ger-man soldiers as well as Lithuanians watched these people being beaten to death. The soldiers did not express assent or disapprobation for what was happening. They did not interfere one way or the other. The Lithuanian civilians could be heard shouting out their approval and goading the men on.

Report of a further member of 562nd Bakers' Company:

In the middle of the square there was a depression in the ground where cars were washed. From the side a man was spraying water on to the people lying on the ground. When they managed to raise themselves slightly they were once again beaten with an iron object. I then saw that they were being beaten with spring-plates.

I . . . arrived when the people were lying on the ground and were being sprayed with water. Then they carried away the bodies and then it all started over again. The new victims came from the group of seventy men who carried away the bodies. They had to line up in a semicircle round the dip in the ground. They were then beaten from all sides. There may have been six people doing the beating. . . . Naturally I asked who the men doing the beating were. Apparently they were Latvian [sic] freedom fighters. I could not comprehend this. The people who were making sure no one entered the square were wearing armbands and carried carbines. At no time were any shots fired. Standing round the square were members of the Wehrmacht, like me. We could not believe what was happening and after some time we went away.

I could only watch the incident up to when the next group of people were beaten to death. Then I had to leave the square because I could not watch any more. My friends left with me.

Report of a medical orderly:

About 150 m from my quarters there was a fort. Looking at the map I think it must have been Fort VII, although up to now I had always thought that there was only one fort in Kovno. From our quarters my mates and I heard shots during the night. The next day and the days after that we went to investigate the matter, climbed on to the ramparts of the fort and saw a crowd of people below us guarded by armed SS or SD men. The guards were all German; there were no Lithuanians. During one of these visits the technical inspector, whose name I do not remember, took these pictures with his camera. . . . At

Kaunas: Fort VII. Three thousand Jews were executed by firing-squad here

that time we didn't see any shootings during the day. We heard that these shootings took place at night. During the day the people – men, women and children – were brought from Kovno to this fort. If I remember correctly they were all Jews, at least, they were the only ones that were talked about.

The bodies were thrown into a large crater that had a diameter of 15 m and was, I should think, about 3–4 metres deep. Each layer of bodies was covered with chloride of lime. People used to say that the next group of Jews always had to throw the last lot to be shot into the crater and cover them with sand. I only went up to this crater once but couldn't see any bodies because everything was covered with sand.

On one of my wanderings through the fort I lost my way as I was not sure where the entrances were. On this occasion a Jewish woman of about thirty ran across my path. She had been shot through both cheeks and the wounds had swollen up considerably. Seeing the red cross on my armband she begged me for a bandage, which I wanted to give her. I was just busy getting the pack of dressings I'd brought with me out of my jacket when an SS or SD guard with a rifle came up to me and told me to make myself scarce, saying that the Jewess had no further need of a pack of dressings. The Jewish woman was then pushed back by the uniformed German.

I was very shaken by this experience and told my colleagues about it – they were shaken too. It would have been pointless and dangerous for me to have disobeyed the SS man – they were very ruthless. He threatened to shoot me down if I didn't get on my way. During my visits to the fort I estimate I saw at least 2,000 people of different ages, both male and female, who were all destined to be shot and indeed certainly were. The people in the pictures are only a small proportion of those shot.

3. 'If they get their revenge, we're in for a hard time'

Soldiers from a motorized column watch a massacre in Paneriai, Lithuania

A driver's statement:

I cannot say whether we arrived in Paneriai on 5 or 10 July 1941. . . . While we were repairing our vehicles – I can no longer tell whether it was on the first or second day of our stay there – I suddenly saw a column of about four hundred men walking along the road into the pine wood. They were coming from the direction of Vilna [Vilnius]. The column, which consisted exclusively of men aged between twenty-five and sixty, was led into the wood by a guard of Lithuanian civilians. The Lithuanians were armed with carbines. The people were fully dressed and carried only the barest essentials on them. As I remember, the guards wore armbands, the colour of which I can no longer recall. I do remember that Hamann and, I think, Hechinger went off after the column. About an hour later Hamann returned to our quarters. He was very pale and told me in an agitated manner what he had witnessed in the wood. His actual words were: 'You know the Jews you saw marching past before? Not one of them is still alive.' I said that this couldn't be the case, whereupon he explained to me that all the men had been shot. Any of them that weren't dead after the shooting had been given the *coup de grâce*. . . .

The very next day – I think it was around lunchtime – once again I saw a group of four hundred Jews coming from the direction of Vilna going into the same wood. These too were accompanied by armed civilians. The delinquents were very quiet. I saw no women and children in either of the two groups.

Together with some of my colleagues from my motorized column I followed this second group. As I recall, the NCOs Riedl, Dietrich, Schroff, Hamann, Locher, Ammann, Greule and possibly some others whom I can no longer remember came with us. After we had followed the group for about eight hundred to a thousand metres we came upon two fairly large sandpits. The path we had taken ran between them both. The pits were not joined but were separated by the path and a strip of land. We overtook the column just before we reached the pits and then stopped close to the entry to one of them (the one on the right). I myself stood about six to eight metres from the entry. To the left and right of the entry stood an armed civilian. The people were then led into the gravel [*sic*] pit in small groups to the right by the guards. Running round the edge of the pit there was a circular ditch which the Jews had to climb down into.

This ditch was about 1·5 metres deep and about the same again in width. Since the ground was almost pure sand the ditch was braced with planks. As the Jews were being led in groups into the pit an elderly man stopped in front of the entrance for a moment and said in good German, 'What do you want from me? I'm only a poor composer.' The two civilians standing at the entrance started pummelling him with blows so that he literally flew into the pit. After a short time the Jews had all been herded into the circular trench. My mates and I had moved up close to the entry to the pit from where we could see clearly that the people in the ditch were being beaten with clubs by the guards, who were standing at the side of the trench. After this ten men were slowly led out from the ditch. These men had already bared their upper torsos and covered their heads with their clothes. . . .

I would also like to add that on the way to the execution area the delinquents had to walk one behind the other and hold on to the upper body of the man in front. After the group had lined up at the

execution area, the next group was led across. The firing squad, which was made up of ten men, positioned itself at the side of the path, about six to eight metres in front of the group. After this, as far as I recall, the group was shot by the firing squad after the order was given. The shots were fired simultaneously so that the men fell into the pit behind them at the same time. The 400 Jews were shot in exactly the same way over a period of about an hour. The shooting happened very quickly. If any of the men in the pit were still moving a few more single shots were fired on them. The pit into which the men fell had a diameter of about fifteen to twenty metres and was I think five to six metres deep.

From our vantage point we could see into the pit and were therefore able to confirm that the (approximately) 400 Jews who had been shot the previous day were also in there. They were covered with a thin sprinkling of sand. Right on top, on this layer of sand, there were a further three men and a woman who had been shot on the morning of the day in question. Parts of their bodies protruded out of the sand. After about one hundred Jews had been shot, other Jews had to sprinkle sand over their bodies. After the entire group had been executed the firing-squad put their rifles to one side.

This gave me an opportunity to talk to one of them. I asked him whether he could really do such a thing just like that, and pointed out that the Jews had done nothing to him. To this he answered, 'Yes – after what we've gone through under the domination of Russian Jewish Commissars, after the Russians invaded Lithuania . . . [1940 – Ed.], we no longer find it difficult.' During the course of our conversation he told me that he had been suspected of spying by the Russians. He had been arrested and had been thrown in and out of various GPU prisons, although he was in no way guilty. He told me he had only been a lorry-driver and had never harmed a soul. One of the methods they used to make him confess was to tear out his fingernails. He told me that each of the guards present had had to endure the most extreme suffering. He went on to tell me that a Jewish Commissar had broken into a flat, tied up a man and raped his wife before the man's very eyes. Afterwards the Commissar had literally butchered the wife to death, cut out her heart, fried it in a pan and had then proceeded to eat it. I was also told by comrades that in Vilna a German soldier had been shot dead from a church tower. For this another 300–400 Jews were executed in the same quarry. In this connection, I would also like to say that the very next day once again about the same number of Jews were led along the road into the wood. Apart from that one day I did not go to the execution area again. . . .

I can only say that the mass shootings in Paneriai were quite horrific. At the time I said: 'May God grant us victory because if they get their revenge, we're in for a hard time.'

Co-driver's statement:

As already mentioned, we arrived in Paneriai one afternoon in the first week of July 1941. The next day we heard rifle and machine-gun fire coming from the woods to the south of Paneriai. Since we were behind the front we wanted to get to the bottom of the matter. I can no longer remember now exactly whether it was during the morning or in the early afternoon that we went off to find out where the shooting was coming from. Anyway, I set off with Greule, Höding, Wahl and Schroff, who were all members of my unit, in the direction of the woods where the shooting was coming from.

When we arrived at the spot, we saw people, who we subsequently learned from the leader of the squad were Lithuanians, in the act of carrying out mass shootings of Jews. On the path which ran between the two pits there was a light-machine-gun, pointing to the left, being used by the Lithuanians. In front of the machine-gun, standing by the edge of the pit, were ten delinquents, who were shot with the machine-gun straight into the pit. I actually looked into the pit and saw that the bottom was already covered with bodies. . . .

In the ditch that had been excavated on the other side of this execution area were the Jews who had not yet been shot. They were all men of different ages. I saw that they had to take off their shoes and shirts and throw them on to the side of the trench. The Lithuanians standing above were rummaging through these things. I also noticed that at one spot in front of the ditch there was a big mountain of shoes and clothes. While the Jews in the trench were getting undressed the Lithuanians beat them with heavy truncheons and rifle-butts. They were then led out of the trench ten at a time to stand in front of the machine-gun.

The leader of the Lithuanians spoke good German and we went up to him and asked what was going on, saying that this was a downright disgrace. He explained to us that he had once been a teacher at a German school in Königsberg. For this the 'Bolsheviks' had torn out his fingernails. Moreover, some of the members of the immediate family – parents, brothers and sisters – of this young Lithuanian who was doing the shooting had been captured at the station by the Bolsheviks before the arrival of the German troops and were to have been transported to Siberia. The transport did not take place because of the arrival of the German soldiers. As a result, all the people who were locked up in the wagons starved to death. Why they were now shooting these Jews, if indeed this Lithuanian's story corresponded with the truth, which I found highly improbable, and whether these particular Jews were the ones who had been involved in that action, he did not tell us. . . .

On one of the last days – it was the third or fourth day of our stay in Paneriai, I can no longer remember exactly now – I went to the execution site once again. If I recall correctly, no more shooting could be heard that day and I wanted to look at the place again. I do not remember who went with me. When I reached the execution area there was a man in a grey uniform standing on the path between the two pits who had been gesturing at us to keep away from a long way off. We kept going, however, and when we got close to him I said to him that there was no need to make such a fuss, as we had already seen everything. As we approached I saw that he was wearing a dark-coloured band on his left forearm with the letters 'SD' embroidered on it. I now saw that slightly to one side there was a coach with two horses, a landau. On the box of the coach stood a second SD man whom I did not look at more closely. In the coach sat two very well-dressed elderly Jews. I had the impression that these were high-class or important people. I inferred this because they looked very well groomed and intelligent and 'ordinary Jews' would certainly not have been transported in a coach. The two Jews had to climb out and I saw that both were shaking dreadfully. They apparently knew what was in store for them. The SS man who had initially gestured to us to keep away was carrying a sub-machine-gun. He made the two Jews go and stand at the edge of the pit and shot both of them in the back of the head, so that they fell in. I can still remember that one of them was carrying a towel and a soapbox, which afterwards also lay in the trench. . . .

I would also like to say that we all said to one another what on earth would happen if we lost the war and had to pay for all this.

A book-keeper's statement:

At about 3.00 in the afternoon on the day after our arrival, Wahl, a member of our unit, came up to me and said that a large column of Jews from Vilna had been sent down to Paneriai. We went to the road and I saw a fairly large column of civilians marching from the north, from the direction of Vilna. As I recall, they were walking four abreast and I estimated that there were at least three hundred of them. They were all men aged between about twenty and fifty. There were no women and children. These prisoners were really quite well dressed and most of them were carrying hand-luggage such as small suitcases, parcels and bundles. . . .

Out of curiosity and to find out if there was a camp close by, Wahl, Corporal Dietrich and some other men from our unit – there must have been about five of us – set off about thirty or forty metres behind the column. . . . After we had walked for about ten to fifteen minutes – I would say we had not gone more than 1 kilometre into the wood – we came to a clearing which looked like a building site. I later learned – I no longer remember from whom – that this building site was the work of the Russians, who had been planning to build a petrol warehouse on it.

From where I was standing . . . in between the other men I took a photograph of a part of the trench with the Jews inside (picture 1). I watched the first ten Jews being led out of the trench. One of the guards held out a club to one side which the first Jew had to hold on to with both hands. The other nine walked one behind the other, stooping and holding on to the man in front with their hands because they could not see. The guard led these ten Jews to the path where they slid down the steep embankment. Some of them lost their footing and fell. When they reached the bottom of the pit they had to line up as before and were then led by the guard to the semicircular embankment of the trench on the east side. I also photographed this situation from where I was standing (picture 2).

The Jews then had to get into a line side by side with their backs to the machine-gun on the path. The guards stepped back a little or moved a little to one side and the order to fire was given in Lithuanian by one of the guards, whereupon the machine-gun started firing. The ten Jews keeled over and those of them not killed by the machine-gun fire were finished off with a bullet in the head by one of the guards.

Exactly the same procedure was followed as each group of ten Jews was led to the execution point and shot. We stayed there for about one hour and during this time some four to five groups were executed, so I myself watched the killing of about forty to fifty Jews.

4. 'Total 137,346'

The so-called 'Jäger Report'*

The Commander of
the Security Police and
the SD
Einsatzkommando 3   Kauen [Kaunas], 1 December 1941

Secret Reich Business!	5 copies
	4th copy

<u>Complete List of Executions Carried Out in the EK 3 Area
up to 1 December 1941.</u>

Security police duties in Lithuania taken over by Einsatzkommando 3
on 2 July 1941.
  (The Wilna [Vilnius] area was taken over by EK 3 on 9 Aug. 1941,
the Schaulen area on 2 Oct. 1941. Up until these dates EK 9 operated
in Wilna and EK 2 in Schaulen.)
  On my instructions and orders the following executions were conducted by Lithuanian partisans:

4.7.41	Kauen–Fort VII – 416 Jews, 47 Jewesses	463
6.7.41	Kauen–Fort VII – Jews	2,514

Following the formation of a raiding squad under the command of SS-
Obersturmführer Hamann and 8–10 reliable men from the Einsatzkommando the following actions were conducted in cooperation
with Lithuanian partisans:

7.7.41	Mariampole	Jews	32
8.7.41	Mariampole	14 Jews, 5 Comm. officials	19
8.7.41	Girkalinei	Comm. officials	6

*The name 'Jäger' means 'hunter' in German.

46

9.7.41	Wendziogala	32 Jews, 2 Jewesses, 1 Lithuanian (f.), 2 Lith. Comm., 1 Russ. Comm.	38
9.7.41	Kauen–Fort VII –	21 Jews, 3 Jewesses	24
14.7.41	Mariampole	21 Jews, 1 Russ., 9 Lith. Comm.	31
17.7.41	Babtei	8 Comm. officials (inc. 6 Jews)	8
18.7.41	Mariampole	39 Jews, 14 Jewesses	53
19.7.41	Kauen–Fort VII –	17 Jews, 2 Jewesses, 4 Lith. Comm., 2 Comm. Lithuanians (f.), 1 German Comm.	26
21.7.41	Panevezys	59 Jews, 11 Jewesses, 1 Lithuanian (f.) 1 Pole, 22 Lith. Comm., 9 Russ. Comm.	103
22.7.41	Panevezys	1 Jew	1
23.7.41	Kedainiai	83 Jews, 12 Jewesses, 14 Russ. Comm., 15 Lith. Comm., 1 Russ. O-Politruk	125
25.7.41	Mariampole	90 Jews, 13 Jewesses	103
28.7.41	Panevezys	234 Jews, 15 Jewesses, 19 Russ. Comm., 20 Lith. Communists	288
		Total carried forward	3,834

Sheet 2

		Total carried over:	3,834
29.7.41	Rasainiai	254 Jews, 3 Lith. Communists	257
30.7.41	Agriogala	27 Jews, 11 Lith. Communists	38
31.7.41	Utena	235 Jews, 16 Jewesses, 4 Lith. Comm., 1 robber/ murderer	256
11/31.7.41	Wendziogala	13 Jews, 2 murderers	15

August:

1.8.41	Ukmerge	254 Jews, 42 Jewesses, 1 Pol. Comm., 2 Lith. NKVD	

		agents, 1 mayor of Jonava who gave order to set fire to Jonava	300
2.8.41	Kauen–Fort IV	170 Jews, 1 US Jew, 1 US Jewess, 33 Jewesses, 4 Lith. Communists	209
4.8.41	Panevezys	362 Jews, 41 Jewesses, 5 Russ. Comm., 14 Lith. Communists	422
5.8.41	Rasainiai	213 Jews, 66 Jewesses	279
7.8.41	Uteba	483 Jews, 87 Jewesses, 1 Lithuanian (robber of corpses of German soldiers)	571
8.8.41	Ukmerge	620 Jews, 82 Jewesses	702
9.8.41	Kauen–Fort IV	484 Jews, 50 Jewesses	534
11.8.41	Panevezys	450 Jews, 48 Jewesses, 1 Lith., 1 Russ. C.	500
13.8.41	Alytus	617 Jews, 100 Jewesses, 1 criminal	719
14.8.41	Jonava	497 Jews, 55 Jewesses	552
15 and 16.8.41	Rokiskis	3,200 Jews, Jewesses and J. children, 5 Lith. Comm., 1 Pole, 1 partisan	3,207
9 to 16.8.41	Rassainiai	294 Jewesses, 4 Jewish children	298
27.6 to 14.8.41	Rokiskis	493 Jews, 432 Russians, 56 Lithuanians (all active Communists)	981

During his sermon Jonas Gylys said, 'Like executioners they beat innocent people, punching elderly and pregnant women. Innocent people suffered like Christ at the hands of Judas. Before their blood had even had time to dry they robbed them of their property.' The priest's words were apparently directed at those who had been involved in liquidating the Jews. Characteristically, G. went to visit the Jews held in the synagogue, without any authorization, to give them solace and courage.

From: *Ereignismeldung UdSSR*, No. 130, 7 November 1941

18.8.41	Kauen–Fort IV	689 Jews, 402 Jewesses, 1 Pole (f.), 711 Jewish intellectuals from ghetto in reprisal for sabotage action	1,812
19.8.41	Ukmerge	298 Jews, 255 Jewesses, 1 Politruk, 88 Jewish children, 1 Russ. Communist	645
22.8.41	Dünaburg	3 Russ. Comm., 5 Latvians, incl. 1 murderer, 1 Russ. guardsman, 3 Poles, 3 gypsies (m.), 1 gypsy (f.), 1 gypsy child, 1 Jew, 1 Jewess, 1 Armenian (m.), 2 Politruks (prison inspection in Dünaburg)	21
		Total carried forward	16,152

Sheet 3

		Total carried forward	16,152
22.8.41	Aglona	Mentally sick: 269 men, 227 women, 48 children	544
23.8.41	Panevezys	1,312 Jews, 4,602 Jewesses, 1,609 Jewish children	7,523
18 to 22.8.41	Kreis Rasainiai	466 Jews, 440 Jewesses, 1,020 Jewish children	1,926
25.8.41	Obeliai	112 Jews, 627 Jewesses, 421 Jewish children	1,160
25 and 26.8.41	Seduva	230 Jews, 275 Jewesses, 159 Jewish children	664
26.8.41	Zarasai	767 Jews, 1,113 Jewesses, 1 Lith. Comm., 687 Jewish children, 1 Russ. Communist (f.)	2,569
26.8.41	Pasvalys	402 Jews, 738 Jewesses, 209 Jewish children	1,349
26.8.41	Kaisiadorys	All Jews, Jewesses and Jewish children	1,911
27.8.41	Prienai	All Jews, Jewesses and Jewish children	1,078

27.8.41	Dagda and Kraslawa	212 Jews, 4 Russ. POWs	216
27.8.41	Joniskis	47 Jews, 165 Jewesses, 143 Jewish children	355
28.8.41	Wilkia	76 Jews, 192 Jewesses, 134 Jewish children	402
28.8.41	Kedainiai	710 Jews, 767 Jewesses, 599 Jewish children	2,076
29.8.41	Rumsiskis and Ziezmariai	20 Jews, 567 Jewesses, 197 Jewish children	784
29.8.41	Utena and Moletai	582 Jews, 1,731 Jewesses, 1,469 Jewish children	3,782
13 to 31.8.41	Alytus and environs	233 Jews	233

September:

| 1.9.41 | Mariampole | 1,763 Jews, 1,812 Jewesses, 1,404 Jewish children, 109 mentally sick, 1 German subject (f.), married to a Jew, 1 Russian (f.) | 5,090 |
| | | Total carried over | 47,814 |

Sheet 4

		Total carried over	47,814
28.8 to 2.9.41	Darsuniskis	10 Jews, 69 Jewesses, 20 Jewish children	99
	Carliava	73 Jews, 113 Jewesses, 61 Jewish children	247
	Jonava	112 Jews, 1,200 Jewesses, 244 Jewish children	1,556
	Petrasiunai	30 Jews, 72 Jewesses, 23 Jewish children	125
	Jesuas	26 Jews, 72 Jewesses, 46 Jewish children	144
	Ariogala	207 Jews, 260 Jewesses, 195 Jewish children	662
	Jasvainai	86 Jews, 110 Jewesses, 86 Jewish children	282

	Babtei	20 Jews, 41 Jewesses, 22 Jewish children	83
	Wenziogala	42 Jews, 113 Jewesses, 97 Jewish children	252
	Krakes	448 Jews, 476 Jewesses, 201 Jewish children	1,125
4.9.41	Pravenischkis	247 Jews, 6 Jewesses . . .	253
4.9.41	Cekiske	22 Jews, 64 Jewesses, 60 Jewish children	146
	Seredsius	6 Jews, 61 Jewesses, 126 Jewish children	193
	Velinona	2 Jews, 71 Jewesses, 86 Jewish children	159
	Zapiskis	47 Jews, 118 Jewesses, 13 Jewish children	178
5.9.41	Ukmerge	1,123 Jews, 1,849 Jewesses, 1,737 Jewish children	4,709
25.8 to 6.9.41	Mopping up in Rasainiai	16 Jews, 412 Jewesses, 415 Jewish children	843
	in Georgenburg	all Jews, all Jewesses, all Jewish children	412
9.9.41	Alytus	287 Jews, 640 Jewesses, 352 Jewish children	1,279
9.9.41	Butrimonys	67 Jews, 370 Jewesses, 303 Jewish children	740
10.9.41	Merkine	223 Jews, 355 Jewesses, 276 Jewish children	854
10.9.41	Varena	541 Jews, 141 Jewesses, 149 Jewish children	831
11.9.41	Leipalingis	60 Jews, 70 Jewesses, 25 Jewish children	155
11.9.41	Seirijai	229 Jews, 384 Jewesses, 340 Jewish children	953
12.9.41	Simnas	68 Jews, 197 Jewesses, 149 Jewish children	414
11 and 12.9.41	Uzusalis	Reprisal against inhabitants who fed Russ. partisans; some in possession of weapons	43
26.9.41	Kauen-F.IV	412 Jews, 615 Jewesses, 581 Jewish children (sick and suspected epidemic cases)	1,608
		Total carried over	66,159

		Total carried over	66,159
October:			
2.10.41	Zagare	633 Jews, 1,107 Jewesses, 496 Jewish chil. (as these Jews were being led away a mutiny arose, which was however immediately put down; 150 Jews were shot immediately; 7 partisans wounded)	2,236
4.10.41	Kauen–F.IX –	315 Jews, 712 Jewesses, 818 Jewish children (Reprisal after German police officer shot in ghetto)	1,845
29.10.41	Kauen–F.IX –	2,007 Jews, 2,920 Jewesses, 4,273 Jewish children (mopping up ghetto of superfluous Jews)	9,200
	November:		
3.11.41	Lazdijai	485 Jews, 511 Jewesses, 539 Jewish children	1,535
15.11.41	Wilkowiski	36 Jews, 48 Jewesses, 31 Jewish children	115
25.11.41	Kauen–F.IX –	1,159 Jews, 1,600 Jewesses, 175 Jewish children (resettlers from Berlin, Munich and Frankfurt am Main)	2,934
29.11.41	Kauen–F.IX –	693 Jews, 1,155 Jewesses, 152 Jewish children (resettlers from Vienna and Breslau)	2,000
29.11.41	Kauen–F.IX –	17 Jews, 1 Jewess, for contravention of ghetto law, 1 Reichs German who converted to Jewish faith and attended rabbinical school, then 15 terrorists from the Kalinin Group	34
EK 3 detachment in Dünaberg in the period 13.7–21.8.41:		9,012 Jews, Jewesses and Jewish children, 573 active Communists	9,585

EK 3 detachment in Wilna:

12.8 to 1.9.41	City of Wilna	425 Jews, 19 Jewesses, 8 Communists (m.), 9 Communists (f.)	461
2.9.41	City of Wilna	864 Jews, 2,019 Jewesses, 817 Jewish children (*Sonderaktion* because German soldiers shot at by Jews)	3,700
		Total carried forward	99,804

Sheet 6

		Total carried forward	99,804
12.9.41	City of Wilna	993 Jews, 1,670 Jewesses, 771 Jewish children	3,334
17.9.41	City of Wilna	337 Jews, 687 Jewesses, 247 Jewish children and 4 Lith. Communists	1,271
20.9.41	Nemencing	128 Jews, 176 Jewesses, 99 Jewish children	403
22.9.41	Novo-Wilejka	468 Jews, 495 Jewesses, 196 Jewish children	1,159
24.9.41	Riesa	512 Jews, 744 Jewesses, 511 Jewish children	1,767
25.9.41	Jahiunai	215 Jews, 229 Jewesses, 131 Jewish children	575
27.9.41	Eysisky	989 Jews, 1,636 Jewesses, 821 Jewish children	3,446
30.9.41	Trakai	366 Jews, 483 Jewesses, 597 Jewish children	1,446
4.10.41	City of Wilna	432 Jews, 1,115 Jewesses, 436 Jewish children	1,983
6.10.41	Semiliski	213 Jews, 359 Jewesses, 390 Jewish children	962
9.10.41	Svenciany	1,169 Jews, 1,840 Jewesses, 717 Jewish children	3,726
16.10.41	City of Wilna	382 Jews, 507 Jewesses, 257 Jewish children	1,146
21.10.41	City of Wilna	718 Jews, 1,063 Jewesses, 586 Jewish children	2,367

25.10.41	City of Wilna	– Jews, 1,766 Jewesses, 812 Jewish children	2,578
27.10.41	City of Wilna	946 Jews, 184 Jewesses, 73 Jewish children	1,203
30.10.41	City of Wilna	382 Jews, 789 Jewesses, 362 Jewish children	1,533
6.11.41	City of Wilna	340 Jews, 749 Jewesses, 252 Jewish children	1,341
19.11.41	City of Wilna	76 Jews, 77 Jewesses, 18 Jewish children	171
19.11.41	City of Wilna	6 POWs, 8 Poles	14
20.11.41	City of Wilna	3 POWs	3
25.11.41	City of Wilna	9 Jews, 46 Jewesses, 8 Jewish children, 1 Pole for possession of arms and other military equipment	64

EK 3 detachment in Minsk from 28.9–17.10.41:

| Pleschnitza, Bischolin, Scak, Bober, Uzda | 620 Jews, 1,285 Jewesses, 1,126 Jewish children and 19 Communists | 3,050 |

| | | 133,346 |

Prior to EK 3 taking over security police duties, Jews liquidated by pogroms and executions (excluding partisans) 4,000

| | Total | 137,346 |

Sheet 7

Today I can confirm that our objective, to solve the Jewish problem for Lithuania, has been achieved by EK 3. In Lithuania there are no more Jews, apart from Jewish workers and their families.
These total:

In Schaulen	c. 4,500
In Kauen	c.15,000
In Wilna	c.15,000

I also intended to kill these Jewish workers plus their families but

Lithuania, summer 1941. Male and female Jews are made to dig a mass grave in a woodland clearing. In the foreground, Jews who have been shot

came up against strong protests on the part of the civil administration (the Reichskommissar) and the Wehrmacht and instructions were issued that these Jews and their families were not to be executed.

It was only possible to achieve our objective of making Lithuania free from Jews by forming a raiding squad consisting of specially selected men led by SS-Obersturmführer Hamann, who grasped my aims completely and understood the importance of ensuring cooperation with the Lithuanian partisans and the relevant civilian authorities.

The execution of such actions is first and foremost a matter of organization. The decision to clear each district of Jews systematically required a thorough preparation of each individual action and a reconnaissance of the prevailing conditions in the district concerned. The Jews had to be assembled at one or several places. Depending on the number of Jews a place for the graves had to be found and then the graves dug. The distance from the assembly point to the graves was on average 4 to 5 km. The Jews were transported in detachments of 500 to the execution area, with a distance of at least 2 km between them. The following example, selected at random, demonstrates the difficulties and the acutely stressful nature of the work:

In Rokiskis 3,208 people had to be transported 4½ km before they could be liquidated. In order to get this work done within 24 hours,

over sixty of the eighty available Lithuanian partisans had to be detailed for cordon duty. The rest, who had to be relieved constantly, carried out the work together with my men. Lorries are only very occasionally available for transporting the Jews. There were a number of escape attempts, which were thwarted single-handedly by my men, whose own lives were at risk. Three men from the Kommando at Mariampole, for example, shot thirty-eight escaping Jews and Communist officials on a path in a wood, with the result that none of them managed to escape. The marching distance to and from each individual action totalled 160–200 km. It was only through the efficient use of time that it was possible to carry out up to five actions per week while still coping with any work that arose in Kauen, so that no backlog was allowed to build up.

The actions in Kauen itself, where there was an adequate number of reasonably well-trained partisans available, were like parade-ground shooting in comparison with the often enormous difficulties which had to be faced elsewhere.

All the officers and men in my Kommando took an active part in the major actions in Kauen, except for an official from the criminal detection department, who was exempted owing to illness.

I consider the Jewish action more or less terminated as far as Einsatzkommando 3 is concerned. Those working Jews and Jewesses still available are needed urgently and I can envisage that after the winter this workforce will be required even more urgently. I am of the view that the sterilization programme of the male worker Jews should be started immediately so that reproduction is prevented. If despite sterilization a Jewess becomes pregnant she will be liquidated.

One of Einsatzkommando 3's most important duties, after the Jewish actions, was to inspect the prisons in each village and town, most of which proved to be overcrowded. In every town there were on average about 600 people of Lithuanian origin held in prison without any real reason. These people had been detained by partisans merely on the basis of denunciations. Many personal scores had been settled in the process. Nobody cared what became of them. You had to visit the prisons and stop for just a moment in the overcrowded cells, which as far as hygiene was concerned defied description, to believe the

---

conditions there. In Jonava – and this is one example among many – sixteen men were kept in a dark room in a cellar 3 m long, 3 m wide and 1·65 m high for five weeks. They could all have been released since there were no charges against them. Girls aged between thirteen and sixteen were incarcerated because they had applied to join the Communist youth in order to get work. In such cases we had to take quite radical measures to hammer the message home into the heads of the relevant Lithuanian authorities. The prisoners were assembled in the prison yard and checked off against lists and documents. Those who had been locked up on spurious charges as a result of quite harmless behaviour were put in a special group. Those whom we sentenced to one to three months and six months for their crimes were also separated into a special group, and those that were to be liquidated, such as criminals, Communist officials, Politruks and other riff-raff, were put into another group. Some of them, depending on their crime, particularly the Communist officials, received an additional punishment of ten to forty lashes with the whip which was meted out immediately. After the inspection was over the prisoners were led back to their cells. Those that were to be freed were led to the market-place in a column where, after a short address in the presence of many inhabitants, they were set free. The content of the speech (it was translated sentence by sentence by an interpreter into Lithuanian and Russian) was as follows: 'If we were Bolsheviks we would have shot you, but as we are Germans we are giving you back your freedom.'

The prisoners were then warned that they were to steer clear of any political activity, that they should report any subversive activities which came to their notice to the German authorities. They were also urged to take part actively in rebuilding local agriculture. They were

---

'I was always a person with a heightened sense of duty . . .'

Former SS-Standartenführer Karl Jäger after his arrest

57

finally warned that should one of them be found guilty again of a crime he would be shot. They were then released.

It is difficult to imagine the joy, gratitude and delight our measures awoke in those released and indeed in the local population. We often had to use sharp words to cool the enthusiasm of women, children and men who with tears in their eyes tried to kiss our hands and feet.

(signed) Jäger
SS-Standartenführer

'Pushed to their psychological limits'

Members of the Einsatzgruppen on the stresses
and strains of killing

1. 'If the victims didn't do as they were told ...'
Problems during mass shootings

Affidavit of Otto Ohlendorf, Head of Einsatzgruppe D:

The Einsatzgruppen and Einsatzkommandos were led by personnel from the Gestapo, the SD or the Kriminalpolizei. Additional men were recruited from the Ordnungspolizei and the Waffen-SS. Einsatzgruppe D consisted of some 400 to 500 men and had about 170 vehicles at its disposal. When the German army advanced into Russia I was the commander of Einsatzgruppe D in the southern sector and during the year that it was under my command it liquidated about 90,000 men, women and children. The majority of those liquidated were Jews but there were also some Communist officials amongst them. For the purpose of carrying out this extermination programme the Einsatzgruppen were subdivided into Einsatzkommandos and these Einsatzkommandos subdivided into smaller units: the so-called Sonderkommandos and Teilkommandos. Generally the smaller units were commanded by members of the SD, the Gestapo or the Kriminalpolizei. . . . In Einsatzgruppe D I never sanctioned shootings by individuals. I always gave orders for several people to shoot simultaneously, in order to avoid any individual having to take direct, personal responsibility.

I would also like to mention that as a result of the considerable psychological pressures, there were numerous men who were no longer capable of conducting executions and who thus had to be replaced by other men. On the other hand, there were others who could not get enough of them and often reported to these executions voluntarily.

Gustave Fix, member of Sonderkommando 6

Statement of Schutzpolizist Tögel, member of Einsatzkommando 10a:

One further incident I remember was a large-scale execution by firing-squad which took place at a well on the way to Kachowka. There was a hole in the steppe measuring about six to seven metres on the upper edge. Near by there were piles of grain in rows.

The grain may have been haystacks or rings of sheaves drying out or something else. We Schutzpolizisten were driven to this well in troop carriers. There was not a village in sight for miles. There was not even a barn in the vicinity. The victims – several hundred, or even a thousand, men and women – were transported in trucks. I cannot recall whether there were any children. These people were made to lie or kneel about a hundred metres from the well in a depression which had been hollowed out by the rain and remove their outer garments there. They were lined up ten at a time at the side of the well and were then shot by a ten-man execution squad, which included myself. When they were shot the people fell forwards into the well. Sometimes they were so frightened that they jumped in alive. The firing-squad was switched a great many times. Because of the psychological pressures to which I too was exposed during the shooting I can no longer say today, try as I might, how many times I stood by the hole and how many times I was relieved from that duty.

Obviously these shootings did not proceed in the calm manner in which one can discuss them today. The women screamed and wept and so did the men. Sometimes people tried to escape. The people whose job it was to get them to stand by the well yelled equally loudly. If the victims didn't do as they were told there were also beatings. I particularly remember a red-haired SD man who had a length of cable on him with which he used to beat the people when the action was not going as it should. Many, however, came without resistance to the execution area. It is not as though they had any alternative. . . .

All the men coped with the tough physical stress well. No less considerable were the extreme psychological demands made on them by the large number of liquidations. The morale and self-possession of the men was kept up by personally reminding them constantly of the political necessity [of what they were doing].

Tätigkeits- und Lagebericht, No. 1, 31 July 1941

The firing-squad at the well consisted of Schutzpolizisten, Waffen-SS personnel and members of the SD. We Schutzpolizisten used our own carbines, the SD men used sub-machine-guns and pistols. At any rate everyone used his own weapon. All the ammunition we needed was kept ready in boxes. The execution area was a terrible sight. The ground round the well was covered in blood; there were also bits of brain on the ground which the victims had to step in when they were brought over. But it wasn't at that point that they first realized what lay ahead for them. They could already hear the shooting and screaming from the place where they were kept waiting. . . .

It took barely an afternoon before the last victim was in the well. Something I still remember clearly about this execution is that afterwards the SD people got drunk, so they must have received a special ration of schnapps. We Schutzpolizisten did not receive anything and I remember that we were very angry about that.

Statement of teleprinter engineer Kiebach, Einsatzgruppe C:

In Rovno I had to participate in the first shooting. . . . Each member of the firing-squad had to shoot one person. We were instructed to aim at the head from a distance of about ten metres. I can no longer say today who gave the order to fire. At any rate it was a staff officer. There were a number of staff officers present at the shooting. The order to fire was 'Ready to shoot, aim, fire!' The people who had been shot then fell into the grave. I myself was detailed to the firing-squad; however, I only managed to shoot about five times. I began to feel unwell, I felt as though I was in a dream. Afterwards I was laughed at because I couldn't shoot any more. A private or lance-corporal from the Wehrmacht, I don't know which unit, took my carbine from me and went and took my place in the firing-squad.

I went and stood about fifty metres away from the firing-squad. It was obvious that I was in no state to go on shooting. The nervous strain was too great for me. When I am asked whether I was reprimanded for my refusal, I have to say that this was not the case.

> I still dimly recall our detachment executing fifteen to twenty Jews, including women and four or five children aged between six and nine months, on the march from Kiev to Poltava. . . . I can no longer describe the execution area today. I think that I also had to do some of the shooting, but I know for sure that I did not have to shoot any children. I still remember today one of the men saying that the children hung on to life like the adults. He must have shot children.
>
> Viktor Trill, member of Sonderkommando 4a

2. 'It took nerves of steel'

The murder of 33,771 Jews in the Babi Yar ravine (29/30 September 1941)

Statement of truck-driver Höfer:

One day I was instructed to drive my truck outside the town. I was accompanied by a Ukrainian. It must have been about 10 o'clock. On the way there we overtook Jews carrying luggage marching on foot in the same direction that we were travelling. There were whole families. The further we got out of town the denser the columns became. Piles of clothing lay in a large open field. These piles of clothing were my destination. The Ukrainian showed me how to get in there.

After we had stopped in the area near the piles of clothes the truck was immediately loaded up with clothing. This was carried out by Ukrainians. I watched what happened when the Jews – men, women and children – arrived. The Ukrainians led them past a number of different places where one after the other they had to remove their luggage, then their coats, shoes and overgarments and also underwear. They also had to leave their valuables in a designated place. There was a special pile for each article of clothing. It all happened very quickly and anyone who hesitated was kicked or pushed by the Ukrainians to keep them moving. I don't think it was even a minute from the time each Jew took off his coat before he was standing there completely naked. No distinction was made between men, women and

The ravine of Babi Yar near Kiev. Execution site

children. One would have thought that the Jews that came later would have had a chance to turn back when they saw the others in front of them having to undress. It still surprises me today that this did not happen.

> Reportedly 150,000 Jews present. Measures taken to register all Jews, execution of at least 50,000 Jews planned. Wehrmacht welcomes the measures and requests radical action.
>
> From: *Ereignismeldung UdSSR*, No. 97, 28 September 1941

Once undressed, the Jews were led into a ravine which was about 150 metres long, 30 metres wide and a good 15 metres deep. Two or three narrow entrances led to this ravine through which the Jews were channelled. When they reached the bottom of the ravine they were seized by members of the Schutzpolizei and made to lie down on top of Jews who had already been shot. This all happened very quickly. The corpses were literally in layers. A police marksman came along and shot each Jew in the neck with a sub-machine-gun at the spot where he was lying. When the Jews reached the ravine they were so shocked by the horrifying scene that they completely lost their will. It may even have been that the Jews themselves lay down in rows to wait to be shot.

There were only two marksmen carrying out the executions. One of them was working at one end of the ravine, the other at the other end. I saw these marksmen stand on the layers of corpses and shoot one after the other.

The moment one Jew had been killed, the marksman would walk across the bodies of the executed Jews to the next Jew, who had meanwhile lain down, and shoot him. It went on in this way uninterruptedly, with no distinction being made between men, women and children. The children were kept with their mothers and shot with them.

I only saw this scene briefly. When I got to the bottom of the ravine I was so shocked by the terrible sight that I could not bear to look for long. In the hollow I saw that there were already three rows of bodies lined up over a distance of about sixty metres. How many layers of bodies there were on top of each other I could not see. I was so astonished and dazed by the sight of the twitching blood-smeared bodies that I could not properly register the details. In addition to the two marksmen there was a 'packer' at either entrance to the ravine. These 'packers' were Schutzpolizisten, whose job it was to lay the

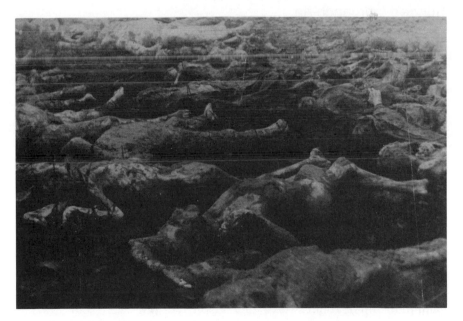

Babi Yar: exhumed corpses

victim on top of the other corpses so that all the marksman had to do as he passed was fire a shot.

When the victims came along the paths to the ravine and at the last moment saw the terrible scene they cried out in terror. But at the very next moment they were already being knocked over by the 'packers' and made to lie down with the others. The next group of people could not see this terrible scene because it took place round a corner.

Most people put up a fight when they had to undress and there was a lot of screaming and shouting. The Ukrainians did not take any notice. They just drove them down as quickly as possible into the ravine through the entrances.

From the undressing area you could not make out the ravine, which was about 150 metres away from the first pile of clothes. A biting wind was blowing; it was very cold. The shots from the ravine could not be heard at the undressing area. This is why I think the Jews did not realize in time what lay ahead of them. I still wonder today why the Jews did not try and do something about it. Masses kept on coming from the city to this place, which they apparently entered unsuspectingly, still under the impression that they were being resettled.

Statement of Kurt Werner, member of Sonderkommando 4a:

That day the entire Kommando with the exception of one guard set out at about six o'clock in the morning for these shootings. I myself went there by lorry. It was all hands to the deck. We drove for about twenty minutes in a northerly direction. We stopped on a cobbled road in the open country. The road stopped there. There were countless Jews gathered there and a place had been set up where the Jews had to hand in their clothes and their luggage. A kilometre further on I saw a large natural ravine. The terrain there was sandy. The ravine was about 10 metres deep, some 400 metres long, about 80 metres wide across the top and about 10 metres wide at the bottom.

As soon as I arrived at the execution area I was sent down to the bottom of the ravine with some of the other men. It was not long before the first Jews were brought to us over the side of the ravine. The Jews had to lie face down on the earth by the ravine walls. There were three groups of marksmen down at the bottom of the ravine, each made up of about twelve men. Groups of Jews were sent down to each of these execution squads simultaneously. Each successive group of Jews had to lie down on top of the bodies of those that had already been shot. The marksmen stood behind the Jews and killed them with a shot in the neck. I still recall today the complete terror of the Jews when they first caught sight of the bodies as they reached the top edge of the ravine. Many Jews cried out in terror. It's almost impossible to imagine what nerves of steel it took to carry out that dirty work down there. It was horrible. . . .

I had to spend the whole morning down in the ravine. For some of the time I had to shoot continuously. Then I was given the job of loading sub-machine-gun magazines with ammunition. While I was doing that, other comrades were assigned to shooting duty. Towards midday we were called away from the ravine and in the afternoon I, with some of the others up at the top, had to lead the Jews to the ravine. While we were doing this there were other men shooting down in the ravine. The Jews were led by us up to the edge of the ravine and from there they walked down the slope on their own. The shooting that day must have lasted until . . . 17.00 or 18.00 hours. Afterwards we were taken back to our quarters. That evening we were given alcohol (schnapps) again.

Anton Heidborn (Sonderkommando 4a) on the days that followed:

The third day after the execution we were taken back to the execution area. On our arrival we saw a woman sitting by a bush who had apparently survived the execution unscathed. This woman was shot by the SD man who was accompanying us. I do not know his name. We also saw someone waving their hand from among the pile of bodies. I don't know whether it was a man or a woman. I should think that this person was finished off by the SD man as well, though I did not actually see it.

67

The same day work began to cover up the piles of bodies. Civilians were used for this task. The ravine walls were also partly blown up.

After that day I never returned to the execution area. The next few days were spent smoothing out banknotes belonging to the Jews that had been shot. I estimate these must have totalled millions. I do not know what happened to the money. It was packed up in sacks and sent off somewhere.

In Kiev, difficulties that arose during the execution of a major action of this type – particularly with regard to registration – were overcome by the use of posters announcing that all Jews were to report for resettlement. Although it was initially thought that the action would only involve some 5,000 to 6,000 Jews, more than 30,000 Jews reported, who as a result of extremely efficient organization still believed they were going to be resettled right up until the time they were executed.

Despite the fact that up to now a total of some 75,000 Jews have been liquidated in this way, it has nevertheless become apparent that this method will not provide a solution to the Jewish problem.

Ereignismeldung UdSSR, No. 128, 3 November 1941

---

3. 'A new and better method of killing had to be found'

The gas-vans

Statement by August Becker, Ph.D., Gas-Van Inspector:

Until about 1941 I was involved in the euthanasia programme in Oberdienstleiter Viktor Brack's department at the Führer's Chancellery. I had been working as a specialist in the gassing processes involved in exterminating the mentally sick in the mental asylums and sanatoriums. Since this action had been suspended a short time before – I do not know why [gassings were suspended: the murders continued by means of drugs – Ed.] – I was transferred to the RSHA in

> I cannot say whether I had misgivings about the use of gas-vans. What was uppermost in my mind at the time was that the shootings were a great strain on the men involved and that this strain would be removed by the use of the gas-vans.
>
> SS-Standartenführer Walter Rauff

Berlin as a result of a private conversation between Reichsführer SS Himmler and Oberdienstleiter Brack. Himmler wanted to deploy people who had become available as a result of the suspension of the euthanasia programme, and who, like me, were specialists in extermination by gassing, for the large-scale gassing operations in the East which were just beginning. The reason for this was that the men in charge of the Einsatzgruppen in the East were increasingly complaining that the firing squads could not cope with the psychological and moral stress of the mass shootings indefinitely. I know that a number of members of these squads were themselves committed to mental asylums and for this reason a new and better method of killing had to be found. Thus in December 1941 I started working in RSHA, Amt II, in Rauff's department. . . . Rauff's deputy at the time was the then Hauptmann Pradel who later became a Major. Although Pradel also had an equivalent SS rank he called himself Major. I did not initially have any personal contact with Rauff. When in December 1941 I was transferred to Rauff's department he explained the situation to me, saying that the psychological and moral stress on the firing squads was no longer bearable and that therefore the gassing programme had been started. He said that gas-vans with drivers were already on their way to or had indeed reached the individual Einsatzgruppen. My professional brief was to inspect the work of the individual Einsatzgruppen in the East in connection with the gasvans. This meant that I had to ensure that the mass killings carried out in the lorries proceeded properly. I was to pay particular attention to the mechanical functioning of these vans. I would like to mention that there were two types of gas-vans in operation: the *Opel-Blitz*, weighing 3·5 tonnes, and the large *Saurerwagen*, which as far as I know, weighed 7 tonnes. In the middle of December 1941, on Rauff's instructions, I left for the East to catch up with Einsatzgruppe A (Riga) . . . to inspect their Einsatzwagen [special vehicles] or gasvans.

On 14 December 1941, however, I had a car accident at Deutsch-Eylau. As a result of this accident, I was sent to the Catholic Hospital in Deutsch-Eylau and following my recovery was discharged from hospital on 23 or 24 December 1941. I am sure of this because I spent Christmas with my family in Berlin.

On 4 or 5 January 1942 I received a message from Rauff asking me to report to him. On reporting to him I was instructed to depart immediately. This time I was to travel directly to Einsatzgruppe D in the south (Otto Ohlendorf) in Simferopol. I was originally to have travelled by aeroplane but this did not work out because of icy weather conditions. I thus left by train on 5 or 6 January 1942 travelling via Cracow and Fastov to Nikolayew. From there I flew in the Reichsführer's plane to Simferopol in the Crimea. The journey took me about three weeks and I reported to the head of Einsatzgruppe D, Otto Ohlendorf, sometime in January. I remained with this group until the beginning of April 1942 and then visited each Einsatzgruppe until I reached Group A in Riga.

In Riga I learned from Standartenführer Potzelt, Deputy Commander of the Security Police and SD in Riga, that the Einsatzkommando operating in Minsk needed some additional gas-vans as it could not manage with the three existing vans it had. At the same time I also learned from Potzelt that there was a Jewish-extermination camp in Minsk. I flew to Minsk by helicopter, correction, in a Fieseler Storch [light aircraft] belonging to the Einsatzgruppe. Travelling with me was Hauptsturmführer Rühl, the head of the extermination camp at Minsk, with whom I had discussed business in Riga. During the journey Rühl proposed to me that I provide additional vans since they could not keep up with the exterminations. As I was not responsible for the ordering of gas-vans I suggested Rühl approach Rauff's office.

When I saw what was going on in Minsk – that people of both sexes were being exterminated in their masses, that was it – I could not take any more and three days later, it must have been September 1942, I travelled back by lorry via Warsaw to Berlin.

I had intended to report to Rauff at his office in Berlin. However, he was not there. Instead I was received by his deputy, Pradel, who had meantime been promoted to Major. . . . In a private conversation lasting about an hour I described to Pradel the working method of the gas-vans and voiced criticism about the fact that the offenders had not been gassed but had been suffocated because the operators had set the engine incorrectly. I told him that people had vomited and defecated. Pradel listened to me without saying a word. At the end of our interview he simply told me to write a detailed report on the matter. Finally he told me to go to the cashier's office to settle up the expenses I had incurred during my trip.

Statement of Wilhelm Findeisen:

I was told that the whole operation and the van itself were secret. It was expressly forbidden to photograph the vans and I was ordered not to let anyone near the van. I then joined Sonderkommando 4 in Einsatzgruppe C. . . .

The van was not used immediately when we arrived in Kiev. When we first arrived they were only carrying out isolated actions. Being a driver, I had nothing to do with these isolated actions. One evening several officers appeared and ordered certain people to go with them. They went into a private flat where they picked up a professor and his daughter. These people were then taken to a spot close to a piece of open land where a grave was dug.

The people, i.e. the officers, then gave orders for these two people to be shot. One of the officers said to me, 'Findeisen, shoot these people in the neck.' I refused to do this as did the other men. The girl must have been about eighteen or nineteen. The officer shot the people himself as the others refused. He swore at us and said we were cowards, but apart from that he did not do anything else.

The gas-van was used for the first time in Kiev. My job was simply to drive the van. The van was loaded at headquarters. About forty people were loaded in, men, women and children. I then had to tell the people they were being taken away for work detail. Some steps were put against the van and the people were pushed in. Then the door was bolted and the tube connected . . . I drove through the town and then out to the anti-tank ditches where the vehicle was opened. This was done by prisoners. The bodies were then thrown in the anti-tank ditches. . . .

A member of Sonderkommando 6 on the deployment of gas-vans in Stalino and Rostov:

I was present at the first execution in Stalino. It took place on Easter Monday, 1942. I know for sure it was Easter Monday because I clearly remember discovering coloured eggs back at the quarters after the execution. This was a gassing of several hundred people in a gas-van. Men, women and children were loaded into it. By no means all of them were gassed that Easter Monday. I think that from the morning, it must have been about 7.00, until about 10.30, when the action ended for the day, I had to load and unload four vans. . . .

These were without a doubt Jews. There was such a range and number of people that they could only have been Jews. You did not get looters and saboteurs in these numbers. It was particularly the presence of children that led me to conclude that they were Jews.

The Jews had to climb into the van fully clothed. There was no sorting out. Men, women and children all had to get in together. I estimate that about sixty people had to get in each time. They had to climb up some steps to get into the van. It did not seem as if the Jews knew that they were about to be gassed. After the doors had been closed we then drove to a disused coal shaft. I do not remember whether the shaft was in front of the van or whether we had to turn round. The gas-van could not be driven right up to the shaft and we had to pull the bodies out of the vans and drag them to the shaft, which was about eight metres away, and then throw them in. . . .

When the doors were opened a cloud of smoke wafted out. After the smoke had cleared we could start our foul work. It was frightful. You could see that they had fought terribly for their lives. Some of them were holding their noses. The dead had to be dragged apart. It was while doing this that I first found out how heavy a human being can be.

There were two gas-vans in use. I saw them myself. They were driven into the prison yard and the Jews – men, women and children – had to get into the van directly from the cell. I also saw inside the gas-vans. They were lined with metal and there was a wooden grille on the floor. The exhaust gases were fed into the inside of the van. I can still today hear the Jews knocking and shouting, 'Dear Germans, let us out.'

Anton Lauer, Police Reserve Battalion 9

[Gas-van work in Rostov:]
The 'prison' was not far from the quarters so it must have been in the middle of Rostov. The gas-van drove up and we had to guard the area. . . .

The captive Jews then had to get into the van. They remained fully clothed. They were brought out [of the prison] by the militia. Men, women and children got in together. I should mention here that the Jews were almost dying of thirst. As far as I know they had only been rounded up the previous night. This was done by the militia. The cellar must have been badly ventilated; it must have also been very warm there. Hence the Jews' poor condition, despite the fact they had been down there only one night. I remember a distressing incident which happened during the loading; a Jewess cried out that her father had died of a heart attack. Nobody took any notice and the dead man was loaded into the van together with his relatives. The gas-van was as usual full, so forty to sixty people must have been loaded.

I also remember fetching two buckets of water and had them brought to the van. As there was almost a fight one of the Jews, an Austrian who spoke very good German, offered to distribute the water and so he handed each of the Jews in the van a mouthful of water. When everyone had had their water he had to get into the van. He was the last in and then the van was shut. The details of what happened then are somewhat blurred. I think that after quite a long drive to a shaft the van was unloaded.

73

I remember saying something like, 'Well, you're more advanced here and do the thing on the way.' Indeed the Jews had already been gassed when the van reached the shaft. In Stalino the gassing only started at the shaft.

The van, as had happened in Rostov, was opened, only with the difference that this happened immediately on reaching the shaft. We had to drag the dead in the usual way out of the van. It was the usual picture. Please spare me from having to keep giving you details.

That day I only had to participate in one loading – the one I have already described – but several unloadings, probably about four or five.

What happened was that we 'unloaders' stayed at the shaft and the gas-van went back to the 'prison' alone. Other men from the Kommando oversaw the loading.

I know that in between each loading the driver of the van had a lot of work to do in order to clean the interior of the vehicle because the people that had been gassed in it had emptied their bowels. Unloading a gas-van was from this point of view not very pleasant. I think that that day executions ended around midday.

Whether there were further gassings that day I do not know. I also think that the cellar was cleaned up when gassing stopped for the day.

In reply to a question: I know for certain that I came to Rostov on 19 September 1942. I do not know today why this date is so clear in my mind since I am certain that nothing special happened to me that day.

'Quite happy to take part in shootings'

Forced to obey orders – the myth

Jews have to undress before they are murdered

A police official from Neu-Sandez Grenzpolizeikommissariat (Cracow District/General-Gouvernement):

Members of the Grenzpolizeikommissariat were, with a few exceptions, quite happy to take part in shootings of Jews. They had a ball! Obviously they can't say that today! Nobody failed to turn up . . . I want to repeat that people today give a false impression when they say that the actions against the Jews were carried out unwillingly. There was great hatred against the Jews; it was revenge, and they wanted money and gold. Don't let's kid ourselves, there was always something up for grabs during the Jewish actions. Everywhere you went there was always something for the taking. The poor Jews were brought in, the rich Jews were fetched and their homes were scoured.

Auxiliary policeman from Einsatzkommando Stalino:

It was made clear to us that we could refuse to obey an order to participate in the Sonderaktionen ['special actions'] without adverse consequences.

A member of Third Squadron Mounted Police, section III, on executions of Jews in Hrubieszow:

I believe it was in autumn 1942 – try as I might, I cannot remember exactly when – that our sarge, Meister Kozar, ordered a group from the platoon that was stationed in Hrubieszow to execute a group of Jews that had been brought in in one or two lorries, which were now parked near the barracks. The Jews were unloaded within the barracks compound behind the prison camp, where the Russian prisoners of war were held, and were to be shot close by to where we were. As I was absolutely opposed to this action, I went and stood behind the lorry in which the Jews had been brought. I did not think I had to take part in the shooting. However, Meister Kozar found me standing there and ordered me to take part in the execution as had been previously planned. I refused, because I had no desire to shoot defenceless people. I had no wish to become a murderer. I said this to Kozar and he did not press me further to carry out this order. . . .

I did not experience any disadvantage as a result of refusing to be involved in the shooting. Although I said to Kozar that he could send me to the front or anywhere else but that I would not shoot any defenceless Jews, there were no such consequences. How many Jews were shot I do not know.

A member of Third Police Battalion 307 on an execution in Brest-Litovsk:

I too was to have been detailed to an execution squad. I received this order either from Leutnant Kayser or from the platoon sergeant, Zugwachtmeister Steffens. I was very disturbed by the sight of the execution areas. I therefore refused to take part in the execution. Nothing happened to me as a result of my refusal. No disciplinary measures were taken; there were no court-martial proceedings against me because of this.

A police reservist (First Reserve Police Battalion 69) on his refusal to take part in cordon duty during a Jewish action:

In the few weeks when I was in Vinnitsa one of these executions took place there. The first platoon of the company was instructed to cordon off the area. It must therefore have been the end of September or the beginning of October 1941. As there weren't enough people in the first platoon some men from the second platoon were also detailed to this action. I was one of them. We were told that a cordon was being set up for an action that the SD was carrying out. The SD, it was said, was planning to draw out all the Jews in the area that we had to cordon off. We were not told that these Jews were going to be shot or whatever else was going to happen to them, though everyone could well imagine what that actually was. For this reason I and some of the other men went to see our sarge, Raderschatt, and asked to be released from having to take part in this action. Although Raderschatt made some scathing remark about my request, he nevertheless gave his permission. Instead I had to do an extra guard duty. I was naturally only too happy to do this swap. Afterwards I did not experience any negative consequences whatsoever as a result.

A police Oberwachtmeister from Police Battalion 322:

Sometimes some of the men refused to participate in shootings. I myself refused a few times. None of my superiors took any action against me and the same applied to other people who refused to carry out orders. We were just assigned different duties. We were not threatened with any kind of punishment, certainly not where the executions were concerned.

An SS-Scharführer and Kriminal-Assistent from Kolomea Grenzpolizeikommissariat (General-Gouvernement):

The only answer I can give to the question what could I have done to be released from taking part in such actions is: there was nothing I could do. During the actions I kept as much in the background as possible, far away from the shootings. There was nothing else I could do. I did not ask Leideritz to be released from certain duties and be given guard duties instead. The reason I did not say to Leideritz that I could not take part in these things was that I was afraid that Leideritz and others would think I was a coward. I was worried that I would be affected adversely in some way in the future if I allowed myself to be seen as being too weak. I did not want Leideritz or other people to get the impression that I was not as hard as an SS-Mann ought to have been. . . .

I carried out orders not because I was afraid I would be punished by death if I didn't. I knew of no case and still know of no case today where one of us was sentenced to death because he did not want to take part in the execution of Jews . . . I thought that I ought not to say anything to Leideritz because I did not want to be seen in a bad light, and I thought that if I asked him to release me from having to take part in the executions it would be over for me as far as he was concerned and my chances of promotion would be spoilt or I would not be promoted at all. That is what I thought at the time and that is why I did not say anything to Leideritz.

A police reservist from Third Police Battalion 91:

After I had returned from Grodno on 1 February 1942 an execution took place near Wolkowysk. . . . I was not present at this execution as

I had not been detailed. . . . The only thing I can say about the selection of men is that people from the first platoon were assigned to these executions, at least to start with. Later, after people had become accustomed to the blood bath enough volunteers could be found. . . .

After the execution described above, the second execution that I knew about in the area close to Wolkowysk took place sometime between 1 February and 31 March 1942. The company had to assemble. Ahrens requested twenty volunteers for an execution that had been planned. No one responded. Ahrens repeated his request. Only after he had asked a further time did the first hands go up timidly. He did not however get his twenty, so Ahrens said, 'Since we're not getting anywhere I'll have to pick them myself.' Whereupon he walked along the ranks of the assembled company and picked out people at his own discretion. When he got to me I tried to make myself inconspicuous because I wished to avoid under any circumstances taking part in the execution squad. Ahrens could see that immediately. He asked my name, which I gave him. He then detailed me for the execution squad. Without hesitation I asked whether he would allow me to be excused from taking part as I could not shoot defenceless people. . . .

Ahrens called me a coward and a cissy and the like. He reprimanded me for unsoldierly conduct etc. It was only when Meister Neubauer whispered something to him, which I could not catch, that he declared he was prepared to release me from execution-squad duty, but he ordered me to stand guard right by the hole (mass grave) in order to harden me up. I did not try to go against this order. Ahrens was probably just trying to show me that a soldier has to do everything he is ordered to do. Finally he said scornfully, 'He is not even worthy of that kind of duty,' by which he wanted to emphasize my uselessness for 'tough action'.

A Kriminalsekretär to the Commander of the Security Police and SD in Riga:

Question: Could you say what disciplinary measures would have probably been taken against Security Police and SD men who refused to take part in shootings of Jews or the planning or running of such operations, or who refused to order such shootings against the will of the Estonia Sicherheitspolizei and SD commander?

Answer: Not a lot. I never knew of such a case at the KdS in Estonia.

I remember in the welcome address he gave, Sandberger [Commander of the Security Police and SD] said: 'If a man does not do his duty here, I will transfer him home.' He then said that this would not exactly help us in our future careers. From this not only I but also the other members of the Criminal Police gathered that we could refuse to carry out an order to take part in a shooting of Jews without coming to any harm.

An SS-Hauptscharführer and Kriminalangestellter (Gorlice branch of Jaslo Grenzpolizeikommissariat):

When the executions of the Jewish population started in an organized way, people in our branch were saying that no one was obliged to take part in a shooting if he could not reconcile it with his conscience. Allegedly there was an order by Reichsführer SS Himmler to the effect that no one could be forced to participate in a shooting. I think that the head of our office, Fundheller, said something like that to me. I do not however remember it exactly. Nevertheless, I was certainly aware of such an order issued by the Reichsführer SS although I never saw anything in writing about it.

One morning, it must have been during the summer or autumn of 1942, I was ordered by Friedrich to go with him to Jaslo. . . . From there we travelled in a column made up of quite a few vehicles to a village not far from Jaslo, at any rate within the area controlled by the Jaslo Grenzkommissariat. . . . As I remember, we did not stay long in the village but went to a place outside where a long grave had been dug. . . . After the execution of the Jews had already begun . . . I was ordered by someone to report to Raschwitz [Head of Jaslo Grenzkommissariat – Ed.]. Raschwitz was already pretty drunk. He ordered me to go to the grave and to shoot Jews there with my pistol. I, however, refused to comply with this order. I gave no reason but just said that I would not do it. Raschwitz then hurled some abuse at me. I still remember the expression he used: 'You Austrian swine.' Apart from that he also, as I recall it, used the word 'coward' and other terms of abuse. He then sent me back to the lorries. Apart from that Raschwitz did not do anything else. At any rate I was not taken to any further shootings and was left in peace.

A member of Einsatzgruppe A:

When the Einsatzgruppen were being assembled, I was discovered by Stahlecker. He knew me from Vienna and asked me to come and see him. He told me he intended to give me the job of administrative officer at the Gruppenstab and later at the Office of the BdS. But in Pretzsch Stahlecker addressed us all, indicating what our future duties would be. He told us that this was no administrative post but a Kriegseinsatz ('war mission'). We would be putting down resistance behind the troop lines, protecting and pacifying the rear army area (the word 'pacify' was used very frequently) and hence keeping the area behind the front clear. Stahlecker also explained that during our assignment we would be exposed to a very great many temptations. He warned us not to fall prey to these temptations. He also told us we would have to conquer our weaker selves and that what was needed were tough men who understood how to carry out orders. He also said to us that anyone who thought that he would not be able to withstand the stresses and psychological strains that lay ahead could report to him immediately afterwards. I can no longer remember today whether Stahlecker delivered this speech to all the men in Pretzsch or just to those who had been selected for Einsatzgruppe A. Stahlecker certainly did not mention shootings of Jews. . . .

I now took up my post [after arriving in Riga] as an office adminis-trator. This, of course, had been my job during the advance but it was only now that I was really doing office work. I was responsible for processing all the incoming and outgoing mail. I also had to record and file all the correspondence. Naturally I got to know about all the secret Reich matters. . . . I clearly remember seeing the first Einsatz orders in these secret Reich papers. . . . One of the first Einsatz orders also gave instructions to treat any Jews that were encountered as enemies of the state, to concentrate them into ghettos and camps, to resettle them periodically and to subject them to a Sonderbehand-lung. The orders for the third or fourth Einsatz were particularly important because they gave instructions for members of the local population to be used to carry out the actual dirty work, to which end special units should be set up. The purpose of this measure was to preserve the psychological equilibrium of our own people. . . .

After the first wave of shootings it emerged that the men, particu-larly the officers, could not cope with the demands made on them. Many abandoned themselves to alcohol, many suffered nervous breakdowns and psychological illnesses; for example we had suicides and there were cases where some men cracked up and shot wildly around them and completely lost control. When this happened Himmler issued an order stating that any man who no longer felt able to take the psychological stresses should report to his superior officer. These men were to be released from their current duties and would be detailed for other work back home. As I recall, Himmler even had a convalescent home set up close to Berlin for such cases. This order was issued in writing; I read and filed it myself. I am sure that Stahlecker made this order known during his briefing sessions with the various officers, because I still remember that this order was put in his briefing file. The group commanders and their deputies and adjutants took part in these briefings. I am in no doubt whatsoever that the commanders in turn passed this order on to the officers under their command. In my view this whole order was an evil trick; I do not think I would be wrong to say it bordered on the malicious – for after all, which officer or SS-Mann would have shown himself up in such a way? Any officer who had declared that he was too weak to do such things would have been considered unfit to be an officer.

SS-Obersturmbannführer Ernst Ehlers:

When the Russian campaign started I was a senior civil servant and member of Einsatzgruppe B. Before that I had been head of the Stapostelle in Liegnitz. In about April or May 1941 I was ordered to report to a police academy, it could have been the Pretzsch Police Academy. I was informed that I had been designated head of Einsatzkommando 8. At the police academy the Einsatzgruppen and Einsatzkommandos designated for the Russian campaign were drawn up. During a briefing session we were told what our future duties would be and it was explained to us quite clearly that the Einsatzkommandos, in addition to combating partisans, agents, etc, would also be responsible for liquidating the Jewish population in the rear army area in Russia. This disclosure hit me like a ton of bricks; I could not believe that such an order could be given. I was frantic with worry as to how I could be released from having to take part in this Einsatz and finally decided to ask my superior, Einsatzgruppenchef Nebe, to release me from my duties as head of Einsatzkommando 8. Nebe made no objections to my request and moved me to his group HQ. He told me that he had decided to make Dr Bradfisch head of Einsatzkommando 8, a man who had up to then been a Referent at HQ. . . .

In the ensuing months I worked as Referent IV to Einsatzgruppe B. Until 14 October 1941 I worked on the Russian programme.

SS-Oberführer Professor Dr Franz Six, Einsatzgruppe B:

During the war a person could at least try to have himself transferred from an Einsatzgruppe. I myself managed to do this successfully. . . . I was not demoted as a result of my transfer and not disadvantaged, apart from remaining on very bad terms with Heydrich until his death. There were without doubt cases where people who were transferred from an Einsatzgruppe suffered disadvantage. I can no longer recall any individual cases. None the less, as far as I know, nobody was shot as a result. One could also apply to the RSHA for a transfer to the front or to be released for service in another field. I was to have been transferred to the front again in mid-1942 but just before my departure I was seconded to the Foreign Office. After working for six months in the information department there I was promoted to head of department. Hence I was not disadvantaged as a result of my transfer.

SS-Obersturmführer Albert Hartl:

Question: As we know, during the Nuremberg trial, amongst other things, you testified that Einsatzgruppenführer Thomas expressly gave the order that people who were either too weak or who could not reconcile themselves for reasons of conscience to take part in shootings should be sent back to Germany or be redeployed for other duties. Please describe what happened and the context in which it happened.

Answer: SS-Gruppenführer Thomas was a doctor by profession; he was very preoccupied with the psychological repercussions of the Einsatz on his people. From my conversations with him I know that these effects took many different forms. There were people whose participation awakened in them the most evil sadistic impulses. For example, the head of one firing-squad made several hundred Jews of all ages, male and female, strip naked and run through a field into a wood. He then had them mown down with machine-gun fire. He even photographed the whole proceedings. Without Thomas's knowledge

Albert Hartl

these pictures fell into the hands of Army Group and they were delivered to him by the liaison officer. The Einsätze also had the reverse effect on some of the SS men detailed to the firing-squads. These men were overcome with uncontrollable fits of crying and suffered health breakdowns. Thomas once told me that a very common manifestation in members of these firing-squads was temporary impotence. It also happened that one member of the Einsatzgruppe who had participated in mass shootings one night suddenly succumbed to a type of mental derangement and began to shoot wildly about him, killing and wounding several men.

On one occasion Thomas asked me whether I would be prepared to take over command of a firing-squad. I replied that this was completely out of the question. Thomas answered that in his view no man should be forced to do this extremely difficult job, which brought with it enormous psychological conflicts and that he had given very clear instructions to this effect. From my position as head of Abteilung I (Staffing) I also know that a number of SS officers and men were sent back to serve at home 'on account of their great weakness' ('wegen zu grosser Weichheit'). During my hearings in Frankfurt and Nuremberg I was able to give examples but I have now forgotten the names.

Question: Was it possible to refuse to take part in a shooting in Einsatzgruppe C?

Answer: In my experience it depended very much on the mentality of the individual commanders of a particular Einsatzgruppe. Thomas was, as I said, a doctor. Some of the individual Einsatzgruppe heads were lawyers, like Dr Stahlecker, some were academics, like Professor Dr Six, who I think lives in either Heidelberg or Darmstadt, or some were economists like Ohlendorf. Some of them were very ambitious and they wanted to report the highest possible shooting figures to Berlin; then there were others who sabotaged the order to shoot as far as possible when the true significance of their squad assignment became clear to them, in order to report back from the Einsatz after a shorter time. An example of the latter type was Brigadeführer Schultz, who, as he told me himself, was against these mass shootings and thus very soon gave up the command of his Einsatzkommando, which if I remember correctly was stationed in the Lemberg [Lvov] area. As far as I know, he did not suffer any serious consequences as a result. It was, however, clear that as a general rule such people could not expect to be promoted in the foreseeable future. . . .

I do not know of any case where the commanding officer of a Kommando . . . was sent to a concentration camp or sentenced to death. At worst he would find his promotion blocked or he would be given a punishment transfer. As far as lower ranks are concerned I do not know of a case where as a result of his refusal to take part in shootings of Jews someone was either sent to a concentration camp or sentenced to death. I am however convinced that very many men of lower rank under the then authoritarian regime and under such strict and tough commanders as Stahlecker never even entertained the thought of giving expression to their inner conflict, fearing privately that a refusal to take part in a shooting would have had very serious consequences. In my experience, amongst the lower ranks there was not so much an objective necessity to obey orders, more of a subjective one. . . .

Erwin Schulz, head of Einsatzkommando 5:

At the beginning of August 1941 the Einsatzkommandoführer of Einsatzgruppe C were ordered to report to Dr Rasch (Head of Einsatzgruppe C) in Zhitomir. There Dr Rasch revealed to us that Gruppenführer Jeckeln had delivered an order from Reichsführer-SS

Himmler that from then on all Jews not engaged in work were to be shot along with their families. I was shattered when I heard this piece of news and I had absolutely no doubt that I could never carry out such an order. For this reason I wrote immediately to Gruppenführer Streckenbach, who was at that time head of personnel at RSHA, and asked him if I could come and see him in Berlin. . . . Once in Berlin I described to Streckenbach what was going on in Russia, to which he replied that what was happening there was nothing short of murder. At the same time I also asked Streckenbach to have me released from my post. He then approached Heydrich.

A few days later I had a further meeting with him during which he disclosed to me that it was too late to change anything and that the course of events could not be halted. He was able to convey the news to me that I had been released from my post. I was also able to return immediately to my earlier position at the Police Academy in Charlottenburg, Berlin. . . . I personally experienced no disadvantage whatsoever as a result of my intervention. . . .

I never knew of any cases where members or heads of the Einsatzkommandos acted in the same way as I did. I believe that things in Russia would never have turned out as they did had a few heads of the Einsatzkommandos and Einsatzgruppen declared that they could not carry out these liquidations. The way I see it, the same applies . . . to the Wehrmacht commanders in whose areas of command the liquidations were carried out and who were fully aware of them. In my opinion, the course of the avalanche could have still been checked if a field marshal or the commanding officer of an army group had intervened. . . .

I do not know of or recall any order that stated that SS chiefs or members of the SD or the police would be sent to concentration camps if they refused to carry out an order. I also never heard of such an order during the course of the conversations I had on the subject or indeed from rumours.

'Once again I've got to play general to the Jews'

From the war diary of Blutordensträger* Felix Landau

Group photo (with persons unknown)

*'Bearer of the Order of the Blood'.

On 25 July 1934 members of the 89th SS-Standarte forced their way into the Bundeskanzleramt (the Austrian Chancellor's Office) in Vienna. Although they fatally injured the Chancellor, Engelbert Dollfuss, the coup failed.

One of those arrested was cabinetmaker Felix Landau, who held up the staff of the Chancellor's office at gun point with a sub-machine-gun [see 'Appendix: Biographical Details' for a detailed biography]. Landau was sent to Wöllersdorf detention camp charged with being an accomplice in the crime. He was released in 1937. He became a naturalized German citizen and obtained a post as a Kriminalassistent. When on 12 March 1938 the German troops marched into Austria he was an SS-Hauptscharführer in a Security Police and SD Einsatzkommando.

Landau was then employed at the Gestapo regional head-quarters in Vienna with the responsibility for 'securing' Jewish property. He married and moved into a villa that belonged to a Jew who had fled. In April 1940 he was assigned to KdS (Commander of the Security Police and the SD) in Radom (Polish General-Gouvernement). He was first sent to participate in the fight against scattered Polish units. Afterwards he worked in the records office. On 31 August 1940 his role in the attempted coup in Vienna and his time spent in imprisonment in Austria were recognized and he was awarded the Blutorden of the NSDAP.

At the office in Radom he met a twenty-year-old shorthand-typist, Gertrude, who was engaged to a soldier from Vienna but wanted to break off the engagement. Landau learnt that Gertrude – despite her promise to him – was still seeing her fiancé. He thus resolved to break off the relationship. On 30 June 1941, just at the start of the Russian campaign, he reported to an Einsatzkommando (EK). At this point the diary begins.

Lemberg, 3 July 1941

On Monday, 30 June 1941, after a sleepless night I volunteered for a number of reasons to join an EK. By 9 o'clock I had heard that I had been accepted. It was not easy for me to leave. Suddenly everything had changed in me. I almost thought that I would not be able to tear myself from a certain person. I felt acutely how attached one can become to another human being.

As usual our departure was delayed several times but at 17.00 hours we finally left. We stopped one more time and once again I saw the person who has become so dear to me. Then we set off again. At 22.30 we finally reached Cracow. The accommodation was good. No creature comforts whatsoever. You can actually become a soldier in just a few hours if you want to. We then passed through Przemyśl. The town was still burning, on the street we saw shot-up German and Russian tanks. It was the first time I had seen two-tier Russian tanks.

After a short time we set off again towards Millnicze. It was becoming increasingly clear that the troops had recently been through. . . . At 21.30 on 1 July 1941 we arrived in M. We stood around aimlessly without any plan. We quartered ourselves in a Russian military school. It was still burning here too. At 23.00 hours we finally went to bed. I set up my bed and kipped down. Naturally I inquired whether it was possible to send letters but unfortunately it wasn't. On 2 July 1941 we were woken at 6.00 as at the front. There were women and children standing by burning houses and rummaging around in the rubble. During the journey we came across more Ukrainian soldiers. As we got closer and closer to the Russians the smell of decaying corpses got stronger and stronger.

At 4.00 pm on 2 July 1941 we arrived in Lemberg. First impression: Warsaw harmless in comparison. Shortly after our arrival the first Jews were shot by us. As usual a few of the new officers became megalomaniacs, they really enter into the role wholeheartedly. We took over another military school in the Bolshevik quarter. Here the Russians must have been caught in their sleep.

We quickly gathered together the bare essentials. At midnight after the Jews had cleaned the building, we went to bed.

3 July 1941. This morning I found out that we can write and it looks as though the post will actually be dispatched.

So while listening to wildly sensual music I wrote my first letter to my Trude. While I was writing the letter we were ordered to get ready. EK with steel helmets, carbines, thirty rounds of ammunition. We have just come back. Five hundred Jews were lined up ready to be shot. Beforehand we paid our respects to the murdered German airmen and Ukrainians. Eight hundred people were murdered here in Lemberg. The scum did not even draw the line at children. In the children's home they were nailed to the walls. Some of the occupants of a prison nailed to the wall.

Today a rumour went round that we are going to return to Radom.

In all honesty I would be happy to see my loved ones again. They mean more to me than I was ever prepared to admit to myself. So far there hasn't been an execution. Today we were on alert all day. It should be happening tonight.

Things are pretty tense. In this confusion I have only written notes. I have little inclination to shoot defenceless people – even if they are only Jews. I would far rather good honest open combat. Now good night, my dear Hasi [bunny].

5 July 1941

It's 11.00 am. Wonderful music, 'Do You Hear My Secret Call' ('Hörst Du mein heimliches Rufen'). How weak can a heart become! My thoughts are so much with the person who caused me to come here. What I wouldn't give to see her even for just ten minutes. I was up all of last night on guard duty, in other words kept watch.

A small incident demonstrated to me the complete fanaticism of these people. One of the Poles tried to put up some resistance. He tried to snatch the carbine out of the hands of one of the men but did not succeed. A few seconds later there was a crack of gunfire and it was all over. A few minutes later after a short interrogation a second one was finished off. I was just taking over the watch when a Kommando reported that just a few streets away from us a guard from the Wehrmacht had been discovered shot dead.

One hour later, at 5 in the morning, a further thirty-two Poles, members of the intelligentsia and Resistance, were shot about two hundred metres from our quarters after they had dug their own grave. One of them simply would not die. The first layer of sand had already been thrown on the first group when a hand emerged from out of the sand, waved and pointed to a place, presumably his heart. A couple more shots rang out, then someone shouted – in fact the Pole himself – 'Shoot faster!' What is a human being?

It looks like we'll be getting our first warm meal today. We've all been given 10 RM so that we can buy ourselves a few small necessities. I bought myself a whip costing 2 RM. The stench of corpses is all-pervasive when you pass the burnt-out houses. We pass the time by sleeping.

During the afternoon some three hundred more Jews and Poles were finished off. In the evening we went into town just for an hour. There we saw things that are almost impossible to describe. We drove past a prison. You could already tell from a few streets away that a lot of killing had taken place here. We wanted to go in and visit it but did not have any gas masks with us so it was impossible to enter the rooms in the cellar or the cells. Then we set off back to our quarters. At a street corner we saw some Jews covered in sand from head to foot. We looked at one another. We were all thinking the same thing. These Jews must have crawled out of the grave where the executed are buried. We stopped a Jew who was unsteady on his feet. We were wrong. The Ukrainians had taken some Jews up to the former GPU citadel. These Jews had apparently helped the GPU persecute the Ukrainians and the Germans. They had rounded up 800 Jews there, who were also supposed to be shot by us tomorrow. They had now released them.

We continued going along the road. There were hundreds of Jews walking along the street with blood pouring down their faces, holes in their heads, their hands broken and their eyes hanging out of their sockets. They were covered in blood. Some of them were carrying others who had collapsed. We went to the citadel; there we saw things that few people have ever seen. At the entrance of the citadel there were soldiers standing guard. They were holding clubs as thick as a man's wrist and were lashing out and hitting anyone who crossed their path. The Jews were pouring out of the entrance. There were rows of Jews lying one on top of the other like pigs whimpering horribly. The Jews kept streaming out of the citadel completely covered in blood. We stopped and tried to see who was in charge of the Kommando. 'Nobody.' Someone had let the Jews go. They were just being hit out of rage and hatred.

Nothing against that – only they should not let the Jews walk about in such a state. Finally we learned from the soldiers standing there that they had just visited some comrades of theirs, airmen in fact, in hospital here in Lemberg who had been brutally injured. They'd had their fingernails torn out, ears cut off and also their eyes gouged out. This explained their actions: perfectly understandable.

Our work is over for today. Camaraderie is still good for the time being. Crazy, beautiful, sensuous music playing on the radio again and my longing for you, the person who has hurt me so much, is growing and growing. Our only hope is to get away from here – most would prefer to be back in Radom. I for one – like many of the other men – have been disillusioned with this Einsatz. Too little combat in my view, hence this lousy atmosphere.

I had a terrible night last night. How true to life and intense a dream can be! The whole Warsaw affair, the reason why I am here, passed before my eyes so clearly there was nothing more I could wish for.

Once again I am psychologically shattered, just as I was then. I feel as if I won't be able to do it – to see beyond it and forget what I have gone through. If I don't meet T. again very soon I will go and do what I planned to do. No one will stop me. My mood is ghastly. I must get to Radom come what may.

Today I managed to send another letter to my Trude. It wasn't a very lovely letter, it expressed my despair to the full. I couldn't help it. I am now more hopeful that we will see each other again. This afternoon we learned that the Kommando will be going to Radom on Monday, 8 July 1941, after it has been to Drohobycz, an industrial town. We all breathed a sigh of relief. If we'd had to go on indefinitely it would have become impossible for us to continue working together. Four lorries have been taken from our EK. We have found some new telephones and gas masks of Russian origin which we took with us.

Things should start moving at our new post, thank God. Today I am reporting for a dangerous special mission [Sonderaufträge]. If we do have to stay there I will arrange things so that Trude can come.

The reveillé came at 8 o'clock. We sleep a long time so that the days are shorter. Once again work to do. Today I went into town for the nth time to look for a stationery shop. I actually managed to find one. Stationery shops have become my great passion. Naturally I rummaged through everything there and even found something usable. Writing paper, as we know it at home, does not exist here. But I finally have envelopes and now don't have to go round scrounging anymore. I also bought myself a lovely big travelling-bag for 32 roubles/3.80 RM.

So we are finally moving on to Drohobycz tomorrow morning at 8.00. We've been told that the area is partly occupied by the Russians. I am glad we are finally moving on a little. Tomorrow there's another post going to Cracow and Lublin from where it will be forwarded. I can write a quick letter to my little Trude. My feelings for all other women have been dead for a long time. I don't actually know myself how it happened.

This morning there was a special announcement that a further 52,000 Russians had capitulated. I should think there'll be a revolution in Russia in under two weeks. By then Moscow will certainly have fallen. Tonight we are having a social evening with our 'Kameraden' from Cracow.

Drohobycz, 7 July 1941

The social evening ended at 6.30 in the morning. There were no incidents. I picked up my two companions at about half past midnight and then we went together to our room to spend the rest of the night there. Our luggage has grown visibly. Oberführer Schönrad is the head of the EK. Sturmbannführer Röck works at the command post. We should have set off at 8.00. We finally left at 10.00 after a lot of quarrelling.

The people of Cracow are almost without exception complete arse-lickers. We had to go back along quite a stretch of the way we had come. We could already smell the prison where hundreds of people were murdered several streets away. There were hundreds of people standing in front of the shops trying to get hold of food of some kind. On our way two Jews were stopped. They said that they had fled from the Russian army. Their story was fairly unbelievable. Six of our men got out, loaded up and the next minute both were dead. When the order to take aim was given, one of the Jews, an engineer, was still shouting, 'Long live Germany.' Strange, I thought. What on earth had this Jew been hoping for?

At 16.00 we reached our destination. We were divided into several teams, in order to look for quarters for all the men. We found three houses which had been barely lived in. Baths everywhere, former Communist Party functionaries' homes. We were also able to establish that the Ukrainians had done a pretty good job plundering. They had really thought they were the masters for a while. There's going to be an almighty clash here – it's inevitable. Another interesting discovery: although there are very few radio sets here, almost every flat has its own speaker. The speakers can be switched on and off and have an adjustable volume so that means there won't be any need to forbid the men to listen to foreign broadcasts. In this case it won't be necessary.

I have a strong feeling that we will not be going back to Radom. My little Trudchen will thus have to come out here instead. We have occupied a Jewish hotel for a few days. I was ravenously hungry, so I have just 'inspected' the kitchen and managed to find a little something to eat. The quarters are very basic. The place is teeming with bugs. Now I must close because I have to report for guard duty. I'll be relieved at 1.00 tomorrow. My darling Trudchen, good night.

Today more crazy toing and froing. The Ortskommandant has said that we should not have been here in the first place, since there's no work for us. Marvellous! In the afternoon our Hauptsturmführer went to the Generalkommando to clarify the situation. The explanation: a misunderstanding on the part of the Ortskommandant. Everything now in order. My explanation: no communication and no cooperation with the Wehrmacht. No further comment necessary.

Around midday we moved into new quarters, a former Communist Party military school. I am to work in the financial running of the place and with the horses. In the stable I discovered three small ponies. Actually a whole family: a male, a female and a foal. A small pony cart and also a saddle, and complete harness. People are strange. When I reported for guard duty there were three ugly dirty women, former chambermaids, standing in the lobby gawping at me. An interpreter came up to us and talked to them. One of these women was asking whether I wanted to go to bed with her. These goddamned people are unbelievable. Of course that had the others clamouring round all the more. I thought she'd end up in bed with someone but she didn't, thank God. Otherwise all hell would have been let loose during room inspection.

In the evening we had another comrades' get-together. During supper a couple of the men wanted to take me to the flat with some women – waitresses from the hotel. I refused point blank. They were both very disappointed. I don't want to and can't. My Trude is far too much on my mind. At the social evening I just could not get her out of my thoughts. I am so worried about her. Who knows whether she is still thinking of me. Still not a word from her and I don't even know if she's been receiving my letters.

Today there were more surprises. In the morning a letter arrived from the Ortskommandantur. In an unfriendly tone we were informed that our work is to be limited merely to checking papers. In addition the letter declared that we were to ask nothing of the Referent for Jewish Affairs. As predicted, an impossible relationship. There was a tremendous amount of work. Once again I have got to play general to the Jews. Today I organized a carriage and harness despite the ban. Today there was beer from the barrel, we could also buy a bottle of Sekt for 1 RM. If only I had post from my Trude. During the day when I am buried in work it is all right but during the night the loneliness and inactivity simply make me despair. Good night Trud-chen. Think a little of your Lexi.

10 July 1941

I left the social evening at 2 o'clock in the morning. I poured as much drink down me as I could to lighten my spirits and forget for a short while. Unfortunately to no avail. Ten litres of beer and a few schnapps as well as a litre of red wine still did not have the desired effect. The next day I felt as if I had been hit around the head with a sledge-hammer. Today I was called to attend the allocation of assignments. I was working with a colleague from the SD [name illegible – Ed.] Department II Economics, in addition I was officially assigned as 'Judengeneral' ('General to the Jews'). I requisitioned two military vehicles for the department. Others have already done so for their own use. I have no time for that. The only thing I wanted was a decent apartment. The arguments with the Wehrmacht continue. The Major in charge must be the worst kind of state enemy. I remarked today that I would apply to Berlin for this M. to be put into preven-tive detention immediately; his actions are a danger to the state. Take his remark that the Jews fall under the protection of the German Wehrmacht. Who could have thought such a thing possible? That's no National Socialist.

14 July 1941

I haven't managed to get round to writing any more in my diary till today. A great many things have happened. New experiences and new impressions.

On 11 July 1941 a vehicle finally left for Radom carrying Dolte, Binder, Gürth and Mireck. Regrettably I could not go with them. At least I was able to give them a letter which I can be sure will arrive. I also have the prospect of hearing from my little Trude to look forward to. Unfortunately I'll be getting other letters as well. Of course, as was to have been expected, our KK [Kriminalkommissar – Ed.] . . . immediately took advantage of Dolte's absence to quench his thirst for action. Barely an hour later his wonderful orders such as 'Get a move on, gentlemen, get that whole pile over here to me' and the like were ringing out. He had arrests and shootings to his heart's desire. The prisoners, mostly Jews but also some Ukrainians, keep on coming. . . . We 'work' right through the night. In the evening a comrade, Urban, and I managed to snatch some time to go and see a cook from whom we can get *Mischlanka*, sour milk and new potatoes. Although the rooms are very small, everything is clean and pleasant. The people were friendly and obliging. There was also a very pretty young Ukrainian girl there. Communication – try as she might – was impossible. The only thing I managed to gather was that she was very interested in me. But my thoughts as ever are still with my Trude. I am not tempted nor do I want to be.

At 11 in the evening we got back to base. A flurry of activity down in the cellar, which I had just cleared up that morning. There were fifty prisoners, two of whom were women. I immediately volunteered to relieve the person who was on guard duty. Almost all of them will be shot tomorrow. Most of the Jews amongst them were from Vienna. Still dreaming of Vienna. I was on duty until three in the morning the next day. Finally went to bed dog tired at 3.30.

12 July 1941

At 6.00 in the morning I was suddenly awoken from a deep sleep. Report for an execution. Fine, so I'll just play executioner and then gravedigger, why not? Isn't it strange, you love battle and then have to shoot defenceless people. Twenty-three had to be shot, amongst them the two above-mentioned women. They are unbelievable. They even refused to accept a glass of water from us. I was detailed as marksman and had to shoot any runaways. We drove one kilometre along the road out of town and then turned right into a wood. There were only six of us at that point and we had to find a suitable spot to shoot and bury them. After a few minutes we found a place. The death candidates assembled with shovels to dig their own graves. Two of them were weeping. The others certainly have incredible courage. What on earth is running through their minds during those moments? I think that each of them harbours a small hope that somehow he won't be shot. The death candidates are organized into three shifts as there are not many shovels. Strange, *I am completely unmoved. No pity, nothing*. That's the way it is and then it's all over. My heart beats just a little faster when involuntarily I recall the feelings and thoughts I had when I was in a similar situation. On 24 July 1934 in the Bundeskanzleramt [Chancellery] when I was confronted with the machine-gun barrels of the Heimwehr [Austrian militia, 1919–38]. Then there were moments when I came close to weakening. I would not have allowed it to show, no, that would have been out of the question with my character. 'So young and now it's all over.' Those were my thoughts, then I pushed these feelings aside and in their

Naked Jews, with a child on the right, just before their murder

place came a sense of defiance and the realization that my death would not have been in vain.

And here I am today, a survivor standing in front of others in order to shoot them. Slowly the hole gets bigger and bigger; two of them are crying continuously. I keep them digging longer and longer; they don't think so much when they're digging. While they're working they are in fact calmer. Valuables, watches and money, are put into a pile. When all of them have been brought to stand next to one another on a stretch of open ground, the two women are lined up at one end of the grave ready to be shot first. Two men had already been shot in the bushes by our KK [Kriminalkommissar] . . . I did not see this as I had to keep my eyes on the others. As the women walked to the grave they were completely composed. They turned round. Six of us had to shoot them. The job was assigned thus: three at the heart, three at the head. I took the heart. The shots were fired and the brains whizzed through the air. Two in the head is too much. They almost tear it off. Almost all of them fell to the ground without a sound. Only with two of them it didn't work. They screamed and whimpered for a long time. Revolvers were no use. The two of us who were shooting together had no failures. The penultimate group had to throw those who had already been shot into the mass grave then line up and fall in themselves. *The last two had to place themselves at the front edge of the grave so that they would fall in at just the right spot.* Then a few bodies were rearranged with a pickaxe and after that then we began the gravedigging work.

I came back dog tired but the work went on. Everything in the building had to be straightened up. And so it went on without respite. In the afternoon the car came back from Radom unexpectedly. Like a small child I couldn't wait to get my post. That was my first question. Unfortunately I didn't get a chance to read all my post, there was so much; no sooner had I begun than the Hauptsturmführer came up to me and asked me to get started on the move to the new offices and set things up there as well.

So I worked until 11 o'clock and had to make myself a plan like a proper little architect. Everyone admired my work.

On Sunday, 13 July 1941, the work started again straight away. I hardly got any sleep. My feet and my head hurt as though I had just been on two pack marches. We also learned that Communists had taken control in the mountainous area behind us. Yet more work. Finally I managed to read all my post. It's strange, my mood completely changed. A lot of what I read gave me great cause for worry. Apart from anything else Trude wrote that she doesn't know whether she can keep her promise and whether she will be strong enough. Why does this have to happen to me with a person I love so much? I have to see her and talk to her, then my little Trude will be strong again. She must come here.

14 July 1941

Attended various meetings. Council of the Jews. Otherwise mostly organized and moved. In the evening found a sheepdog bitch.

20 July 1941

Today is Sunday. Once again I worked until 8 o'clock. It is now 10.00 and I have finally managed to find the time to record in my diary the few events which, in the larger context of what is happening in the world, are so insignificant.

[On] 15 July 1941 I went together with a comrade to the afore-mentioned Ukrainian family. It was very cosy and also very interesting for someone who is interested in the ways of another people. We talked over just about everything. The only subject I thought it better not to touch upon was religion, as it would be easy for misunderstandings to arise when communication was somewhat limited. We were still talking at 11.00. On the way there – we had gone there in our pony and trap – something very funny happened to us. First we were caught in a downpour, although that did not last long. Then when we turned into a real Russian track we were confronted by potholes over a metre deep. Naturally we were jolted out of our seats on quite a number of occasions. Then we got to a particularly fine spot and my cart bounced backwards slightly while the pony kept on going. All of a sudden I heard a splash and when I turned round I saw my comrade in a pretty deep puddle, with his legs sticking up in the air. Despite the unpleasantness of the situation I couldn't help roaring with laughter. The trip back looked like becoming even more tragic; had the farmer not taken us to the main road we would have certainly ended up, pony, trap and all, in a ditch.

Because of this delightful track we didn't get back until midnight. As we rode through the gate a car was just starting up. Soon I realized that things were pretty lively for this time of night. My first thought was that something was up. Obviously people were worried on our account and thought that something had happened to us. . . . The next morning we were informed that all social intercourse with the Ukrainians was forbidden. He, that is the Hauptsturmführer, had no objections if any of us spent the odd night with an *U-Mädel* [Ukrainian girl] but all other contact was forbidden. Odd attitude. Well as far as I am concerned that is out of the question, since all I wanted was to get to know the people. My small young dog is coming along fine. As each day passes she is becoming more and more devoted but she's still as nervous as ever.

On 16 July 1941 more moving again. My role here is more one of architect than of official. I am now, in addition, responsible for overseeing and conducting the training of 150 Ukrainians. I'm quite happy to play at being master builder and architect, the only thing I wish is that I had workmen and not Jews to carry out the work. Still, that's the way it has to be.

On 17 July 1941 nothing much happened. I messed around with the Jews some more – and that's my work.

18 July 1941. The question of the day is who will travel to Radom. All of a sudden everybody has got to go there. They've all left things they can't do without there. Nobody has a suitcase, nobody has clean laundry. Usually in the military, failure to carry out orders is punished harshly; here, however, it's rewarded with a Sunday excursion to Radom. At midday there was a meeting and yes, as expected, once again I was not amongst those who were to go. I was bursting with rage. Here I am slaving away day and night so that everyone has

a nice apartment and is assured every comfort, and then when I make the smallest request others are given preferential treatment.

19 July 1941. The entire day I could not get the thought out of my head that at that very moment I could have been with Trudchen in R. Try as I might to push these thoughts to one side I still imagine my little Trudl there waiting and hoping to see me. What use is my fine apartment fitted out with every comfort if that very thing is missing? Everything is dead in my flat.

19 July 1941. So I was not able to travel to Radom. The way I feel I could kill everyone. I of all people was not permitted to go. I am not very optimistic about my chances next time. Spent the whole day working solidly. How disappointed my little Trude will be when instead of me only a letter arrives. In the evening we had another visit, only a day after the Oberführer arrived without any prior warning. He was very pleased with the rooms and the buildings. As usual others took all the credit. That's the way it will always be given human nature. In the evening as I was lying in bed I was filled with a tremendous yearning, yearning for quiet, peace and love.

21 July 1941

After waiting in vain yesterday for the men to return from Radom, all I could do again today was wait. Every five minutes I asked whether the vehicles had returned from Radom. Again and again my question was in vain. Finally towards midday the car arrived. By that time I no longer needed to ask for they all shouted to me in unison, 'Felix there's a packet for you.' I breathed a sigh of relief. When I read the letter I locked myself in my room. It was short and sketchy. I began to worry and think dark thoughts. Could Trude have been unfaithful after such a short time? I am uneasy. What I would give for Trudchen to be with me. Well, this is how I wanted it, only I thought it would turn out differently. Oh well, ordinary life is far too tame for me. I don't understand Trudchen. She sent me the pictures of my children and my wife. I could understand why she'd send the former, but the latter is beyond me. The men had the day off today, some of them went hunting. I had to work here. Thanks and praise is sure to come my way. The above-mentioned Sturmbannführer went off hunting once again with his five men. The work is going ahead well. I have just been informed by the Hauptsturmführer that I am to take over the training of the militia. Apparently I have the right attitude. Today I answered my wife's letters and sent her 180 RM. Trudchen got a short letter from me.

Another eventful day. In the morning the workers I had ordered failed to appear. Just as I was about to go to the Jewish Committee one of my colleagues from the council came and asked me for my support as the Jews were refusing to work here. I went over. When those arse-holes saw me they ran in all directions. Pity I did not have a pistol on me or else I would have shot some of them down. I then went to the Council of Jews and informed them that if 100 Jews did not report for work within an hour I would select 100 of them *not for work but for the firing-squad*. Barely half an hour later 100 Jews arrived together with a further seventeen for those who had run away. I reported the incident and at the same time gave orders for the fugitives to be shot for refusing to work, *which happened precisely twelve hours later. Twenty Jews were finished off.*

Another incident. I sent one of the men off with two Jews to get hold of some material we needed. He took the keys from the usual place and went off. While we were clearing up one of the Ukrainians started pestering the Jews, who were carrying out our orders, naturally with the full agreement of the Germans. Amongst other things he asked the Jews who they thought they were, letting on to the Germans what was in the storeroom. He said he would come and find them in the evening and beat them to death. Well, that really got my blood up. Such people in my opinion are the real enemies of the state, so I had the lad brought in. In my room he received by way of introduction a little bit of my special treatment. After the first beating, blood was spurting. First he tried to deny he had done anything. After the fourth beating however he gave up this tactic. I gave orders for him to be arrested for having an anti-German attitude.

In a village near Drohobycz four released convicts were shot on the spot. This time the Slovaks dug the graves and did the burying.

I am very curious to know how the Council of Jews will take it. They'll all be wailing and gnashing their teeth tomorrow. We also found that No. 13 barracks had been broken into again, and an attempt had been made to steal the rubber tyres from our vehicles. One of the tyres had been sliced right through with a sharp knife. So in the evening I made yet another arrest.

Tomorrow I am going to make a concerted effort to ask about my Trudchen coming here. As a final resort, if I get a refusal I am going to ask for a transfer or obtain one somehow. At the same time I'm also going to sort out the Radom trip. Then tomorrow I'll write a long letter to Trudchen. Good night my dear little rascal, please still love me, think of me and stay true to me. Now I am going to bed, to look at your picture and read your book. When my eyes begin to get tired I shall put the book aside and look at your picture again, give you a big kiss, switch off the light and go to sleep.

23 July 1941

Well, I was not able to put yesterday's plans into action. The reason is simply the unbelievable amount of work. I sometimes wonder how much more I can take of this. At 8 o'clock this morning I should have detailed the Jews for various tasks and drilled the Ukrainian militia at the same time as well. In the afternoon I was given a lot more jobs but I am determined to write the letter to Trudchen. I must see her, speak to her come what may. Today I found quite a few Communist Party banners and weapons. Work is progressing quickly on all the buildings. The new militiamen certainly seem to be finding it difficult to adjust to my tempo and tone. Today ten out of forty men failed to report.

Our chief once again threatened some of the comrades with execution and again for no reason whatsoever. He said to Urban, 'If you don't change your tone with me you will be included in the next execution.' There have already been complaints about him. He has been nicknamed 'Revolverkommissar' and 'Sonnensoldat' ('Sunshine Soldier'). He is the only one who goes about with a white battle tunic and long trousers. It's now already 23.00 but I must write the letter without fail.

28 July 1941

All of my good intentions – come what may – to write my diary every evening have come to naught. It's midnight and I have finally got round to writing a few lines. I was quite amazed when I discovered on Saturday morning what day it was. I had intended to approach Dolte again on Friday about going to Radom. I was devastated and spent the rest of the day in a frightful frame of mind. I worked until 11 at night. What else can I do? Some of the other men went out at midday and returned towards 7.00 in the evening with some Ukrainian girls whom they took up to their quarters. I was still clearing the place and having carpets laid. On Sunday I worked until 3.00 and then for the first time since my Einsatz I am having a break.

On Friday and Saturday there was an interesting development on the work front. Some Ukrainians brought a report from a neighbouring village which went more or less as follows: Someone had discovered the bodies of twenty-four Ukrainians who had been murdered by the Russians in the woods. The bodies were almost unrecognizable. As this was a murder case the criminal police took it up immediately and went to the place in question. There they were solemnly received by a cleric who told them how pleased he was to see them. The cleric said that it was extremely kind of the Germans to take such an interest in the murder and fate of the Ukrainians. The bodies were solemnly buried and our officials had no choice but to take part. On the way the cleric said to me, 'Do you know, the vilest thing about it is that Jewish passes and papers were put in their pockets.' Now this is unbelievable! These supposed Ukrainians were in fact the very twenty-three Jews plus, I think, two Ukrainians we ourselves had shot! Cheers, bon appetit. The papers on the bodies stank terribly. I had petroleum poured over them, then ordered them to be burnt and buried in the grave. . . .

30 July 1941

I had a wonderful surprise. Post from Trude. I had been waiting for so long! Her post arrived just as I was writing a letter. My mood shot up 100%. What a funny girl my Trude is. In her letter she wrote a philosophical treatise about my love life and marriage, utterly serious as though her life depended on it. Full of intellectual utterances like a wise and experienced woman. There was not a thought or a word about herself. She had excluded herself entirely from the letter. Sometimes there is a slight sense that she wants to convince me of something so that she can be rid of me more easily. But then when I read the letters from the day before and the day after I cannot help smiling at these thoughts, for out of these lines emerges a hot and passionate love, like the one I feel for her. Sometimes I begin to feel afraid, as though in a dream. She has no idea what she has come to mean to me. Also she does not realize what has happened inside me recently. If she, who has come to mean so much to me, disappointed me I would be completely devastated. I think that I would lose my belief in humanity right up to the day I died. Yesterday evening, despite the ridiculous amount of work, I wrote Trudchen another six-page letter. Today I was summoned in confidence to D. who informed me that the GG [General-Gouverneur] will be coming on Saturday. So no trip once again. I am not giving up hope. I sent Trudchen a letter and a small miniature – a baroque love scene.

Today, 31 July 1941, there was a crazy amount of work again. The letter left today with the vehicle for Radom.

1 August 1941

Yesterday I managed to have my much requested conversation with Dolte. This time I refused to let myself be fobbed off. At 8.00 in the evening I went to Dolte's apartment, which is above mine, and asked him whether he had time to see me. He did and asked me to come in and sit down at the table. He had Briese with him. He was just in the middle of reading out a ten-page letter from his girlfriend in Radom to Briese. I was initially slightly embarrassed but in this respect Dolte is as open as I am and does not have any secrets. So much the better for me and my affair. I could not have hit on a better moment. He told me he has not got any further with his divorce and that he has now engaged four lawyers. Then good old Briese left. Dolte offered me some wine and cigarettes and we sat together like old chums. Then I fired away. I no longer had any need to mention what I wanted because it is so widely known and has already been referred to. His position was the following: Every support . . . of course. First of all Trudchen must come here and only then will we take it further. As far as going to Radom was concerned I received a promise that I could travel on Saturday, 9 August 1941. So something is fixed. I was very satisfied with the outcome. My spirits were finally restored after so long. My Ukrainian militia got a 'honeymoon period'. The Jews were 'more considerately' treated. I gave away more cigarettes than usual. You could tell by my whole behaviour that something pleasant had happened to me. However during supper I couldn't avoid getting angry.

A certain Herr Gabriel, a man with an inferiority complex and bulging eyes, became angry because I had dismissed for incompetence a Jewess who was working for me. The gentleman forgets that we have introduced the race law into the National Socialist state. I'd already caught him once tenderly stroking the chin of a Jewess and given him a thorough talking-to. At the time he was pretty discomfited. The gentleman must have already forgotten this.

Once again plenty of work, until 22.00. The General-Gouverneur is due to arrive tomorrow, so my militia have to be properly kitted out. At 7.00 in the evening I went to their barracks and established that out of sixty men only twelve are fully kitted out. About forty tailors had been working for almost three days and could not finish the uniforms. I was furious. Of course, most of the blame lay with the leadership of the militia. I immediately summoned the Council of Elders to me and told them that all the remaining uniforms had to be ready by midday the following day or else I would have five tailors executed for sabotage by firing-squad.

A man was brought before me who wanted to report his sixteen-year-old daughter for whoring. According to his own account his daughter has been on the make since she was thirteen. So now it's up to the police to teach the child how to behave! I gave the father who wanted to put his own flesh and blood in prison such a good clip round the ear that he lost his balance five times. . . .

2 August 1941

Work goes on. This morning we started at 6. The GG is not coming. At 12.00 the Council of Elders reported to me that all the uniforms were ready. *Since I had twenty of its men shot for refusing to work,* everything's been running smoothly. This evening four of the men are off to Radom. So that means a quick letter to my Trude. I also have to send the money, 180 RM, to my wife. I've written the letters and given them to Laufmann. Will Trudchen be pleased? I also sent some toys to my wife for the children. The men left for Radom at 22.00 hours. . . .

5 August 1941

Today we took over four buildings for the women and wives who are due to arrive. Dolte is sometimes too weak, not ruthless enough. . . .

6 August 1941

I already know that it is going to take a tough and difficult fight to make her strong enough to get her to assert herself against her parents. She should not simply stumble into a marriage as I did. I will not let her. She is worth more than I am. She is far too good to be thrown away for something which offers her nothing. She will gain far more if she is allowed to love the person who can love her back completely. Today some of the men and I got the Jewish housemaid to roast some chickens for us. We also had new potatoes, cucumber salad and raspberry compote. I contributed the wine. Everything was perfect except for the empty places on my right and left. I looked at both chairs and said to my companions that all that was missing was our sweethearts. Then one of the men talked about his wife and their happy life together. Whether I like it or not I always become dejected and sad during such conversations. There is nothing I can do about it.

105

For the time being there is no happy family life for me. Perhaps somebody will help me to become happy. Good night, Trudchen. Please remain true to me. . . .

> Despite the extreme stress, which every single SS and police member had to contend with during these actions, the mood and morale of the men from the first to the last day was exceptionally good and praiseworthy. It was only by a personal sense of duty that every officer and man was able to overcome this pestilence in the shortest space of time.
>
> SS- und Polizeiführer of Galicia, SS-Gruppenführer Friedrich Katzmann, in a report dated 30 June 1943

8 August 1941

. . . My first thought when I awoke and dawn was breaking: tomorrow at this time we could already be leaving for Radom and if all goes well we could be there at 11 or 12 in the morning. Once I had begun to think about this subject naturally I could not go back to sleep. I imagined where I'd meet T., whether she would be able to go with me straight away or if I didn't arrive until the afternoon where I would find her. At her apartment, at the hairdresser's, at the sports centre, at German House, or – I hope not – out with one of my dear comrades. Then I thought about where I would actually be sleeping. If [illegible name – Ed.] is not at my apartment, or rather his apartment, then there. If he's at home then I will ask him to let me borrow my former flat for the night. I have so much to tell T. and I want my Hasi [bunny] to tell me everything on her mind. I fear a lot of unpleasantness. If only she had a quarter of my decisiveness and strength of will. I would love to give her everything and transfer [some of] my will to her. I still have more than twenty-two hours to wait. I am already more nervous than I have ever been in my entire life. . . .

'Execution as popular entertainment'

The murder of Jews as a public spectacle

1. 'Soldiers sitting on rooftops and platforms watching the show'
An execution on 7 August 1941 in Zhitomir

Herbert Selle, commander of Pioneer Regiment 604:

In August 1941 my Pioneer Regiment was under orders to make preparations for crossing the Dnieper and was stationed in readiness in and around Zhitomir. I recall that in August 1941 a public hanging of two people took place in Zhitomir. The people were two Jews who, it was said, had ill-treated the Ukrainians in the most horrible manner during the Russian domination. I did not see the hanging itself but was told that there were soldiers sitting on rooftops and platforms watching the show. The execution was arranged as a form of popular entertainment. I could not comprehend this at all, since right from the start I had been an opponent of the National Socialist Jewish policy and for this reason and because of holding views opposed to the regime my family and I suffered persecution. The army staff used this incident as an opportunity to issue an order to the effect that members of the Wehrmacht were not to participate in the racial struggle because this was the duty of the SS and departments associated with it.

A truck-driver from Technical Battalion 6:

One day a Wehrmacht vehicle (police vehicle?) drove through Zhitomir with a megaphone. We had been lodged in the electrical plant where we were working. Over the loudspeaker we were informed in German and Russian (Ukrainian) that at a certain time that day Jews would be shot in the market-place or something to that effect. As I had that particular day off I went at the appointed time to the market-place. I was alone. Upon arriving there I saw that fifty to sixty Jews (men, women and children) had assembled there and were being held under SS guard. There were about eight guards. Round and about stood about 150 civilians watching. There were also, of course, members of the Wehrmacht among the onlookers. The Jews

Der Tschekajude **WOLF KIEPER** der Mörder von 1350 Volksdeulschen u. Ukrainern

Zhitomir: mass murder as public entertainment. German soldiers even sit on the roofs so as not to miss the spectacle

sat on the ground. I had made my way through the spectators and had stopped about two metres away from the Jews. I can therefore say with certainty that they were all wearing civilian dress and could therefore not have been prisoners of war. The guards asked the people

109

standing around if they had any scores to settle. Thereupon more and more Ukrainians spoke up and accused one or other of the Jews of some misdemeanour. These Jews were then beaten and kicked and ill-treated where they were, mostly by Ukrainians. This went on for about forty-five minutes. Then three [two – Ed.] from this group were taken out and executed on a gallows. The wooden structure was ready and waiting. There were three nooses hanging from it. The three delinquents had to climb on to a truck. After the nooses had been put round the necks of these males the truck drove away. That is how the execution was carried out. This part was also carried out by SS people. Finally all of the Jews assembled there had to get on to the truck. They stood herded tightly together. Then an announcement came over the loudspeaker that we should all follow the lorry to the shooting. This announcement was directed towards the spectators.

Then the truck set off, stopping about 150 metres further on. On a stretch of open ground there was a ditch, filled with water, about 150 cm long and about 80 cm wide. It must have been about 50 cm deep. SS men stood at either side of this ditch. One by one the Jews had to jump over the ditch. Because of their bad physical condition – partly due to undernourishment but mostly as a result of the ill-treatment and also because a lot of them were very old – only a few managed to clear it. . . . Those who fell in the ditch were beaten with various types of blunt instruments by the SS men and driven or pulled out of the ditch. Many could not get out of the ditch. The ditch had to be kept clear because it was only 80 cm wide and the other people had to cross it.

> After the German troops arrived in the Zhitomir district the Jews were mobilized to clean the barracks. Their behaviour was extremely impudent and they even refused to carry out the work. . . . The requisite reprisal measures were immediately enforced.
>
> *Tätigkeits- und Lagebericht*, No. 3 of the Sipo and SD Einsatzgruppen in the USSR (period covered 15 to 31 August 1941)

About thirty metres behind the ditch I saw a stack of logs. The stack was about 10 m long, 1·5–2 m high and about 1·5 m wide. This wooden wall was used as a bullet butt. Little by little the Jews had to line up facing this wall. There must have been five or six people lined up there each time. They then received a shot in the neck from the carbines. Row upon row were shot in the same way. The dead from each row were dragged away immediately and taken behind the stack of logs. There was a large grave there that I only saw from afar. . . .

I stood about twenty metres from the ditch and about fifty metres from the wood-stack. A cordon was stretched across for the spectators. The spectators were not permitted to come any nearer.

SS-Obersturmführer August Häfner, Sonderkommando 4a:

At what must have been the beginning of July 1941 I returned to Lutsk from a journey. When after much questioning I found my unit, they were all running around like lost sheep. I realized that something must have happened and asked what was wrong. Someone told me that [Standartenführer] Blobel had had a nervous breakdown and was in bed in his room. I went to the room. Blobel was there. He was talking confusedly. He was saying that it was not possible to shoot so many Jews and that what was needed was a plough to plough them into the ground. He had completely lost his mind. He was threatening to shoot Wehrmacht officers with his pistol. It was clear to me that he had cracked up and I asked [Obersturmführer] Janssen what had happened. Janssen told me that Reichenau had issued an order, according to which 3,000 Jews had to be executed by firing-squad in retaliation for 2,000 bodies which had been found in the castle court-yard in Lutsk. No preparations to carry out this order had yet been made. At least none was known to me. I had someone call a doctor. I no longer know who fetched him. When the doctor saw the condition Blobel was in he gave him an injection and instructed us to have him taken to Lublin to a hospital. While he was being examined Blobel kept on reaching for his pistol. By talking to him I managed to calm him down enough so that he did not fire. I said that I was prepared to take him to Lublin together with a driver called Bauer. We officers were somewhat at a loss what to do. It was not clear who would take over command in Blobel's absence. As far as I can remember, [Obersturmführer] Hans, Janssen and I urged [Hauptsturmführer] Callsen to take over command since as a Hauptsturmführer he was the most senior officer present. Callsen put up a lot of resistance to this suggestion as he was well aware that the execution of the Jews lay ahead. Someone then suggested notifying [Brigadeführer] Rasch. I think it may even have been me. I then went with Bauer to Lublin.

111

We bundled Blobel into the [Opel] 'Admiral'. In Lublin we delivered him to a hospital which was known as a loony bin by the conscripts. Then we went back. You can ask Bauer about that.

When we got back to Lutsk there were masses of conscripts standing in a square which must have been the market-place. There were people from all branches of the armed forces as well as the Organization Todt. As I got closer to the square I realized that Jews were about to be executed there.

As soon as I saw the troops I knew that this must be what was happening. I went towards the ditch. I saw a major from the Wehrmacht being handed a heavy-machine-gun by some privates, which he pointed straight at the ditch, firing a whole round of bullets into it. If I remember correctly he shouted out, 'Some of them are still alive!' Then an elderly man rose up from the pile of corpses near him and shouted, 'Give me another one!' I do not know who then shot this man. I was appalled that many people were left lying wounded in the grave. These people were left to die wretchedly. When I saw this I tried to find someone from our Kommando. I assumed that our Kommando had carried out this order. I walked along a bit but could not see anyone. Back at headquarters I then met various members of our Kommando. If I remember correctly I met Callsen, Janssen and Hans there. I said to them, 'What in God's name is going on over there?' I also asked, 'Who carried out the execution? Who was in command?'

I did not receive a direct answer. One of them said that it had been Dr Rasch [Head of Einsatzgruppe C] and that he had ordered the shootings. . . .

Question: Herr Häfner, you mentioned that it was terrible to see people dying in the ditch. Did you yourself give any *coups de grâce* in order to curtail the suffering of the victims?

Answer: Not in Lutsk.

Question: Did you ever give *coups de grâce* on other occasions?

Answer: Probably in Kiev.

Question: While you were a member of Sonderkommando 4 did you ever hear of any of the officers or men being splattered with bits of a victim's brain during a shooting with the result that this person suffered an infection and had to be treated back home?

Answer: In Zhitomir the victims' brains sprayed in the faces of the firing-squad. I did not hear anything about a firing-squad member having to be treated back home. . . .

112

Question: What happened during the shooting in Zhitomir?

Answer: I went to the HQ in Zhitomir one day in August. There I was told that the Soviet judge, Kieper, and his aide were to be hanged. The hanging was to be public. I think that there was even a poster campaign to publicize it. At that time I knew nothing about it.

Two days later Blobel ordered me to report to the execution site and to make contact with the officers from Army HQ. When I arrived at the square I found a gallows had been set up there. There were a lot of people there. They were mostly Wehrmacht, but there were also some civilians I believe. The Jews were sitting near the gallows. You could tell they were Jews because many of them had long beards and were wearing kaftans. A lorry drew up and stopped under the gallows. The victims stood in the truck. I then saw the lorry move away and the people were hanged at the gallows. I do not know who put the noose round the people's necks. At that point I thought that it must all be over.

Then Blobel said to me, 'Now 400 Jews are going to be shot.' I went by car to the spot where the grave had already been dug. Several cars must have gone to this grave. I no longer remember who was with me in the car. As we stood by the grave the Jews were brought in on

---

I can remember that the Jewish functionary Kieper and his aide fell into the hands of Sonderkommando 4a. Who tracked down these men I no longer know. I think that Dr Boss, who was working with us, had something to do with it. Blobel gave orders that both were to be hanged publicly in the market-place in Zhitomir. The Wehrmacht, our unit and the civilian population were notified. On the day of the hanging the entire unit marched to the market-place in closed formation. Some of our truck-drivers had erected a gallows there.

Before the hanging Untersturmführer Müller gave a speech in Ukrainian to the big crowd of civilians gathered there. In front of the gallows sat a largish crowd of Jews huddled together. These Jews had to keep their hands above their heads and watch the proceedings. I do not know whether the Jews were made to say anything during the execution. If I am challenged with the witness Jordan's statement that the Jews had to say, 'We want to go to the Promised Land', I cannot tell you if this is true. After the hanging the Jews were shot outside Zhitomir at the so-called Pferdefriedhof [horse cemetery].

Heinrich Huhn, member of Sonderkommando 4a

---

trucks. A group of Jews was lined up by the edge of the grave. There were about ten to twelve of them. They were standing facing the marksmen. There was one marksman for each Jew. Then the platoon-leader of the Waffen-SS platoon gave the order to fire. The victims fell backwards into the grave. When it became apparent that many of the victims did not die immediately the method of execution was changed.

Then a discussion was held between Blobel, the army judge of the 6th Army, myself and I think, but am not completely sure, the army doctor. The outcome of this discussion was an order to the Waffen-SS platoon to aim at the head for the rest of the execution. The result of this was that if the marksmen hit their target the tops of the victims' skulls flew into the air and bits of their brains were spattered in the faces of the firing-squad. Kompanie-Führer [company commander] Grafhorst, who felt responsible for his men, was strongly opposed to this type of execution. And so once again the method of shooting was changed.

Question: Did you give *coups de grâce?*
Answer: I cannot remember.
Question: After this execution were these events discussed with the Wehrmacht? If they were, what was said?
Answer: We left the execution area and went home. Then a discussion took place at which members of the Wehrmacht were also present. There were also men who had been at the execution, amongst others the army judge. During this discussion it was said that this type of shooting was intolerable for both victim and firing-squad members. This was because when the firing squad aimed at the heart, in my view, about twenty-five per cent were off the mark and when the victims were shot in the head, not only did the victims have to look at the firing-squad but in addition five per cent were not killed outright. I no longer remember whether the legality of executing Jews was discussed. It is however likely. My understanding is that the army judge, by citing a number of cases, made it clear that Reichenau was a merciless overlord. I can no longer remember the army judge's name.

Dr Artur Neumann, military judge:

I was a military judge on active service and in the spring of 1940 was transferred to the HQ of Sixth Army as Oberstkriegsgerichtsrat. I had authority over the courts of the divisions and corps which were under the supervisory command of the army. I was also with Sixth Army for the Russian campaign, indeed right from the start until Stalingrad. . . .

In the summer of 1941 when the Army headquarters were in Zhitomir, one day one of my drivers reported to me that a Russian was to be publicly hanged in one of the town squares. I no longer remember whether it was my chief driver Boettcher or not. Boettcher was from Saxony. I immediately drove to the square, which was already full of locals. Around the square stood sentries. As I recall there were no members of the Wehrmacht present. In the middle of the crowd of people there was a type of gymnastics apparatus from which a noose hung down. Underneath the structure there was a lorry (it may have driven to the structure), on which as I recall a man stood. I do not remember who put the noose around his neck. At any rate the lorry then started its engine and moved away and the man hung from the noose. As a result of his death throes his trousers fell down around his ankles.

I remember it was said that the man being hanged was a Russian spy (or saboteur or partisan). It was also said that he may have been quite a high-ranking Russian official from the judiciary or the GPU. The latter seems to me more likely. When I wanted to leave the square after this execution I could not get away immediately because my car had been surrounded by newly arrived locals or perhaps they were blocking the road. It is possible that these people had been forced to attend the execution. At any rate I then saw local inhabitants being marched away in columns. Together with other members of the staff of Sixth Army who were also present we then started off towards the outskirts of the town with these columns. After a time I saw a group of people gathered some distance away from the road, towards whom the groups of locals were marching. When I reached the spot I discovered the following scene:

A trench between ten and fifteen metres long and about four metres wide had been dug out in the earth. I cannot say how deep it was. About fifteen metres away from it stood a row (which may have been two deep) of members of an SS formation. Ten to twelve local people at a time were led to the front of this grave and made to line up facing it with their backs to the SS firing-squad (they may even have had to kneel down). The order to fire was given and they were shot by the firing-squad. They fell immediately into the grave. I watched some three or four executions at a distance of perhaps twenty metres to the side of the firing-squad. I remember that the members of the firing-squad were young and some of them were upset. I also remember an SS officer bawling something out to one of these young men who was agitated. I can no longer remember what this SS officer looked like or what accent he spoke in. I also no longer remember what rank he was. The people being shot were of all ages. There were also women among them. I then realized that because of their appearance these people could not be partisans, spies or the like but that they were almost certainly all Jews.

I also remember hearing yelling and screaming further back among the crowd from where each group was led for execution. I can no longer remember whether the people being executed were beaten or bore signs of ill-treatment, or more particularly traces of blood. I also remember one or two SS marksmen firing *coups de grâces* into the trench after the executions. While I was present at these executions the then

Adjutant (IIa) of the army, Oberst von Schuler, was certainly also present. Other members of the staff were also present, but I can no longer say today who they actually were.

Question: Did you or another staff officer discuss the particularly cruel execution method with the SS officer in charge, as the SS officer in question claims?

Answer: No, I didn't.

Question: The SS officer in question also claims that the military judge was not only present, but that together with other staff officers had a part in the decision that the young marksmen had to aim not at the forehead but at the neck. What do you say to this?

Answer: No, that is not true, as far as I'm concerned. I refrained from any type of involvement in the events. . . .

During dinner at the officers' mess – presumably before and after the actual meal – this incident was discussed, which – as it then transpired – a large number of members of the staff had seen.

We all voiced our uneasiness about these events. It was also said that members of the Wehrmacht had taken part as marksmen at similar executions in the area controlled by the Sixth Army, in fact on the orders of the SS marksmen or their officers. The whole matter was brought to the attention of the Oberbefehlshaber der Armee [Commander-in-Chief of the Army], Field Marshal von Reichenau. I also think that I talked to him about it once when he came to address us. At any rate an army order was issued to the effect that all members of the army were expressly forbidden to take part in executions of this type.

2. 'Scores of soldiers, some in bathing trunks, watching the proceedings'
Major Rösler to Infantry General Schniewindt, 3 January 1942

At the end of July 1941 Infantry Regiment 528 was on its way to Zhitomir from the west, where it was to move into resting quarters. At that time I was regimental commander. On the afternoon of the day we arrived I was taking up my staff quarters with my staff when we heard rifle salvoes at regular intervals, followed after some time by pistol fire. The shots were not coming from far away. I decided to go and look into this matter and so together with the Adjutant and the Ordonnanzoffizier (Lieutenant von Bassewitz and Second Lieutenant Müller-Brodmann) set off in the direction of the rifle fire to find out what was happening. We soon realized that a cruel spectacle was taking place out there for after a while we saw numerous soldiers and civilians pouring on to an embankment in front of us, behind which, as we were informed, executions were being carried out at regular intervals. We were not able to see over the embankment; however, at intervals we kept hearing the sound of a whistle, followed by a ten-volley rifle salvo, followed after a while by pistol shots.

When we finally climbed on to the embankment we were completely unprepared for what we saw. We were confronted by a scene that was so abominable and cruel that we were utterly shattered and horrified. In the earth was a pit about seven to eight metres long and perhaps four metres wide. The earth that had been dug out was piled up to one side of it. This pile of earth and the wall of the pit were stained red by streams of blood. The pit itself was filled with innumerable human bodies of all types, both male and female. It was hard to make out all the bodies clearly, so it was not possible to estimate how deep the pit was. Behind the piles of earth dug from it stood a squad of police under the command of a police officer. There were traces of blood on their uniforms. In a wide circle around the pit stood scores of soldiers from the troop detachments stationed there, some of them in bathing trunks, watching the proceedings. There were also an equal number of civilians, including women and children. By going up very close to the pit I saw something that to this day I can never forget. Among the bodies in the pit lay an old man with a white beard, who still had a small walking-stick hanging over his left arm. It was clear that the old man was still alive as he was panting for breath and so I asked one of the policemen to kill him once and for all, to which he replied in a jocular fashion, 'I've already shot him seven times in the belly, don't worry, he'll snuff it soon enough.'

In the pit the dead were not laid out in any orderly way but were left where they happened to land after being shot down from the top of

---

On some occasions members of the Wehrmacht took the carbines out of our hands and took our place in the firing-squad.

Erich Heidborn, Member of Sonderkommando 4a

the pit. All these people were first shot in the neck and then finished off with pistol shots from above.

3. 'When the Jews saw how easy it was to be executed . . .'

A customs official on murders in Vinnitsa and Brailov:

In April 1940 I was called up to Kassel and drafted into the infantry. After my training I was posted to the customs service. Our unit was assembled in Kassel and then sent to Poland and later to Russia. I went with the unit to Vinnitsa via Kamenets Podolsky. Our unit, consisting of about 120 men, arrived in Vinnitsa just after the troops. . . .

My first stay in Vinnitsa lasted about four weeks. During this time mass executions took place. The people who were shot there were without a doubt Jews: men, women and children. In fact anyone Jewish was executed. I too was present at such executions. It was terrible. The executions took place a little way outside Vinnitsa at graves which the Jews themselves had to dig beforehand – though they did have the right equipment like shovels and pickaxes for this purpose.

What happened at the executions was that the offenders positioned themselves with their backs to the firing-squad at the edge of the ditch and were killed with a shot in the back of the neck from a submachine-gun. Anyone who did not fall into the trench was kicked in. The firing-squad consisted of police officers in all cases. You could tell they were police officers as they wore a green uniform. There were also only two marksmen carrying out the execution. . . .

About fifteen to twenty people had to line up at the edge of the trench. The two marksmen then shot them individually. There were some frightful scenes. When the Jews saw how easy it was to be executed they ran to be executed of their own accord. They even pushed in front of each other to get there sooner. I should also add that the Jews were half-starved when they were shot. They had probably not had anything to eat for weeks. I can say that in the four weeks that I initially spent in Vinnitsa executions were carried out on a daily basis. Over the total period some thousands would have been executed. . . .

After about four weeks – the executions had by no means stopped by this point – I was sent to Brailov on the Romanian border. Our role there was to take everything away from people crossing the border. After a short time I was, however, transferred back to Vinnitsa to the command post. This was before Christmas 1941. I then stayed there until about 1944.

Back in Vinnitsa I worked as Schirrmeister (motor transport sergeant) at the customs command post. I was responsible for about fifty vehicles and in addition had to undertake tours of inspection of the vehicles at the Bezirkskommissariaten. During one of these trips I once got snowed in. It was in Brailov. I had to stay there for a few weeks. At that time Jews in Brailov were engaged in digging large graves just outside the village. It could not have been that cold as it was still possible to dig the soil. One evening I visited the graves with several colleagues, who were full of indignation. At that point only the graves had been dug. The Jews were allowed to live for a while longer. They probably wanted to starve them to death completely.

After a few days the executions started. It was said that the Jews had been rounded up in the market-place. Members from our Dienst-stelle were also used to guard these Jews. I would like to say that more than 500 Jews had been rounded up in the market-place. Here too there were men, women and children. I saw children who tried to escape being shot at as though they were hares and you could see a number of bloody children's bodies lying round this crowd of people. They were then led to the graves under guard. The way to the grave was strewn with torn-up paper money. The Jews had probably torn up the money so that it would not fall into the hands of their killers.

When they had reached the execution area the Jews had to get completely undressed. They then had to throw their clothes on to a pile. The clothing was then sorted by the militia. The Jews then had to climb naked into the grave and lie face downwards on the earth. Here a single policeman fired the shots from above with a sub-machine-gun. The policeman also climbed into the trench so that he stood right behind the offenders. When he had riddled them all with bullets it was the turn of the next lot. They had to lie down on those who had already been shot. When the pile of bodies had grown too high the policeman took a few steps back and the next offenders had to go and lie on a new part of the grave behind those who had already been executed. And so it went on. . . .

I cannot say whether this one policeman carried out the execution alone or whether he was later relieved. The only thing I can remember is that after a little while he lit a cigarette and had a break. I actually spoke to him and asked him whether he didn't find it hard to carry out something like this. He told me that he had two children but that he had got used to this work which he seemed to do with the utmost satisfaction.

4. 'Present at the execution with heads of other authorities'
A Wirtschaftsführer on mass killings in Bobruisk

In March 1942 I went as a Wirtschaftsführer [lit. economics officer] to the Central Russia zone (Russland-Mitte). My job was to get the businesses and factories left behind by the Russians up and running again. My work took me to among other places the towns of Bobruisk, Borissov and Minsk right on into the Gomel area. I spent about six months in this area and in about September 1942 went to the southern zone and the Caucasus. My rank was equivalent to that of Oberstleutnant [lieutenant-colonel]. The headquarters of the Wirtschaftsinspektion [economics inspectorate] were in Borissov. The office was headed by Lieutenant-General Wagner. During the course of my work I came into contact with Lieutenant-General von dem Bach-Zelewski on numerous occasions.

During his time in Bobruisk 12,000 to 15,000 Jews were executed. On the first day, when the action began, exactly 2,500 Jews (men, women and children) were executed by firing-squad. I was present at this execution with heads of other authorities. In a sense we were really ordered to be present: we had received a memorandum or telephone call asking for us to be present at the beginning of the action. The various offices must have sent delegations in order not to give the impression that they were opposed to National Socialism. The action took place in April or May of 1942 within the boundaries of the town and began at 6 o'clock in the morning. It lasted the entire day though there was a break because some members of the squads carrying it out were cracking up and had to be relieved. The execution squad consisted only of young and inexperienced policemen. . . .

This first action was followed by others until some 12,000–15,000 people had been exterminated. I was, however, not present at the later executions.

121

After this execution, von dem Bach-Zelewski held a briefing session in Bobruisk. I and others who were present told him that we needed the manpower which was being lost by the executions. Von dem Bach-Zelewski voiced his opposition to this notion and stated he was fulfilling a duty of the fatherland.

5. 'The Twelve Toppers and a Little Hat'
A 'Troop Welfare Kamerad' reports

When the war started I was drafted into the Reserve Corps of the Schutzpolizei at Regensburg and a few days later was sent to Hof am Saale. Before I finished my training I was discharged from the police service on the grounds that musicians were not needed in this unit. . . . In June 1941 I was called up once again. This time I had to go to Zirndorf where I stayed for eight to ten days. I was then transferred to Würzburg. At that time an order had been issued that a 'song leader' was to be detailed to each battalion. The role of these leaders was to rehearse songs in the individual companies and also to organize the social evenings. In summer 1941 I thus went with the (motorized) Reserve Police Battalion under the command of Major Englisch from Würzburg to Galicia. The unit was stationed in Stanislav. I myself belonged to the company which had a Sarge by the name of Stumm and an officer named Schlüter.

I then spent between four and five months in Stanislav. During this time I reported to the Truppenbetreuung ('Troop Welfare Bureau') in Berlin-Mariendorf, circumventing the usual channels. Not long after, I was summoned by the Truppenbetreuung to Berlin where I spent about nine months. I was given four weeks to devise a programme for the Truppenbetreuung and to select people from the many Kameraden there who seemed suitable for my programme. I found a group of thirteen men and that is how 'The Twelve Toppers and a Little Hat' crystallized. This group made its first appearance on 22 December 1942 in the Berliner Sportpalast [Berlin Sports Palace] or Reichsportfeld [Reich Sports Field]. I ran this group until the end of the war. I was never imprisoned.

I belonged to the reserve Schutzpolizei throughout the war. My last rank was Oberwachtmeister Schutzpolizei der Reserve. I would, however, like to point out that the members of the Truppenbetreuung

Kameraden der Frontbetreuung.

Winniza, die Stadt an des Buges Strand,
in aller Welt nun ist sie bekannt,
jeder vernahm es mit Schrecken.
Durch Mord, Sadismus der Juden Hand,
geschändet ist das ukrain'sche Land.

Im tiefsten Frieden dies'Schandwerk gelang,
da wird es dem Mutigsten fast bang,
uns könnte ein Gleiches geschehen.
Doch wer mit eigenen Augen gesch'n diese Post,
stehet für alle Zeiten fest.

Und nun kamt Ihr, Kameraden aus gleichem Blut,
brachtet uns mit, deutsches, heiliges Gut,
den unbändigen Willen zum Leben.
Brachtet Frohsinn, Laune in schwerster Zeit,
wie machtet Ihr unsere Herzen weit.

Wir sahen zwei Welten
und lassen drum eines nur gelten,
dem Führer sei es geschworen;
Einen Frieden den unser Schwert beschützt,
Einen Frieden der unserem Volke nützt.

Oberw. Freytag

SS und Polizei-Standortführer.

Winniza
im August 1943.

Hauptmann d. Schußpolizei.

123

To the Comrades from Troop Welfare

Vinnitsa, the town on the edge of the Bug,
is famed throughout the world.
Nobody could hear its name without terror.
Through murder and sadism at the hands of the Jews
the Ukrainian land was tainted.

These vile deeds were allowed to go on completely unhindered
as even the most courageous were afraid –
the same could have happened to us.
But he who has seen this pest with his own eyes
stands firm for ever more.

And then you came, comrades of one blood,
brought with you German, holy goodness,
the fearless will to live.
You brought cheer, good spirits in the most difficult of times,
how full you make our hearts.

We saw two worlds
and will allow only one to hold sway,
this we have sworn to the Führer;
a peace which our sword protects,
a peace which serves our people.

Oberwachtmeister Freytag

(Stamp)
Vinnitsa,
August 1943

SS and Police Garrison Commander
[sig. illeg.]
Hauptmann of the Schutzpolizei

The war has not taken away our cheer and good spirits

This says it all

This 'Paradise'

Der **Krieg** selbst
uns Frohſinn und Laune
noch liess?

Hier
sagt
alles

dies „Paradies"

were treated as Sonderführer, that is, we had the same rights as a Sonderführer as far as accommodation, rationing, etc. were concerned. We did not wear the insignia of a Sonderführer, however. We only had a pass, which was issued by the relevant commander of the Ordnungspolizei.

I think that our unit spent most of its time in exercises. It is correct that the members of our unit were called in for the so-called Jewish actions. I, however, never participated in any of these actions. Whenever an action took place I was detailed by Schlüter, with whom I had a very good relationship, to guard duty. I personally neither participated in nor watched mass shootings in Stanislav and other places. Nevertheless, I do remember certain executions, which occurred when the Jews who had been rounded up were loaded into the waiting wagons. Then I saw the escort personnel – these were SS members and Ukrainians – shooting individual Jews. I heard from members of our battalion that Meister Zimmermann was always looking for volunteers for what was called a Sonderkommando. These Sonderkommandos had the task of carrying out executions. The remaining battalion members were partly detailed to cordon duty and transport escort duty, as I myself was. Whether some also had to round up the Jewish population is beyond my knowledge.

6. 'The execution area was visited by scores of German spectators'

'Execution tourism' in Liepaja, Latvia

A security-police interpreter in Liepaja:

I would like to say that at the beginning executions of Jews took place every two weeks, if not more frequently. All of these early executions took place in the area to the south of the lighthouse. Later the execution area was moved to the north of the port among some dunes. Although I did not have to take part in every single shooting I had orders to be there pretty often. I would also like to state at this point that I was the only man in our section without any rank whatsoever. . . . It was only in the early days that members of our section had to man the firing-squad. Later we had a Kommando of Latvians who made up the firing-squad.

126

A boatman working for the harbourmaster:

I have had a lot of trouble with my memory and I forget things very easily. When I am asked whether I knew something about the executions of Jews I have to say that Fahlbusch and I once received orders to attend an execution of Jews as spectators. . . . I still remember that we both had to be at the execution area at 20.00 hrs on the appointed day. We walked there and back. When we arrived at the appointed place a number of German soldiers were already there. There may have been over a hundred men. I still remember that they were not SS men but soldiers from the Wehrmacht. I think I would be correct in saying that men from all the units stationed in Liepaja were ordered to report to this execution area.

The head of 2nd Company, Reserve Police Battalion 13:

I heard about the executions of Jews shortly after our arrival [July 1941] in Liepaja. We were still clearing up in our quarters when some marines from the naval unit came past. When I asked them whether they wanted to help us, they answered that they had heard that Jews were always being shot in the town and that they wanted to see this for themselves. . . . Some days later, if I remember correctly it was 24 July 1941, a Saturday, I had the following experience:

Together with the naval unit 2nd Company had to carry out some searches in the new part of Liepaja, that is, north of the canal. The company had already marched on ahead. I followed with Leutnant Haufschild and my driver in a vehicle. In a street in the new part of the city I saw some Jews crouched in the back of a lorry guarded by uniformed Latvians. You could tell they were Jews by the yellow patches on their clothing. Out of curiosity and in order to see what was happening I followed this lorry in my car. We travelled in a northerly direction as far as the area round the naval port. We stopped near the beach. There I saw [SS-Untersturmführer] Kügler with some SD men and a number of Jews. The Jews were crouching down on the ground. They had to walk in groups of about ten to the edge of a pit. Here they were shot by Latvian civilians. The execution area was visited by scores of German spectators from the Navy and the Reichsbahn (railway). I turned to Kügler and said in no uncertain terms

Libau (Liepaja), 15 December 1941: Jewish women are made to undress in the cold before the very eyes of their murderers

that it was intolerable that shootings were being carried out in front of spectators.

A war correspondent on the 'unfortunate' murderers:

In July 1941 I was stationed as a naval correspondent on board a minesweeper in Liepaja harbour. One day while we were on board we heard rifle salvoes ringing out at intervals of a few minutes. I got somebody to row me across the harbour in the direction of the lighthouse. Thanks to the pass I had obtained from Armed Forces High Command, which every war correspondent carried with him, I was allowed to cross the lines of Latvian auxiliary police. There I became an eyewitness to the executions of Jews. The way these executions were conducted is well known, so there is no need for me to go into that.

As a journalist what interests me are the people who had to carry out such an action and I had the opportunity to study these people closely. The reason . . . is that I saw SD personnel weeping because they could not cope mentally with what was going on. Then again I encountered others who kept a score-sheet of how many people they had sent to their death. During the course of long conversations I learned that they had been ordered to join this firing-squad and that there was nothing left for them but suicide, and that some indeed had already committed suicide. They said that if they had refused they themselves would have been shot or sent to the Sonderkommandos, where their days would be numbered. Death was certain for them, they said, and they would not survive the war since such afflicted people would never be permitted to return to the homeland. I spoke for a long time with these unfortunate people. . . .

Who today can determine which were those who wept as they carried out their duties and which the ones who kept a score-sheet?

A boatswain's mate from harbour surveillance:

I had been hearing continuous rifle salvoes for some time in the harbour area, so I decided to see what was happening there. After finishing work some time between 17.00 and 18.00 hours, I went by boat to the other bank, in the direction of the shots. With me was a member of our section, I no longer remember his name. It may have

Several thousand Jews lived in Libau (Liepaja), the second largest city in Latvia. Gradually, they were all executed. The photographs are of a 'Murder Action' between 15 and 17 December 1941. The victims reached the execution site in Skeden, to the north of Libau, after a march by foot on icy roads. The site was right on the Baltic

The victims had to undress. Clothes can be seen that belonged to Jews already murdered

Women and girls photographed before being shot. The murder squad consisted of a Latvian SD guard platoon, SS- und Polizeistandortführer Dr Dietrich's Schutzpolizei-Dienstabteilung and Latvian Police Battalion 21

A group of women and children above the death trench, just before they were murdered

The victims fell into the mass grave. On 31 December 1941 SS-Untersturm-führer Kügler [Security Police, Liepaja branch] reported to SS- und Polizeistandortführer Dr Dietrich, that twenty-three Communists and 2,731 Jews had been 'executed'

been around August 1941. When we reached the other bank we went to the bunkers at the old citadel. We stayed there a while and climbed on to a bunker so that we could see better. . . . I saw a long deep trench which was said to have been dug by the Jews the previous day. By the trench stood members of the SS and Latvian plain-clothes police wearing armbands. The execution area was cordoned off by the Latvians. We had a good view of the trench, so we were able to observe everything well.

The execution area was about a kilometre from the lighthouse. The land was overgrown with bushes and the ground was sandy. We watched the execution for about an hour and a half. During this time three or four trucks each holding five men were brought from the town to the execution area. The victims had to lie down in the back of the truck during the transport. It was driven right up to the trench and then the victims were herded into the trench from the truck like cattle. This was done by the Latvian police. They were holding clubs and were armed with carbines. I saw the victims being struck by the clubs. Each time, the five had to walk single file into the trench. Then they had to line up in the trench with their backs to the five marksmen. The five marksmen stood with their rifles on the side of the trench. I clearly remember that an SS officer stood by the trench. Apart from him there were also some SS or SD men. The shooting took place under the supervision of the SS. I no longer know for sure today whether the firing-squad was made up of Latvians or SD men; I think however that they were SD men. One of them gave a command and a salvo was fired.

The victims stood facing us. I still remember clearly that after the salvo the victims collapsed. They were shot in the head. Blood spurted out. I can still very well remember the SS officer finishing them off with his pistol. . . .

I clearly recall one elderly man who was wearing a white coat, from which you could tell that he was a Jewish minister. I must mention that apart from me there were also other members of the Wehrmacht (army and navy) watching the execution. One of the other soldiers who was also watching told me that this man was a Jewish man of religion. As he was walking to the trench the man collapsed. The other Jews had to take him to the trench, where he was shot.

An adjutant from Naval Anti-Aircraft Detachment 707:

Two or three days before our unit was transported to France . . . Jews – men, women and children – some 200–300 metres away were led past our quarters in Liepaja in a northerly direction on the road to Windau. There were people of all ages. The column was under guard. Later on, we learned that the guards were Latvian members of the SS who wore the German field-grey SD uniform. The men were armed with carbines. I would estimate that there were about 300 to 500 people in the group that was led past our quarters on the said street. The column marched about one to two kilometres north of our quarters to a little wood where a fairly large wide ditch had already been dug. As I still recall I had seen these ditches, correction, this ditch a couple of days before. The terrain was bumpy and could not be seen from our quarters. The execution area was overgrown with pines. The trench was situated in this wooded hilly area. The trench was about two to three metres wide, about three metres deep and about fifty to seventy-five metres long. I only saw one such trench.

On the day that the above group was led past our quarters there was black ice on the roads and people were falling all over the road on the ice. The Jews were not beaten or ill-treated. At any rate I did not see anything of this sort happening. I still remember that this group to my knowledge was shot later that day, in the afternoon I believe. Not only I but also other people from our unit later heard the sound of rifle fire coming from the direction of the said grave for quite a long time. . . .

The following day I went with several members of our unit . . . to the execution area on horseback. When we arrived at the said hills we could see the arms and legs of the executed Jews sticking out of the inadequately filled-in grave. After seeing this we officers sent a written communication to our headquarters in Liepaja. As a result of our communication the dead Jews were covered properly with sand.

Letter of 3 January 1942 from the Liepaja SS and Police chief to the Livonia SS and Police chief, commander of Riga Ordnungspolizei:

The execution of the Jews which was carried out during the period covered by this report is still the main topic of conversation among the local population. Regret about the fate of the Jews is constantly expressed; there are few voices to be heard which are in favour of the elimination of the Jews. Amongst other things a rumour is abroad that the execution was filmed in order to have material to use against the Latvian Schutzmannschaft. This material is said to prove that Latvians and not Germans carried out the executions.

'In the interest of maintaining military discipline . . .'

The massacre of children in Byelaya Tserkov, military chaplains and the Wehrmacht

Street in Byelaya Tserkov, August 1941

Byelaya Tserkov (Bialacerkiew) is a Ukrainian village, 70 km from Kiev. In August 1941 the Feldkommandant of Byelaya Tserkov requested the intervention of Sonderkommando (SK) 4a to kill its Jewish inhabitants. The extermination orders were received by a unit ('Teilkommando') of SK 4a which was under the command of SS-Obersturmführer August Häfner. The unit consisted of regular members of SK 4a and a platoon from 3rd Company, SS Special Operations Battalion (Waffen-SS) under the command of SS-Oberscharführer Jäger. Between 8 and 19 August the Waffen-SS platoon – with the help of the Ukrainian militia – executed several hundred Jewish men and women by firing-squad. Scene of the crime: a rifle-range near the barracks (see witness report).

The children of those murdered were initially locked up in a building on the edge of the village. On the evening of 19 August some of the children were transported in three full lorry-loads to the rifle-range and killed there. Some ninety children were kept back in wretched conditions. The following day, 20 August, the Catholic military chaplain, Ernst Tewes, and his Protestant colleague, Gerhard Wilczek, were having lunch together in the mess. Both were soldiers of officer rank. A distraught non-commissioned officer came and pleaded with Tewes (who was ordained a bishop after the war) to take 'remedial action'.

The military chaplains visited the children and informed the divisional chaplain of 295th Infantry Division (ID), who was in the area for a few days. Then the Catholic divisional chaplain, Dr Reuss, (who was ordained bishop in Mainz after the war) and his Protestant colleague Kornmann (presumed dead), together with Tewes and Wilczek, visited the awful scene. In the afternoon divisional chaplains Dr Reuss and Kornmann reported to the Generalstabsoffizier of the division, Lieutenant-Colonel Helmuth Groscurth (killed in action) on their visit.

What follows – the actions of the Wehrmacht up to the officially condoned murder of the children on 22 August – can be found in the passages printed below.

1. An officer cadet on the killing of the adults

From the middle of July until the second half of August I was in Byelaya Tserkov with my unit. I know for certain that on 15 August we were still in B.T. In fact I remember that some of us had been saying that the sun was not strong enough to tan us any more and that autumn must be on its way. We were so tanned, we suddenly realized that the sun was no longer changing the colour of our skin. We were stationed in the grounds of a genetics institute. I had spoken to the professor of the institute about genetic mutation because I was interested in the subject. I remember that the medical officer at that time was a doctor from Bad Mergentheim. I went round the institute with him to look for some spare parts for X-ray equipment. During the evenings when we had nothing to do we used to go for a stroll in the grounds. I know that one evening I was walking past a barracks, at the back of the institute grounds, when I saw a sentry standing in front of a tiny house with, if I remember correctly, a fixed bayonet. He was an SS man. He was not very old; I think he must have been about twenty-six. This guard was standing at one corner of the house. Near by sat three young girls. One of these girls was answering a call of nature. This particularly stuck in my mind. I found it hilarious that the SS man was guarding the girl with his bayonet fixed while she relieved herself. The girls were also laughing and giggling about it. The guard called over to me and said, 'You cannot come through here, an execution is taking place.' I laughed at this and said, pointing to the girls, 'Not the girls by any chance?' I thought he would say that the girls had nothing to do with it. But he only said, 'They have got to watch.' I said to him, 'Many thanks.' I then turned back. I could not get the thought of this execution out of my mind and so I went over there to see what was going on.

Access to the execution area was blocked by a wall and the way in was through a high iron gate with railings, which was locked. I could not get through so I stopped with other soldiers and civilians in front of the gate and looked through the railings at the execution area, which was about eighty metres away. I saw about nine girls or women kneeling in front of a deep ditch. They were kneeling with their faces towards the ditch. A further nine girls were waiting in front of the little house where the girl who had been guarded by the SS man had relieved herself. What struck me particularly was the calmness and discipline of these people. Behind the kneeling girls stood the marksmen: two for each person. The marksmen were members of the SS.

On the orders of a superior they fired shots at the heads of these people with their carbines. When hit, these people fell forwards into the ditch. Some of them went head over heels. Sometimes the tops of their skulls flew up into the air. Some of the marksmen were sprayed with blood. They were shooting from a distance of about five metres. It was a terrible scene. I remember an SS officer walking along the edge of the ditch and firing shots into it with a sub-machine-gun as he went along. First he went along the length of it and then across the breadth of it. He had first taken up a position on the right side of the trench from where he also gave the orders to shoot. As far as I can remember the SS officer had three stars and a stripe on his collar patch. He was a tall man in his mid-thirties, I would guess. Later, after the execution, the iron gate was opened and I went across to the ditch. In front of the grave there were pools of blood. I didn't climb into the grave. It was about seven or eight metres long, about two and a quarter metres wide, and I would estimate that it had originally been four metres deep. When I looked into it that day there were still two and a half metres clear up to the edge of the ditch. In this grave the bodies lay in layers. The bodies were covered with earth.

While I was standing at the grave the SS officer with the three stars and stripe was still walking round the grave firing the last shots to finish the people off. When he went away I could still see them moving. That first evening I saw some 162 people being executed in the way I have described. Nine people were shot at a time while a further nine had to wait their turn. They were then led over to the grave. The people who were to be shot walked towards this grave as though they were taking part in a procession. They walked in a line, each person with their hands on the shoulders of the person in front. They went composed and quietly to their deaths. I saw only two women weep the whole time I observed such executions. I found it simply inexplicable.

After that first evening I went past that spot from time to time. The executions took place every evening at about 18.00 hours. I was in B.-T. for about six weeks and personally saw about six executions. I heard about others when some of the other cadets came in and said, 'They're shooting again.' At the six executions I saw, altogether some

800–900 people must have been killed. It was always the same picture that presented itself. One concentrated more on the victims than on the marksmen. I can still picture the whole scene in my mind's eye today. It was always so strange when the victims toppled over into the trench. The victims did not collapse regularly but sometimes stumbled, sometimes they also fell higgledy-piggledy into the pit. I once even held a piece of scalp with greying hair in my hand that was lying near the pit. That was on the first evening I was there. [That evening] women had been shot. As far as I can recall I saw two children. They were boys. . . . It was not curiosity which drove me to watch this but disbelief that something of this type could happen. My comrades were also horrified by these executions.

The soldiers knew about these executions and I can remember one of my men saying that he had been permitted to take part in one. Whether or not he did I do not know. I forbade my men to take part in them.

I don't want to end without mentioning that all the soldiers who were in B.-T. knew what was happening. Every evening the whole time I was there rifle fire could be heard, although there was no enemy in the vicinity.

2. Report by the military chaplain, Dr Reuss, to Lieutenant-Colonel Groscurth, 1st Generalstabsoffizier, 295th Infantry Division

Catholic Divisional Chaplain
to 295th Infantry Division

Division command post
20 August 1941

I submit the following report to 295th Infantry Division:

Today in the afternoon towards 14.30 hours Military Chaplains Tewes and Wilczek, Military Hospital Division 4/607, came to the Protestant divisional chaplain and myself and reported the following:

They told us that German soldiers had drawn their attention to the fact that Jewish children aged between a few months and five or six years, whose parents are said to have been executed, are locked up in a house in intolerable conditions under guard by Ukrainian militiamen. These children can be heard whimpering continuously. They said that they went there themselves and had confirmed this fact but had not seen any members of the Wehrmacht or any other authority responsible for keeping order here or carrying out guard duty. They reported that there were only a few German soldiers there as spectators, and that these men had expressed their indignation at this state of affairs. They asked us to report to our headquarters.

Their description of these incidents made it reasonable to suspect that this was an arbitrary action on the part of the Ukrainian militia. In order to be able to report the matter accurately, I myself, accompanied by the two military chaplains and the Protestant Divisional Chaplain, Wehrmachtsoberpfarrer Kornmann, paid a visit to the house, where we discovered the following:

In the courtyard in front of the house the crying and whimpering of children could be heard very loudly. Outside there were a Ukrainian militiaman keeping guard with a rifle, a number of German soldiers and several young Ukrainian girls. We immediately entered the house unobstructed and in two rooms found some ninety (I counted them) children aged from a few months to five, six or seven years old. There was no kind of supervision by the Wehrmacht or other German authorities.

A large number of German soldiers, including a sanitation officer, were inspecting the conditions in which the children were being kept when we arrived. Just then a military policeman, who was under the command of the Ortskommandantur or the Feldkommandantur, also arrived. He stated that he had come only in order to investigate a case of looting which was said to have been carried out by guards from the Ukrainian militia.

The two rooms where the children had been accommodated – there was a third empty room adjoining these two – were in a filthy state. The children lay or sat on the floor which was covered in their faeces. There were flies on the legs and abdomens of most of the children, some of whom were only half dressed. Some of the bigger children (two, three, four years old) were scratching the mortar from the wall and eating it. Two men, who looked like Jews, were trying to clean the rooms. The stench was terrible. The small children, especially those that were only a few months old, were crying and whimpering continuously. The visiting soldiers were shaken, as we were, by these unbelievable conditions and expressed their outrage over them. In another room, accessible through a window in one of the children's rooms, there were a number of women and older children, apparently Jews. I did not enter this room. Locked in a further room there were some other women, among them one woman with a small child on her arm. According to the guard on duty – a Ukrainian boy aged about sixteen or seventeen, who was armed with a stick – it had not yet been established whether these women were Jews or not.

When we got back into the courtyard an argument was in progress between the above-mentioned military policeman and the Ukrainian sentry who was guarding the house. This guard was being accused of the looting and also of destroying several passes which had been issued by the German military authorities to other Ukrainians (who were in fact women). The pieces still lay scattered on the ground. The military policeman disarmed the Ukrainian guard, had him led away and then went away himself. Some German soldiers who were in the courtyard told me that they had their quarters in a house right next door and that since the afternoon of the previous day they had heard the children crying uninterruptedly. Sometime during the evening of the previous day three lorry-loads of children had already been taken away. An official from the SD had been present. The lorry-driver had told them that these were children of Jews and Jewesses who had already been shot and the children were now going to be taken to be executed. The execution was to be carried out by Ukrainian militia. The children still in the house were also to be shot. The soldiers expressed extreme indignation over the conditions in which the children were being kept; in addition, one of them said that he himself had children at home. As there were no Germans there in a supervisory role I asked the soldiers to make sure that nobody else, particularly members of the local population, entered the house, in order to avoid the conditions there being talked about further.

Meanwhile a senior medical officer from the Wehrmacht whom I did not know had visited the children's rooms and declared to me that water should be brought in urgently. In such conditions the risk of an epidemic could not be excluded.

I consider it necessary to report this matter to my HQ for two reasons: first, there is no German watch or supervision at this house and second, German soldiers are able to enter it any time. This has indeed already happened and has provoked a reaction of indignation and criticism.

Dr Reuss
Military Chaplain

3. Report by Wehrmachtoberpfarrer Kornmann

Wehrmachtoberpfarrer Kornmann   O.U.
Protestant Divisional Chaplain   21 August 1941
to 295th Infantry Division

I submit the following report to 295th Infantry Division:

Yesterday (20 August) towards 1500 hours two military chaplains from a military hospital unit in this area came to see me and the Division's Catholic Military Chaplain and reported to us that near by, some 500 m away, about 80 to 90 children from babies to school-age were being held in the upper storey of a house. The children could be heard from a long way off shouting and crying and as they had already been there 24 hours, the soldiers quartered in the neighbouring houses were being sorely disturbed at night. The two military chaplains had been made aware of the presence of the children by the soldiers themselves. Together with the two chaplains and my Catholic colleague, I went to the house in question and saw the children lying and sitting about in two small rooms. They were partly lying in their own filth, there was not a single drop of drinking water and the children were suffering greatly due to the heat. A man from the Ukrainian militia was standing guard downstairs. We learned from him that these were Jew children whose parents had been executed. There was one group of German soldiers standing at the watchpost and another standing at the corner of the house. Some of them were talking agitatedly about what they had heard and seen.

As I considered it highly undesirable that such things should take place in full view of the public eye I hereby submit this report. The two military chaplains were from Military Hospital Unit 4/607 and were named Wilczek (Protestant) and Tewes (Catholic).

                                             Kornmann
F.d.R.   Wehrmachtoberpfarrer
signed: signature
Lieutenant and O.1 (1. Ordonanzoffizier)

4. Lieutenant-Colonel Groscurth's report to C.-in-C. Sixth Army, Field Marshal von Reichenau

295th Infantry Division
1. Generalstabsoffizier

Division Command Post
21 August 1941

Report on events in Byelaya Tserkov on 20 August 1941

On 20 August at about 16.00 hours the two divisional chaplains reported to me that some ninety Jewish children had been locked up in a house in the town for twenty-four hours without any food or water. They reported that they had gone to investigate the conditions there after they had received reports from chaplains from the military hospital. These conditions, they told me, were intolerable and an attempt to induce the Ortskommandant to intervene had not met with success. The divisional chaplains recommended that the conditions should be remedied urgently as numerous soldiers were visiting the house and the sanitary conditions were liable to have dangerous repercussions. This was confirmed by a senior medical officer from the military hospital.

Upon receiving this report I went at 16.30 hours together with the ordnance officer, Lieutenant Spoerhase, Divisional Chaplain Dr Reuss, and an interpreter, Sonderführer Tischuk [Pyszczuk – Ed.] to the house, which was situated down a side road set back some fifty metres from the road. From the road one could see the house and hear children whimpering. There were about twenty NCOs and men standing in the courtyard. There was no guard post in front of the house. A few armed Ukrainians were standing about in the yard. There were children lying on the window-sills, but the windows were not open. On the landing on the first floor stood a Ukrainian guard who immediately opened the door of the rooms in which the children were accommodated. In the three interconnecting rooms there was a further Ukrainian guard armed with a rifle. There were about ninety children and several women crammed into the rooms. A woman was cleaning up in the farthermost room, which contained almost only babies. The other rooms were unbelievably filthy. There were rags, nappies and filth all over the place. The half-naked children were covered in flies. Almost all the children were crying or whimpering. The stink was unbearable. A German-speaking woman was claiming she was completely innocent, had never had anything to do with politics and was not Jewish.

Meanwhile an Oberscharführer [Jäger] from the SD had entered the house. I asked him what was going to happen to these children. He informed me that the children's relatives had been shot and the children were also to be eliminated. Without making any comment I went to the Ortkommandantur and demanded an explanation from the commandant. He told me that the matter was out of his competence and that he had no influence over measures being taken by the SD, although he was aware of them. He suggested discussing the matter with the Feldkommandant, Lieutenant-Colonel Riedl. I then went to see him accompanied by the Ortskommandant and the O.1. The Feldkommandant reported that the head of the Sonderkommando had been to see him, had notified him about the execution and was carrying it out with his knowledge. He stated that he had no power to change the Obersturmführer's instructions. I asked the Feldkommandant whether he thought that the Obersturmführer had also received orders from the highest authority to eliminate children as well; I had heard nothing about this. The Feldkommandant replied he was convinced of the correctness and necessity of this order.

I then requested that the area around the house be sealed off so that the troops would have no possibility whatsoever of seeing what was happening inside. I pointed out that the soldiers who were quartered in the vicinity of the house had heard the children whimpering throughout the night, which had already given rise to considerable criticism on their part. I further asked that the transport to the execution should be conducted inconspicuously. I also offered some of the men from the division for guard duty if the Feldkommandantur did not have sufficient manpower. I further stated that I would immediately instruct Army Group to come to a decision as to whether the execution of the remaining children should proceed or not. (According to the Feldkommandant, a number of children had already been eliminated the previous day by the Ukrainian militia on SD orders.)

The Feldkommandant gave his agreement to this arrangement and emphasized that the divisional commander was the most senior officer in the area and had the competence to issue all the necessary orders. He said he intended to 'adjourn' carrying out any further measures until Army Group's decision was known. He added that he would be requesting an order in writing as a matter of urgency. I had misgivings about interrupting the measures as I thought that the children would not be transported until the evening, by which time Army Group would have made its decision known. I was aware that suspending the measures would inevitably lead to complications with the political authorities and wanted to avoid this if possible. However, the Feldkommandant stated that the transport would take place shortly. I then instructed the Feldkommandant to inform the Head of the Sonderkommando that he would have to postpone the transport until a decision had been taken by Army Group.

I did not go to see the Head of the Sonderkommando myself because I wished to establish contact with Army Group as quickly as possible. I was of the opinion that Army Group should be instructed of the very great importance of this matter immediately and of the fact that the division was not capable of making this decision on its own. The operations officer of Army Group, whom I immediately contacted, stated that the matter had to be handled by Sixth Army HQ. It took me some time to contact the operations officer there. Finally I was told that he would not be able to have a decision from the Commander-in-Chief until the evening. Meanwhile Obersturmführer Häfner, the head of the Sonderkommando, came to see me asking for confirmation of the division's order, which had been communicated to him. He asked for an order in writing. I refused this, remarking that a definitive decision could be expected very shortly. He declared in a rather unmilitary tone that he would have to report these instructions to his commanding officer. He had clear orders to carry out the measures. I stated that I had to stick to my instructions and would back them with force if necessary. I said once again emphatically that the instructions of the political authorities were known to me but that I had to demand that the measures be carried out appropriately, in the interest of maintaining the military discipline of the troops. We would have to wait for the army's decision.

At 19.00 hours I reported the proceedings and measures taken so far to the divisional commander; these met with his approval.

At about 20.00 hours we received the army's decision. The measures were to be postponed. Meanwhile during the late afternoon a truck had already been loaded up with children and was standing in front of the house. The Feldkommandant was immediately notified by the O.1 and then the Obersturmführer was brought by the O.1 to Divisional HQ where I communicated the army's instructions to him.

An officer from Divisional HQ was responsible for ensuring that the orders were executed correctly. Meanwhile access to the house was cut off on the orders of the Feldkommandant. The barricade consisted partly of armed Ukrainians without papers. This blockade by Ukrainians against German soldiers was not permitted to continue. Meanwhile, the Feldkommandant arranged for water and bread to be supplied to the children.

On 21 August at about 11.00 hours Captain Luley (Abwehr-Offizier AOK 6) came together with Standartenführer Blobel and Obersturmführer Häfner to a meeting which had been called by the army. This meeting took place at the Feldkommandant's office. Captain Luley had had a look at the neighbourhood before his arrival at the division but had not gone into the house and the children's accommodation. I conveyed the views of the division and made it very clear that the division had only intervened because of the way in which the action was being carried out. The Standartenführer and the Obersturmführer admitted there had been shortcomings in the way things had been run and stated that a way had to be found to settle the matter quickly on the basis of the prevailing conditions. He did not now see himself as still in a position to be able to carry out the shooting. The Feldkommandant noted critically that the first report on the conditions at the house had come from the divisional chaplains. To this Captain Luley observed that although he himself was a Protestant he considered it preferable for chaplains to limit themselves to the spiritual welfare of the soldiers. To judge from the nature of the comments made by both the Feldkommandant and Captain Luley, they were, first, questioning the credibility of the divisional chaplains and, second, treating the matter as a case of 'stirring up trouble'. They regarded the report as an exaggeration and an impertinent interference on the part of the divisional chaplains. The Standartenführer made no comment on this.

The O.1 [1. Ordonnanzoffizier] and I rejected these outrageous accusations, pointing out that the divisional chaplains must have initially thought that this was another case of the sort of high-handed behaviour on the part of the Ukrainians which had already forced the division to intervene in Zloczow. During the rest of the conversation the Feldkommandant tried to steer the matter into an ideological [weltanschaulich] context and to start a discussion on fundamental questions. He declared that he considered the extermination of Jewish women and children to be pressingly urgent and to be carried out in whatever form it took. He was at pains to point out that as a result of the division's actions the elimination of the children had been delayed unnecessarily by twenty-four hours. The Standartenführer said he was of the same opinion and added that it would be best if those troops who were nosing around carried out the executions themselves and the commanders who were stopping the measures took command of these troops. I quietly rejected this view, without taking any position as I wished to avoid any personal acrimony. When we discussed what further measures should be taken the Standartenführer declared that the Herr Oberbefehlshaber recognized the necessity of eliminating the children and wished to be informed once this had been carried out. The Intelligence Officer of Sixth Army High Command had already confirmed that this indeed was an accurate reflection of Herr Oberbefehlshaber's position.

We then settled the details of how the executions were to be carried out. They are to take place during the evening of 22 August. I did not involve myself in the details of this discussion. The measures that I ordered to keep the troops away will be carried out.

Afterwards Hauptmann Luley reported the outcome of the discussion to the divisional commander.

Members of the Ortskommandantur

Where on earth would we have found enough bread for ninety children? Even in the unlikely event that we had succeeded in doing so and we had managed to bring over some water, we would have only slowed down the whole action. Our priority was to try to effect an order that could help the children. It was not that we wanted to protect our own lives. It was also not the case that if someone had refused to carry out an order he would have been immediately put against the wall. What was needed then were stronger steps. We could have coped with the difficulties. By difficulties I mean that we assumed that we would have been reprimanded for our actions. What they would have done with us, I do not know, nevertheless I don't suppose it would have been something particularly awful. We had nothing to do with the SD; we belonged to the army.

Former military chaplain Gerhard Wilczek

Conclusion:

1. The troops have been trained by their officers to have a decent soldierly attitude and to avoid violence and roughness towards a defenceless population. They are fully aware of the need for the toughest intervention against *franc-tireurs* [= guerrillas]. In the case in question, however, measures against women and children were undertaken which in no way differ from atrocities carried out by the enemy about which the troops are continually being informed. It is unavoidable that these events will be reported back home where they will be compared to the Lemberg (Lvov) atrocities. The troops are waiting for their officers to intervene. This is particularly true for the older married men. An officer is therefore forced to intervene out of consideration for his troops when such things take place in public. In the interest of maintaining military discipline all similar measures should be carried out away from the troops.

2. The execution could have been carried out without any sensation if the Feldkommandantur and the Ortskommandantur had taken the necessary steps to keep the troops away. This unfortunate state of affairs was caused by the failure of both commanders to take the necessary action. During all the negotiations the impression was given that all the executions could be traced back to an initiative of the Feldkommandant. Following the execution of all the Jews in

the town it became necessary to eliminate the Jewish children, particularly the infants. Both infants and children should have been eliminated immediately in order to have avoided this inhuman agony. The Feldkommandant and the Obersturmführer declared that it was not possible to provide alternative accommodation for the children and the Feldkommandant declared several times that this brood had to be stamped out.

(signed) Groscurth

5. Report by military chaplains Tewes and Wilczek

Protestant and Catholic   O.U.
Military Chaplains   22 August 1941
to Military Hospital 4/607

We hereby submit the following report to 295th Infantry Division as instructed:

On 20 August 1941 at 13.00 hours we heard from German soldiers that quite a large number of children had been locked up in intolerable conditions in a house near our quarters. A Ukrainian was said to be guarding these children. As we suspected this to be some arbitrary action on the part of the Ukrainians we went over there straight away. We found about ninety children packed together into two small rooms in a filthy state. Their whimpering could be heard in the vicinity of the house. Some of the children, mainly infants, were completely exhausted and almost lifeless. There was no German guard or supervision present, only a Ukrainian guard armed with a rifle. German soldiers had free access to the house and were expressing outrage over these frightful conditions. As these events were taking place under the aegis of the German Wehrmacht and would therefore damage its reputation, we immediately went and reported to the Ortskommandantur. The Ortskommandant went with us to the house, inspected the conditions and then took us to report to the Feldkommandantur.

At the Feldkommandantur none of the competent gentlemen was available for us to talk to and we were advised to call later. As the matter seemed to us to be one of utmost urgency and we assumed that the divisional commander of 295th Infantry Division stationed in the area was the most senior-ranking officer, we went to see the two divisional chaplains of 295th Infantry Division and informed them of what was happening so that they could report to their HQ.

Tewes, Military Chaplain
Wilczek, Military Chaplain

F.d.R.
(signed) Spoerhase
Lieutenant and O.1

6. Statement by C.-in-C. Sixth Army, Field Marshal von Reichenau

From the Commander-in-Chief
of Sixth Army

Army Headquarters
26 August 1941

1c/A.O.
No. 2245/41
9. Kdos

3 copies
copy 2

Statement on the report of 295th Division
on the events in Bialacerkiew [Byelaya Tserkov]

The report disguises the fact that the division itself has ordered the execution to be interrupted and has requested the consent of the army to do so.

Immediately after the division's telephone inquiry, after consulting Standartenführer Blobel I postponed the carrying out of the execution because it was not organized properly. I gave instructions that on the morning of 21 August, Standartenführer Blobel and a representative of Army Headquarters should go to Bialacerkiew to inspect the

152

conditions. I have ascertained in principle that once begun, the action was conducted in an appropriate manner.

The conclusion of the report in question contains the following sentence, 'In the case in question, measures against women and children were undertaken which in no way differ from atrocities carried out by the enemy about which the troops are continually being informed.'

I have to describe this assessment as incorrect, inappropriate and impertinent in the extreme. Moreover this comment was written in an open communication which passes through many hands.

It would have been far better if the report had not been written at all.

(signed) von Reichenau

Distribution:
Army Group South = 1st copy
295th ID = 2nd copy
Files = 3rd copy

f.d.R.d.A.

(signed) Groscurth
Lieutenant i.G. (im Generalstab)

7. SS-Obersturmführer August Häfner on the killing of the children

. . . Then Blobel ordered me to have the children executed. I asked him, 'By whom should the shooting be carried out?' He answered, 'By the Waffen-SS.' I raised an objection and said, 'They are all young men. How are we going to answer to them if we make them shoot small children?' To this he said, 'Then use your men.' I then said, 'How can they do that? They have small children as well.' This tug-of-war lasted about ten minutes. . . . I suggested that the Ukrainian militia of the Feldkommandant should shoot the children. There were no objections from either side to this suggestion. . . .

August Häfner

I went out to the woods alone. The Wehrmacht had already dug a grave. The children were brought along in a tractor. I had nothing to do with this technical procedure. The Ukrainians were standing round trembling. The children were taken down from the tractor. They were lined up along the top of the grave and shot so that they fell into it. The Ukrainians did not aim at any particular part of the body. They fell into the grave. The wailing was indescribable. I shall never forget the scene throughout my life. I find it very hard to bear. I particularly remember a small fair-haired girl who took me by the hand. She too was shot later. . . . The grave was near some woods. It was not near the rifle-range. The execution must have taken place in the afternoon at about 3.30 or 4.00. It took place the day after the discussions at the Feldkommandanten. . . . Many children were hit four or five times before they died.

'Practical work for our Führer'
Daily life during the Holocaust

Group photograph with unknown persons

1. Letters by Gendarmerie chief Fritz Jacob

Jonsdorf spa, 24 April 1941

Dear Herr Lieutenant-General Querner,
Since 11.4.41 I have been back at our garrison in Jonsdorf and I am going about my duties once again. I graduated from Bad Ems as fifth best cadet, which I was very pleased about. I did not manage 'Good' all round as I only scored about 103 points. The two best graduated with 113. Herr Oberstleutnant Bardua spoke to me during the graduation celebration and told me that he would have very much liked to have placed me higher. This had not been possible, however, for reasons of fairness. I entirely understand that and am therefore satisfied. I earned my marks honourably. To come top out of the Saxons and above all to be higher than so many Prussians is already quite something. About six weeks before the end of the course my nerves suddenly fell to pieces. I could hardly cope with the most basic things. Had that not happened I would certainly have come a lot higher up.

But I believe that even this mark, Herr Lieutenant-General, will give you pleasure.

And now I have to wait. I will be a match for my future role as Bezirksleutnant and as always will try to win the trust of my future superiors. . . .

I permit myself, Herr Lieutenant-General, to present my warmest compliments to you and to your esteemed family.

Heil Hitler
Fritz Jacob, Gendarmerie-Meister

Ebersbach, 29 October 1941

Dear Herr Lieutenant-General,
Before I depart from Ebersbach, I would like to pay my respects to you. Your picture, which is still hanging in the upper corridor, is a

constant and happy reminder of your esteemed personage.

Together with Meister Kluge and others I have been detailed for service in the East. I am truly pleased about this as I can now get down to doing some good practical work for our Führer. I hope that we shall be going to a region which will suit my love of nature, and that this opportunity will finally permit me to advance myself. In Saxony promotion is slow to say the least and almost impossible if a person does not have connections.

I hope as ever that you and your esteemed family are well. I shall permit myself to send written greetings from the realms abandoned by the Red Tsars.

I send best wishes to you and your most worthy family,

Heil Hitler
Jacob, Meister der Gendarmerie

Kamenets Podolsky, 5 May 1942

Dear Herr Lieutenant-General,

I have been here in K. for a month. I have been meaning to give you a sign of life for a long time, but there seems to be no end to work. No wonder either. The region which I have to look after together with 25 Gendarmes and 500 Schutzmännern (Ukrainians) is as large as a *Regierungsbezirk* in Germany. The Schutzmänner cause me the most work, the good-for-nothings. Hardly surprising really. Yesterday semi-bolsheviks and today wearers of the honourable uniform of the police. But some of them are capable chaps. Nevertheless the percentage is small. In my capacity as station chief I act as executioner, lawyer, judge, etc.

Naturally, there's a good deal of mopping up taking place, particularly amongst the Jews. As you can imagine, the population has to be kept on a tight rein. You have to be very careful. Well, we just get on with it. That way we'll all be home quicker. My family is not happy. Almost two years in Ebersbach and now here in the East on the Romanian border. . . .

Permit me, Herr Lieutenant-General to send you my best wishes,

Heil Hitler
Jacob, Meister der Gendarmerie

Dear Herr Lieutenant-General Querner,

I have good cause to answer your first letter of 10 June 1942 promptly. For one thing I forgot your birthday, which my wife drew my attention to, and for another it was a great pleasure to receive your letter. It is such a comfort when you are the only Saxon in a foreign country to hear from a familiar person.

Please excuse my omission, Herr Lieutenant-General. Please accept belatedly my very best wishes for your birthday (your fiftieth, I believe). I wish you all the very best, in particular health for you personally and also for your dear family.

I can just picture your Barbary stallion. It must be a fine beast. Doesn't your wife wish to ride on its noble back? I almost envy her. Our nags are mostly a hotchpotch, like the local population. But up till now I've been surprised at their lack of criminality. You can ask anything of them, just like horses. They work until they drop and make no demands.

Thank you for your reminder. You are absolutely right. We men of the new Germany have to be very tough with ourselves even when we are forced by circumstances to be separated from our families for quite a long time. This is the case right now. We have to settle up with the war criminals once and for all so that we can build a more beautiful and eternal Germany for our children and our children's children. We're certainly not being idle here: three or four Actions a week. First gypsies then Jews, partisans and other such riff-raff. The good thing is that we now have an SD branch here with which I have an excellent working relationship. A week ago a Ukrainian Schutzmann was brutally murdered. The reason? He had made the Jews work in a minefield and so the Jews banded together with partisans and murdered him. In addition, twenty Hungarian soldiers who were running the technical side of the work on the minefield are said to have been murdered. Although they had the Romanian and Protectorate borders in their favour all four criminals were caught, thanks to speedy action. In connection with this crime, fifty people were executed that very evening. We do not exercise wild justice here. However, in cases where a crime demands an immediate punishment we get in touch with the SD and a proper court is immediately set up. Obviously, in an ordinary court of law, it would not be possible to stamp out an entire family if only the father was the criminal.

I do not know whether you too, Herr Lieutenant-General, saw such frightful Jewish types in Poland. I thank my lucky stars that I've now seen this mixed race for what it is. Then if life is kind to me I'll have something to pass on to my children. Sick with venereal disease, cripples and idiots were the norm. Materialists to the last in spite of everything. Every one of them without exception said things like, 'Sei'mer Spezialisten, werd'n sie uns schiess'n nicht' ['We're specialists, you're not going to shoot us, are you?']. These were not human beings but ape people.

Well, there is only a small and rapidly dwindling percentage left of the 24,000 Jews originally living in Kamenets Podolsky. Those little Jews living in the Rayons [the lowest administrative district – Ed.] are also some of our best clients. We are forging ahead and suffer no pangs of conscience and then 'Die Wellen schlagen zu, die Welt hat Ruh' ['the waves will claim what is theirs and the world will have peace'].

And now for my girlfriend. She has chosen the profession of pharmacist. I wish I'd once gone to a certain pharmacy in Hamburg, to buy some acid drops for 5 pfennigs. I don't know what kind of a reception little Dittsch would have given me. He might have shown me the door and told me I was a rotten old so-and-so.

I hear that Tommy is keeping you on your toes. But one of these days he'll run out of ammunition. I find it quite remarkable when you say he cannot affect morale, despite your own personal losses. We all hope that this once Nordic race will disappear into the waves lock, stock and barrel.

Herr Lieutenant-General, please excuse my stupid prattle. I got completely carried away. When that happens 'Jacob Fritze' isn't quite as restrained as usual.

I have a further request, Herr Lieutenant-General: please write to me now and again. It does one so much good to receive a friendly word from home.

So that I don't forget. Today Herr Bezirks-Leutnant Sofka writes that he has been appointed Kreisführer in Zittau Kreis. I envy him. . . .

Permit me, Herr Lieutenant-General, to send you and your esteemed family my warmest greetings from far away.

Heil Hitler
Jacob, Meister der Gendarmerie

2. A Gendarmerie Oberwachtmeister's photographs

The 14th of October 1942, before a mass shooting in the Sdolbunov
(Ukraine) Gebietskommissariat

Jewish women from the Misotsch (Misocz) Ghetto, required to undress

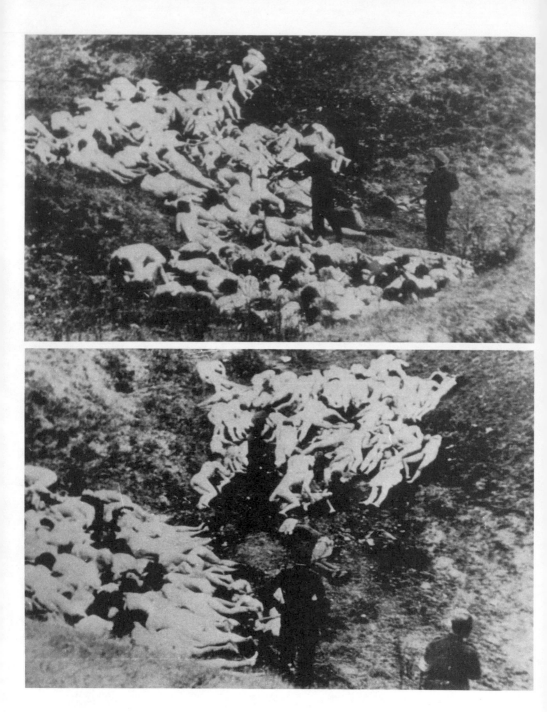

Those women still alive were finished off like wounded game (the *coups de grâce*)

3. Letters of SS-Obersturmführer Karl Kretschmer (SK 4a)

Sunday, 27 September 1942

My dear Soska,
You will be impatient because you have received no letter from me since Monday, 21 September 1942 but I really could not write sooner. First because I once again travelled a thousand kilometres during the past few days (this time by car, two days of dust and rattling) and second because I'm ill. I am feeling wretched and am in horribly low spirits. How I'd like to be with you all. What you see here makes you either brutal or sentimental. I am no longer in the area of Stalingrad but further north in the middle of the front. Not directly at the front but close enough for an aerial bomb to hit me one of these days. But then I have as much chance of being hit by one here as I do in Karlsruhe. As far as I know, up to now you have been spared by the English. Let's hope that's how it stays. After my experiences in Russia, my lovely home means more to me than anything else in the world. If I could pray, I would ask for you and the Homeland to be kept safe. It will be wonderful to be reunited. I know you will be surprised to hear me say that.

As I said, I am in a very gloomy mood. I must pull myself out of it. *The sight of the dead (including women and children) is not very cheering.* But we are fighting this war for the survival or non-survival of our people. You back home, thank God, do not feel the full force of that. The bomb attacks have, however, shown what the enemy has in store for us if he has enough power. You are aware of it everywhere you go along the front. My comrades are literally fighting for the existence of our people. The enemy would do the same. I think that you understand me. *As the war is in our opinion a Jewish war, the Jews are the first to feel it. Here in Russia, wherever the German soldier is, no Jew remains. You can imagine that at first I needed some time to get to grips with this.* Please do not talk to Frau Kern about this.

I am also ill (diarrhoea, fever, cold shivers). It seems that everybody here has got it. The change in diet and no water to boot. After you have the great cities of Western Russia behind you you come to the endless steppe. Africa can't be worse. The country is terrible. Just dust, dust and more dust. The people vegetate in it. The damage caused by the war is soon repaired as the houses are nothing but a few beams and boards. Everything else is made out of mud, which is provided by nature. The roofs are covered with straw and hay and then mud is smeared over them. The sun bakes everything hard. As there is also a lot of chalk, everything is painted white and that's it. The women do all these jobs. There are also men about, but they must work somewhere where you can't see them. Everybody spits. Old and young. You see people taking a mouthful of sunflower seeds and then out it all shoots. The whole day. Like parrots. In the cities I encountered some kind of culture still. In the country there's nothing more to see. Everything is primitive. The only thing I still don't understand is where Stalin got his military power and arms from. The only answer must be that the entire population has been engaged in the war effort and nothing else over the last twenty years. It could not have been possible any other way.

So much for that. Now to food. I always said to you that a soldier does not go hungry. There's just one catch: food is obtained from the countryside and when you leave the rich fields of the Ukraine behind and get to the steppes some things are in short supply, e.g. butter. The army command then helps by providing us with canned and preserved food. *I personally have been lucky, because we are able to buy food in view of our hard work.* Buy is not the right word, the money is worth nothing, we barter. *We happen to be in possession of old clothes, which are very much sought after. We can get everything here. The clothes belonged to people who are no longer alive today. So you don't need to send me any clothing or the like.* We have got enough here to last us for a year. Please could you get hold of some salt for me – the white *Kaisers-Kaffee* type in packets. When I go on leave I'm going to bring back at least fifteen kilos of it. It is more valuable than money here.

I wrote to you that I might be able to find you a Persian rug. It now turns out that it won't be possible. First I'm no longer in the right area and second *the Jewish dealers are no longer alive.* What is more, a lot of people are trying to obtain carpets like that. I also heard people have paid a fortune for them. Obviously that's not something I can do. Perhaps, though, fortune is smiling on us. This is my sixth letter. Today I dispatched parcels no. 2 (butter) and 3 (two tins of sardines in oil, 2 rubber balls, 1 × tea and 2 packets of sweets for the children). . . . Once the cold weather sets in you'll be getting a goose now and again when somebody goes on leave. There are over 200 chattering around here, as well as cows, calves, pigs, hens and turkeys. We live like princes. . . . Today, Sunday, we had roast goose (1/4 each). This evening we are having pigeon. I spread butter thick on bread. We sweeten everything with honey because there is no sugar available. Please send me your empty cans with lids (not more than 100g in weight) but no large ones. We have them filled and sealed here. We can send parcels weighing up to 1 kg in any quantity. You can send me a parcel weighing up to 1 kg with the enclosed stamps. I am just in the process of taking over the business. At the moment I have counted over 110,000 in the kitty – RM in roubles. . . .

Take care of the children for me
With longing and love
in my heart,
your Karl

Please send me the *Führer* and other newspapers every day. We can't get any of them here.

[Date not known]
. . . When the cold sets in don't be surprised if one day you receive a parcel containing a goose. When one of the men goes on leave he will take it along with him and post the parcel to you. Even if you receive a parcel from Hungary go and pick it up. I have lent money to Germans from Hungary who volunteered to serve in the SS and I gave them my home address as well. When they go on leave they will remember me. You see, I'm taking care of you. No doubt you gathered from Göring's speech that we are allowed to send packages. The Führer has given his approval. Even if the end result is that the people here die of hunger, we will still take the food for ourselves. But it need not go that far. That would only be if the worst came to the worst. We have got to appear to be tough here or else we will lose the war. *There is no room for pity of any kind.* You women and children back home could not expect any mercy or pity if the enemy got the upper hand. *For that reason we are mopping up where necessary* but otherwise the Russians are willing, simple and obedient. *There are no Jews here any more.*
　Up to now I have sent you the following parcels. For you all:
(1)　Tin of meat, fish, sweets.
(2)　Tin of butter.
(3)　2 tins sardines in oil, 2 packs sweets, 2 balls, 1 tea.
(4)　Tin of butter.

(5) Tin of butter.

(6) Sardines in oil, 1 fish, 1 soap.

(7) 1 tin of salami.

(8) Volkmar's birthday parcel: 800 g French chocolate.

(9) Package: tin of butter.

(10) Package: tin of butter.

Wednesday, 7 October 1942

No. 8

Dear Sonja, dear children,

It's now a whole month since I had to leave you. I am very sad and lonely. At the moment it is raining heavily. The world is gloomy. The city is a frightful dump. Even the footpaths are in a state. When you walk along you have to keep looking out. Everything that the Russians made or built is shoddy and poorly finished. We Germans will have to work for decades to put things in order. . . .

Kursk, 15.10.1942

No. 11

Beloved wife, dear children,

You will be very surprised to receive a letter from me from Germany. The reason for this is that someone who is going on leave is taking it with him and he'll post it from there. I am also giving him a parcel (8 kg) which he's going to post in Koblenz. It contains 5 kg butter, 2·5 kg wheatflour and a bar of washing soap. . . .

Of my life today I can tell you that things are going more or less smoothly. We have got hold of a little house similar to the one in Gartenstr. only not as nice. It's dilapidated and has had a lot of shoddy building work done to it. More than forty families used to live here but they had to make way for us. I now have my own two-room apartment. I work in the living-room, which is also where I keep the war kitty (150,000 RM) and I sleep in the kitchen. The apartment is heated from the kitchen. Until now it has not been very cold so it's been bearable. We are having wood brought in by the ton. I hope it will last the winter. The prisoners have to chop it up and put it into stacks. I'll survive. If you were with me now it would be wonderful. The reveillé is at 6.00 but I always wake up earlier because up to now I have not been able to sleep more than five hours, though I sometimes go to bed early.

At 7.00 we have coffee (as much bread as you want, a blob of butter – about 60 g – sometimes purée or artificial honey. When we first arrived there was always real honey. I always have four slices of bread. Then we work until 12.00. There is always good food for lunch – a lot of meat, a lot of fat (we have our own livestock, pigs, sheep, calves and cows). We have also arranged for lots of potatoes, so everybody has plenty to eat. We have pickled our own tomatoes and cucumbers. Our cook has a sideline at home running a delicatessen and really knows what he's doing. Depending on my mood and appetite I can eat up to three helpings. Then back to work again until 18.00. For supper there is either something hot: roast potatoes with scrambled eggs or other dishes, or something cold: bread and some salami. You can see that our bodily needs are taken care of. We receive Wehrmacht rations, which are not excessive but nevertheless adequate, and get ourselves something extra. I think there will be enough for the winter. At the moment there are 600 geese making a terrific racket in the yard. Your Christmas goose (geese?) are, I hope, amongst them. If things work out I'll bring them myself. If not, I'll make sure that you receive them in good time.

We spend the evenings either playing cards, boozing or sitting together with the boss. *I have to spend a lot of time with the boss.* When he wants to play cards, drink coffee or schnapps some of the officers have to keep him company. One can't keep oneself to oneself. I think I have made a good impression so far. The first few days I was tired and could not take very much but after that I managed to see the night through and was actually the last to quit the field.

I have already told you about the shooting – that I could not say 'no' here either. But they've more or less said they've finally found a good chap to run the administrative side of things. The last one was by all accounts a coward. That's the way people are judged here. But you can trust your Daddy. He thinks about you all the time and is not shooting immoderately. So that's our life. We don't get out of the building except for visits to the pictures, theatre or invitations to the staff offices [*Dienststellen*] or officers. There's absolutely nothing going on in town. Sundays are just like weekdays. How I love being at home with you all. How is the garden? . . .

It's nice that Herr Kern is going to France. I think he would have been too weak for the East, though people do change here. People soon get used to the sight of blood, but Blutwurst [blood sausage] *is not very popular round here.*

I send you lots of love. I hope my parcels (ten packages, two parcels) will reach you very soon. At the moment I can't send anything else but what I've sent you should last for a while. By then there'll be another opportunity.

I hope the package for Wurzel will get there in time for his birthday. It would make me very happy.

Lots of kisses and greetings for the children
For their dear mummy a long deep kiss
You are my everything
Your Papa.

O.U., 19 October 1942

Dear Mutti, dear children,

I'm sending you a quick letter so you don't think that Papa has forgotten you. I have a great deal to do at the moment but I hope that it'll have let up within a couple of weeks. Then the decks will be cleared and according to my calculations I'll be able to live a little bit and get my work organized. *If only one did not have to spend so much time with the top brass.* Last Saturday once again it went on the whole night. The whole of the next day you're tired and weary. The boss is quite amenable when he's not asking for the impossible, and apart from that he's very pleasant. On Sunday we had a feast. There was roast goose. I had roast goose for breakfast, for lunch and (cold) for tea. Then in the evening I had fish. Even the best roast does not go on tasting good indefinitely. Anyway you need not worry that we are living badly here. *We have to eat and drink well because of the nature of our work, as I have described to you in detail. Otherwise we would crack up. Your Papa will be very careful and strike the right balance. It's not very pleasant stuff. I would far rather sleep. This week I've got a staff officer here and have to make several inspections at night. We cannot really trust the Russians in our region. Up to now nothing has happened; they have too great a respect for us. We are more notorious than their old Cheka or GPU.* [The OGPU, the political police of the USSR, was formed in 1922 from the Cheka. – Ed.]

If only I were back at home with you. Life here is monotonous and desolate. Apart from *a few exceptions* I spend the whole day in my office. Even skat is not as much fun as it was in the beginning. I think about you all a lot and hope that the first parcels will have finally reached you by now. What would give me the most pleasure would be if the packet for Wurzel got there in time. I have already got either a Christmas present – if I come myself – or otherwise a birthday present for darling Dagi-Muckerle. Mutti mustn't let on what it is (a children's bike, old but reconditioned here). I think she'll be very pleased with it. But she'll only receive it if she's a good girl and does the shopping.

I have sent all kinds of requests with my colleagues who are going on leave. The children may even get some shoes from the Protektorat. Mutti should accept all parcels even if they come from strangers. I have only given our home address to people whom I know will keep their word. There are men here from all over Greater Germany. One or other of them can always get hold of something without coming up against the law, but you should not talk too loudly about it. Dagi must get used to talking less on the street. We are in fact allowed to send our own personal parcels but people can get too envious, so it's better not to talk about it. Up to now I have sent you ten small one-kilo parcels. There are also two large parcels from Germany and a special surprise on their way. Whether the surprise will come off I don't know. The men left in the dead of night and I did not get a chance to speak to them again before they went, but they are the type who will keep their promise. One of them may even come and say hello to you personally from me. As they are coming via Berlin they will also call on mother and father and stop in Reinickendorf. You see, I'm also thinking of Oma [granny], even if I don't write all that often. To date I have sent mother and father a packet of butter, a packet of cigarettes and special greetings. I won't be able to get hold of so much in the winter but you'll manage for a good while with what I have already sent. We ourselves had a stroke of bad luck. We filled two large barrels which used to contain oil and petrol with honey. Although according to the Russians the barrels had been scoured and rinsed with warm water, the whole thing tastes strongly of petrol and is inedible. *That smacks of sabotage. When we catch the scoundrels they'll be treated without mercy. . . .*

We have been to the cinema twice and once to the theatre. Here we are thankful for every diversion. Up to now I have received letters one to ten but not two and nine, also parcel number one, from Mutti. Only don't send me too much. No Christmas parcels because I'm going to try and come home on leave. We haven't been able to raise the question of leave so far, because it's too early and as a newcomer here I am not in a position to express a preference. However, none of the men here have been on leave for a long time, and they are going now. Because of this a gap has arisen at Christmas which I am going to take advantage of. In addition, Christmas, as a religious festival so to speak, is not particularly popular. We celebrate the winter solstice. If the holiday does not work out Mutti will have to write me letters saying she is ill, so that I have to go home urgently to make sure everything is all right. But you must put it in such a way that I see through it and do not worry needlessly. It's only the end of October and I cannot, as I said, discuss Christmas.

Are the children still behaving? Is Muckerle working hard at school? Has Volkmar stopped wetting his bed? He'll soon be a big man and should not be doing a thing like that any more. And how about washing hands and brushing teeth? You know how important it is not to be sloppy. Dagi too should now become accustomed to sitting properly at table and not put her elbows on the table. When she's grown up she'll move around the world a lot as a German girl. Everyone will be watching her and learning from her. Foreigners immediately notice any weaknesses and then take advantage of them. It starts with small things and ends with big things. That is why we have to make a big effort with ourselves and always take care. *After all, fate permitting we Germans are the people of the future.* The future depends on how we bring up our children and their understanding that all those who were killed in battle did not die in vain. So teach Dagi that she must study hard and always obey her parents and her teachers. *Only a person who has himself firmly under control can judge or rule over others.* The girl will soon be eight and must slowly gain an understanding of such matters. She will get to know the world and experience great joy. . . .

To judge by recent Wehrmacht reports, you have so far been left in peace or else have only had to go into the shelter without actually being attacked in the end. I hope you continue to be spared the raids so that the window panes stay intact and you won't get too cold. Please send my best wishes to the Polizeirat. Tell him I've had a lot of work and have not had a chance to write. If you consider it necessary to get on the right side of his wife then why not curry favour with her and take over half a pound. If not, it does not matter too much to me. I've already got to know some other gentlemen here who will get me transferred to Berlin (that is, if they keep their word, which one cannot always be sure of), so there's room for hope. In any case they have all already noticed that I know what I'm doing. That's the main thing. Up to now they only had idiots as administrators and thought they would have to deal with me in the same way as they did with them. They were partly very surprised and partly very satisfied since everyone likes to have an efficient administrator. I gain from it personally, too, because the men like to fulfil my wishes, as you will soon find out.

If it weren't for the stupid thoughts about what we are doing in this country, the Einsatz here would be wonderful, since it has put me in a position where I can support you all very well. Since, as I already wrote to you, I consider the last Einsatz to be justified and indeed approve of the consequences it had, the phrase: 'stupid thoughts' is not strictly accurate. Rather it is a weakness not to be able to stand the sight of dead people; the best way of overcoming it is to do it more often. Then it becomes a habit. I am on tenterhooks to know how you received my letter of 13 October. It would perhaps have been better if I had not written it or had written it only later. For the more one thinks about the whole business the more one comes to the conclusion that it's the only thing we can do to safeguard unconditionally the security of our people and our future. I do not therefore want to think and write about it any further. I would only make your heart heavy needlessly. We men here at the front will win through. Our faith in the Führer fulfils us and gives us the strength to carry out our difficult and thankless task. For everywhere we go we are looked upon with some degree of suspicion. That should not however divert us from the knowledge that what we are doing is necessary.

It is very late. I'll close here. Tomorrow morning, 20 October, the letter will be leaving. With luck it may be with you on the 25th. It will show you that all my thoughts revolve around you. You are the very substance of my private life.

You deserve my best wishes
and all my love
Your Papa

. . . .

'His attitude towards the Jews is quite impossible'

Documents on persecution in the White Russia Generalbezirk

A Jewish mother before being shot

1. 'The bodies piled up in the streets'
Communication of Slutsk Gebietskommissar to the Generalkommissar in Minsk, 30 October 1941

Secret!

Re: Action against the Jews

With reference to our telephone conversation of 27 October 1941 I hereby submit the following written report:

In the morning of 27 October at about 8.00 hours an Oberleutnant of Police Battalion No. 11 from Kaunas (Lithuania) arrived saying he was the Security Police Battalion commander's adjutant. The Oberleutnant explained that the police battalion had received orders to carry out the liquidation of all the Jews here in the town of Slutsk over the next two days. The battalion commander, he said, was on his way with his four-company battalion, two companies of which were made up of Lithuanian partisans, and the action had to begin immediately. My reply to the Oberleutnant was that I would have to discuss the action first with the commander. About half an hour later the police battalion arrived in Slutsk. As I had requested, I had a meeting with the battalion commander as soon as he arrived.

First of all I explained to the commander that it would simply not be possible to carry out the action without prior preparation. Everyone had been sent off to work and it would create chaos. I told him that it had been his duty at least to have given one day's advance warning of the action. I then asked for the action to be postponed for one day. This he, however, refused informing me that he had to carry out similar actions in all the towns and only had two days available for Slutsk. At the end of those two days the town of Slutsk had without fail to be free from Jews. I immediately raised very strong objections and made it very clear that a liquidation of the Jews should not take place in an arbitrary manner. I told him that a large proportion of the Jews still present in the town were craftsmen or the families of craftsmen. These Jewish craftsmen simply could not be spared, as they were vital for the economy. I further stated that there were absolutely no White Russian craftsmen to speak of and that all the crucial factories and workshops would have to cease operations in one fell swoop if all Jews were liquidated. At the end of our interview I also said that all the craftsmen and specialists that were indispensable had passes and that these people were not to be taken from the factories and workshops. It was then agreed that all those Jews still present in the town should first of all be brought to the ghetto for the purpose of selection, in particular on account of the families of craftsmen, whom I did not wish to be liquidated either. Two of my officials were to be responsible for the selection. The commander raised no objection and I with the best of faith believed that the action would be conducted in this way.

A few hours after the action started acute difficulties arose. It became clear to me that the commander had in no way kept to our agreement. All Jews without exception were removed from the factories and workshops and sent off in a transport. Although a number of Jews were taken to the ghetto, where I was able to identify and pull out many of them, the majority were loaded directly on to trucks and liquidated outside the town without further ado. Shortly after midday complaints started coming in from all sides that it was impossible for the factories and workshops to continue to function because all the Jewish skilled workers had been removed. The commander had left for Baranovichi and it was only after numerous attempts that I contacted his deputy, a Hauptmann [captain] whom I asked to suspend the action immediately, pointing out that my instructions had been ignored and that the economic losses suffered were totally irreparable. The Hauptmann was very surprised by the view I expressed and said that he had received orders from the commander to clear the entire town of Jews with no exceptions, as they had done in other towns. This mopping up had to be carried out for political reasons and economic considerations had not played a role anywhere. As a result of my energetic intervention he did, however, stop the action towards evening.

As far as the manner in which the action was carried out, it is with deepest regret that I have to state that this bordered on the sadistic. The town itself presented a horrific picture during the action. The Jewish people but also White Russians were taken from their homes and rounded up with indescribable brutality by both the German police officials and in particular the Lithuanian partisans. Gunfire could be heard everywhere in the town and the bodies of the executed Jews piled up in the streets. The White Russians experienced tremendous problems escaping as the police closed in from all sides. Apart from the fact that the Jewish people, including the skilled workers, were brutally ill-treated before the eyes of the White Russian people, the White Russians themselves were also beaten with rubber truncheons and rifle butts. There was no longer any question of this being an action against the Jews; it more closely resembled a revolution. I personally spent the whole day uninterruptedly with my officers trying to save whatever could be saved. On numerous occasions I literally had to force German police officials and Lithuanian partisans to leave the workshops by threatening them with my revolver. My own Gendarmerie had been instructed to do likewise but in many cases were forced to leave the streets because of the wild shooting, in order to avoid being shot themselves. The whole scene was unspeakably appalling. In the afternoon there were a large number of horse-drawn carts left unattended in the streets, so that I had to request the town authorities to take steps to deal with the vehicles straight away. It was later established that these were Jewish vehicles which the Wehrmacht had used for transporting ammunition. They had simply offloaded it from the carts and left, without even bothering about the vehicles.

I was not present at the shooting which took place outside the town. I cannot therefore make any remarks about the brutality. It should however suffice to say that some time after the graves had been filled up victims managed to work their way out of them. With regard to the economic losses, my view is that the tannery has been hardest hit. Twenty-six craftsmen worked there. Of these people alone, fifteen of the best specialists have been shot. Four others jumped from the lorry during the transport and escaped, and a further seven avoided capture. The workshop is only barely running. There were five cartwrights working in the cart-making workshop, four of whom were shot. The shop now has to be kept going with just one cartwright. Further craftsmen are lacking such as carpenters, blacksmiths, etc. It was, however, not possible until today for me to obtain a clear picture of the situation.

As I mentioned above, the families of the craftsmen were also to have been spared. Today, however, it looks as though there are people missing from all of these families. There are reports coming in from all sides indicating that in some families the craftsman himself, in other families the wife and in yet others the children are missing. Almost all families have been torn apart in this way. It is very doubtful whether under these circumstances the remaining craftsmen will still work willingly and productively, particularly since some of them are still going around today with faces beaten bloody in the brutality.

The White Russian population, whose full trust we had managed to gain, is completely stunned. Although they are intimidated and dare not speak their mind freely, the view that this day was no glorious chapter in Germany's history and is not to be forgotten can already be heard. I am of the view that a great deal of what we achieved over the past months has been destroyed and that it will take a long time for us to regain the trust we have lost with the local population.

In conclusion I feel myself compelled to state that during the action the police battalion plundered in an outrageous manner not only Jewish houses but also houses belonging to White Russians, taking with them anything usable such as boots, leather, cloth, gold and other valuable things. According to reports by members of the Wehrmacht, Jews had watches torn from their wrists and rings pulled off from their fingers in the most brutal fashion openly in the streets. An Oberzahlmeister [paymaster] reported that a Jewish girl was ordered by the police to fetch 5,000 roubles immediately and they would set her father free. The girl indeed is said to have run around everywhere to try to obtain the money.

Inside the ghetto the police even broke into and robbed the individual houses containing Jewish property which had been boarded up by the civilian authorities. In the barracks where the unit was accommodated window frames and doors were ripped out and used for a camp-fire. Despite the fact I once again raised the matter of the plundering with the commander's adjutant on Tuesday morning, who during the course of our meeting gave me his word that no police officer would enter the town, some hours later I was compelled to arrest two fully armed Lithuanian partisans who had been caught looting. On Tuesday night the battalion left town for Baranovichi. The local population was visibly happy when the news spread through the town.

That is the report so far. I will be coming to Minsk soon in order to discuss this matter in person. I am currently not in a position to continue the action against the Jews. Things must first of all be allowed to calm down. I hope to be able to restore calm as soon as possible and, despite the difficulties, get the local economy back on its feet again. I have only one request to ask of you: 'Please spare me from this police battalion in future!'

(signed) Carl

2. 'The action rid me of unnecessary mouths to feed'

From the situation report of Gebietskommissar Gerhard Erren, 25 January 1942

The town of Slonim is a haphazard jumble of a few good stone buildings, quite a few serviceable wooden houses and a good many dilapidated log shacks ripe for demolition. There are no uniformly well-maintained enclosed quarters which would be suitable as areas for Germans to live in. One-third of the town has been completely destroyed. As a result of this and the heavy influx of refugees, when I arrived Slonim was severely overpopulated and the housing situation in some places catastrophic. The Judenaktion on 13 November alleviated the situation perceptibly. It resulted in our being able to clear a street completely and set up homes and offices for Germans there. Work to clean this street and the surrounding quarter is continuing in preparation for the future SS base. Operating on the premise that my colleagues need the highest standard of overall living conditions in order to maintain peak performance I saw to it from day one that each of our men not only has decent accommodation and enough to eat but that his whole lifestyle embodies German culture and the prestige appropriate to it. Our accommodation is such that members of all the German services, including Sonderführer and police, eat together but in separate dining-rooms. Standards of conduct are adhered to, with the result that even people with little upbringing soon learn manners which command the respect of the local serving staff towards the German master race.

Upon my arrival there were about 25,000 Jews in the Slonim area, 16,000 in the actual town itself, making up over two-thirds of the total population of the town. It was not possible to set up a ghetto as neither barbed wire nor guard manpower was available. I thus immediately began preparations for a large-scale action. First of all property was expropriated and all the German official buildings, including the Wehrmacht quarters, were equipped with the furniture and equipment that had been made available. . . . Any articles which could not be used for Germans were handed over to the town for sale to the local population. Proceeds from their sale were sent to the finance department. The Jews were then registered accurately according to number, age and profession and all craftsmen and workers with qualifications were singled out and given passes and separate accommodation to distinguish them from the other Jews. The action carried out by the SD on 13 November rid me of unnecessary mouths to feed. The some 7,000 Jews now present in the town of Slonim have all been allocated jobs. They are working willingly because of the constant fear of death. Early next year they will be rigorously checked and sorted for a further reduction.

The plains were extensively cleansed for a time by the Wehrmacht. Unfortunately, however, this only took place in villages with fewer than 1,000 inhabitants. In the Rayon towns [the lowest administrative districts in the USSR – Ed.] all Jews will be eradicated with the exception of all but the most essential craftsmen and skilled workers, after auxiliary work for the east–west movement has been carried out.

Since the Wehrmacht is no longer prepared to carry out actions on the plains I shall concentrate all the Jews of the area into two or three Rayon towns. They will work in closed columns only, in order to stamp out once and for all illicit trading and support for the partisans among them. The best of the skilled workers among the Jews will be made to pass their skills on to intelligent apprentices in my craft colleges, so that Jews will finally be dispensable in the skilled craft and trade sector and can be eliminated.

> I was holding a whip or a pistol. I was loading or unloading. The men, children and mothers were pushed into the pits. Children were first beaten to death and then thrown feet [first] into the pits. . . . There were a number of filthy sadists in the extermination Kommando. For example, pregnant women were shot in the belly for fun and then thrown into the pits. . . . Before the execution the Jews had to undergo a body search, during which . . . anuses and sex organs were searched for valuables and jewels.
>
> Alfred Metzner, Gebietskommissar's driver and interpreter

3. 'Eliminate the Jews once and for all'

Generalkommissar for White Russia Wilhelm Kube, 31 July 1942, to the Reichskommissar for the Ostland, Hinrich Lohse

Secret!

Re: Combating partisans and Judenaktion in the White Russia Generalbezirk

It has become apparent during the course of all clashes with partisans in White Russia, in both the former Polish and the former Soviet parts of the Generalbezirk, that the Jews, together with the Polish resistance movement and the Moscow Red Army in the east, are the principal supporters of the partisan movement. Consequently, the question of how the Jews in White Russia should be handled is a political matter taking priority over all considerations about risks to the economy as a whole. Accordingly, it has to be solved not from an economic but from a political point of view. During the course of extensive discussions with SS-Brigadeführer Zenner and the very competent Leiter of the SD, SS-Obersturmbannführer Dr jur. Strauch, it was established that we have liquidated about 55,000 Jews in the past ten weeks. In the Minsk area ['Gebiet Minsk-Land'] the Jews have been completely eradicated, without any negative effect on the workforce. In the mainly Polish area of Lida 16,000 Jews have been liquidated, in Slonim 8,000 Jews. Our preparations for the liquidation of the Jews in the Głębokie area were disrupted when the rear army area pre-empted us, liquidating 10,000 Jews whom we had been due to eradicate systematically, without any prior liaison with us. (A report on this incursion has already been submitted.) On 28 and 29 July about 10,000 Jews were liquidated in the city of Minsk, 6,500 of them Russian Jews – for the most part old people, women and children – and the rest Jews unfit for work, who had mostly been sent from Vienna, Brünn, Bremen and Berlin in November of last year to Minsk on the Führer's orders.

In addition, the Slutsk area has been alleviated of several thousand Jews. The same applies for Nowogrodek [Novogrudok] and Wilejka [Vileyka]. Radical measures have yet to be taken in Baranovichi and Gantsevichi. There are still some 10,000 living in the city of Baranovichi alone, of whom 9,000 will be liquidated next month.

There are 2,600 Jews from Germany left in the city of Minsk. In addition to these, there are a total of 6,000 Russian Jews and Jewesses still alive, left over from the labour units in which they were employed during the action. Minsk will continue to retain the largest Jewish workforce. This is currently necessary because of the high concentration of armaments factories and work related to the railway. In all the other areas the SD and I have limited the number of Jews coming for Arbeiteinsatz to a maximum of 800 and, where possible, 500. Thus, at the conclusion of the actions we have reported, we retain in the city of Minsk 8,600 Jews and in the other ten areas, including the Minsk-Land Gebiet which is free of Jews, some 7,000 Jews. This means the risk that partisans will continue to gain vital support from the Jews has been removed. Naturally the SD and I would prefer to eliminate the Jews in the Generalbezirk of White Russia once and for all as soon as the Jews are no longer needed by the Wehrmacht for economic reasons. For the time being, the Wehrmacht's requirements, as the principal employer of Jewish labour, are being taken into account.

Coming into conflict with this clear brief regarding the Jews is the difficult task the SD in White Russia is faced with of having to ensure that the continuous flow of Jewish transports reaches its destination. This takes a terrible toll on the physical and mental strength of the men of the SD as well as distracting them from their duties, which lie within the area of White Russia itself.

I should therefore be grateful if Herr Reichskommissar could arrange for further Jewish transports to Minsk to be suspended, at least until the danger from the partisans has been overcome

Wilhelm Kube

conclusively. I require the SD for 100 per cent deployment against the partisans and the Polish resistance movement, both of which demand all the strength of the not exceptionally strong SD units.

Tonight, after the Minsk Judenaktion was over, SS-Obersturmbannführer Dr Strauch reported to me with justified anger that a transport of 1,000 had suddenly arrived from Warsaw for the district air command here without any instructions from the Reichsführer-SS or prior notification from the Generalkommissar.

I would ask Herr Reichskommissar, as the most senior authority in the Ostland (my request is already prepared by teleprinter) to call a halt to such transports. The Polish Jew is as much an enemy of the German people as the Russian Jew. He poses a political danger far more significant than his worth as a skilled worker. Under no circumstances in an area under civil administration can army or air force personnel bring Jews from the General-Gouvernement or elsewhere without authorization from you, Herr Reichskommissar, as they jeopardize all the political work and the security of the Generalbezirk. I am fully in agreement with the commander of the SD in White Russia that we should liquidate every Jewish transport which has not been ordered by our superiors or for which we have not received notification from our superiors, in order to prevent further unrest in White Russia.

> Generalkommissar for
> White Russia
> (signed) Kube

4. A 'quite literally slavish' attitude to the Jews

SS-Obersturmbannführer Dr Strauch on Gauleiter Kube

The Reichsführer SS and
  Chief of the German Police
The Chief of the Guerrilla
  Combat Units 1c Daily
  Rept No. 2/43

O.U., 25 July 1943

[Stamp:]
Personal Staff of Reichsführer-SS
Schriftgutverwaltung [Secretarial
Department]
File No. Secret

To the
Chief of the Guerrilla Combat Units
SS-Obergruppenführer and General
of the Police von dem Bach

Re: Generalkommissar for White Russia, Gauleiter Kube
Previous correspondence: none

Dear Obergruppenführer
    Permit me to submit the following report regarding the General-
kommissar for White Russia, Gauleiter Kube.
    I have composed the report from documents in the files at the office
of the Commander of the Security Police and the SD in White Russia.
    As is known, there are a great many rumours surrounding
Gauleiter Kube. In my report I have therefore almost exclusively
limited myself to mentioning facts for which there exists documentary
evidence or which I myself have witnessed. I have attempted to
demonstrate that Kube is wholly incompetent as both a leader and
administrator, that he has a hostile attitude towards the SS and police
and that in the Jewish question he displays an absolutely impossible
attitude.
    White Russia is currently in administrative chaos. The administra-
tion is at most in control of one-third of the area. It has relinquished
control over the remaining two-thirds of the zone with resignation and
no longer dares penetrate this area, although the guerrilla situation
there is not particularly serious. All attempts to bring the area back

under civil administration have been stopped. It is indicative that the administration is never at hand during major SS and police actions and only resumes its work once a trouble spot has been pacified. As a result almost all actions are ineffectual. . . .

The administrative deficiencies described above in White Russia are for the most part to be attributed to a deficient staff policy on the part of the Generalkommissar. This policy can be described succinctly as follows: any strong and competent men to be appointed have been removed while dim-wits and bootlickers, most of whom have some past connection with the Gauleiter and who have now once again latched on to him, are retained. The category of decent men includes Landrat [District Administrator] Eger, Hauptabteilungsleiter II, the Head of the Propaganda Department, Dr Scholz, the 2. Staatsanwalt Assessor [assistant public prosecutor] Scheid, who was transferred after being commended highly, and Inspector Weich, whose trust was lost for the simple reason that he had dared to put a 'former acquaintance' of the Gauleiter's on night duty.

By contrast everything is done to retain for example a man like Stadtkommissar Janetzke. Janetzke is an extremely weak human being given to heavy drinking. He runs his office in a disturbingly negligent and disorderly manner. His wife, who likewise consumes too much alcohol, has committed the most serious appropriation of essential foodstuffs. She was also involved in a fight with the Stadtkommissar's driver. At a 'party' in the presence of her husband she undid the clothes of a drunken party guest and blackened some parts of his body with shoe polish. All these things are known to the Gauleiter. Although he could not prevent legal proceedings from being brought against her he managed to ensure that these only resulted in a rehabilitation order or a transfer from Minsk to Nowogrodek [Novogrudok].

Landrat z.D. Schröder, Head of the Procurement Office was, to my knowledge, already connected with the Gauleiter in Brandenburg. Schröder's way of life from an alcoholic and erotic viewpoint is also unworthy of a German person in the East. His 'business dealings' as Head of the Procurement Office are so shady that the entire department is accusing him of misappropriation. He is constantly saying that a word with the Gauleiter is enough to render any reproach invalid. Although he was stripped of his title Landrat by the Ministry for the Interior and the Ministry for the Eastern Territories refused Schröder's appointment as Gebietskommissar in principle, the Gauleiter appointed him as deputy Stadtkommissar and requested the Reichkommissar to give its final approval of his appointment as Stadtkommissar.

The Gebietskommissar in Głębokie is a further member of the former Kube circle, Paul Hachmann. Before Hitler came to power and for some time afterwards this man worked as a private detective and chorister. He has numerous convictions for robbery and embezzlement, but his criminal record was destroyed after Hitler came to power. Hachmann is utterly unsuited to the job of Gebietskommissar. His conduct towards the Jews is unbelievable. Despite warnings from a number of quarters he has nevertheless been retained by the Gauleiter. . . .

Rumours surrounding the personal conduct of the Gauleiter are particularly wide-ranging. There is however no reliable proof for these. Kube once told a small group of people with visible pleasure how he had personally fitted underwear for female artists who were passing through town. It is also fairly certain that from time to time he had relations with his female employees before his wife arrived in Minsk.

The following incident can be verified. The Gauleiter once noticed a White Russian woman doctor because of her beauty but subsequently lost track of her. When he could not establish the identity of the doctor he called a White Russian doctors' convention in Minsk at which he gave a talk. There he discovered her and ordered his adjutant to take her photograph and find out her personal details. The next day the doctor was ordered to the head of the local self-help centre, who revealed to her that the Gauleiter had requested her as his domestic servant. When she refused to go, it was explained to her that one had to make sacrifices for the White Russian cause. Upon refusing a second time she was told that criminal proceedings would be considered. Only following this threat did the White Russian declare herself prepared to work for the Gauleiter. It is not known to date whether or not there was any intimacy in this case. This is currently being determined. In conclusion it can be said that since Frau Kube's arrival in Minsk criticisms in this regard can no longer be made.

As far as the Gauleiter's attitude to the SS and the police is concerned, it can be established that he has had a very negative attitude towards them. It is extremely difficult to provide precise proof as he gives a show of being amicably disposed towards the SS and holding the Reichsführer in high esteem. He asked the SS and Polizeiführer, Brigradeführer Zenner and v. Gottberg if he could use the informal 'Du' to address them and even used 'Du' during high official occasions.

> I can say that I have succeeded in gaining the Gauleiter's trust and I can present him reports which often do not correspond to his innermost views but which he nevertheless accepts without any rancour.
>
> From a report written by Obersturmbannführer Dr Strauch on 10 April 1943

In daily life, however, particularly during police actions against Jews, which will be gone into in more detail later, his negative attitude has been repeatedly made evident. While he behaved in an outwardly friendly manner towards Brigadeführer Zenner, behind his back he made verbal and written reports to the Reichskommissar and to the Minister [for the Eastern Territories] in which he was at pains to draw attention to the Brigadeführer's alleged incompetence.

After 'Operation Malaria' SS-Obergruppenführer Jeckeln was of the view that White Russia was to a large extent pacified. The Gauleiter expressed his agreement and sent a letter of gratitude to him. However, in private circles he made fun of the Obergruppenführer and maintained that the report the Obergruppenführer had submitted to the Reichsführer was incorrect. . . .

The attitude of Generalkommissar Kube to the Jews is quite literally slavish. Here, too, his duplicity is clearly discernible, despite the fact he stresses in all his official speeches and written communications that the Jewish question must be settled as quickly and radically as possible. The following letters, comments and orders I cite shed light on his real attitude. I will let the substantive writing speak for itself.

I would like to venture that the most serious document is a communication from the late chief of the Security Police, SS-Obergruppenführer Heydrich. Obergruppenführer Heydrich's letter is dated 21 March 1942.

Dear Pg. Kube,

Gauleiter and Reichsstatthalter Dr Meyer came and handed over to me a list of persons about whose cases, as he informed me, there had been numerous complaints. These complaints had been raised as, allegedly, in their cases the relevant guidelines were not adhered to during the evacuation of the Jews from the Reich territory to Minsk.

186

Although I had been previously convinced that the guidelines I had issued regarding the practical procedure for the evacuation of Jews from the Reichsgebiet were observed rigorously in every case, I nevertheless ordered a thorough and *time-consuming* check of cases you had complained about. As can be seen from the attached report on our findings, all the cases are *without exception* legally determined Jews, i.e. Jews and Jewesses who as a result of divorce and the like no longer have relations with their German-blood spouses and therefore can be equated entirely with the Jews.

I was not informed of the circumstances under which this list was compiled. Really, the only explanation I can give for the compilation of the list is that the accounts of the evacuated Jews were believed blindly.

There seems to have been an inclination to give the accounts of the Jews more credibility than the German authorities, which act in accordance with highly detailed instructions issued after the most thorough examination of each individual case. And this at a time when the clearing up of the Jewish problem in the Reich etc. has been tackled in earnest.

Many of the Jews in the above-mentioned list are already known for their repeated attempts to deny their Jewishness, on all kinds of possible and impossible grounds. It is also natural that first-degree half-castes [*Mischlinge*] in particular try to deny their Jewishness at every available opportunity.

You will agree with me that, in the third year of the war, even for the Security Police and the Security Service there are tasks which are more important for the war effort than running about pandering to the bellyaching of Jews, making time-consuming lists and distracting so many of my colleagues from other far more important duties. If I instigated an investigation into the persons on your list at all this was only in order to prove such attacks wrong once and for all in writing. I regret to have to write yet another such justification six and a half years after the enactment of the Nuremberg laws.

Heil Hitler!
(signed) Heydrich

The following file note shows the circumstances in which this list, for which Obergruppenführer Heydrich reprimanded Kube, was compiled:

On 29.11.1941 the ghetto was visited by Gauleiter Kube.
Present were SS-Brigadeführer Zenner, General of the Police Herf and some political leaders. The Jew Frank acted as guide. During the conversation Frank mentioned that there were people here whose brothers were engaged in active service. Kube stated that he would immediately report these cases to the Führer. He asked Frank for a list of names of these cases. In the Berlin section of the ghetto Kube stopped two girls who in his view had an Aryan appearance and had their personal details taken down by a political *Leiter*. The whole proceedings took place in the presence of the Jew, Frank.

So it was the Generalkommissar himself who had ordered the Jews to draw up such a list of allegedly unfairly resettled Jews.

The following letter, dated 15 January 1942, to SS-Brigadeführer Zenner reveals a strange attitude towards the Jewish question:

My dear Carl,

Today my transport officer reported to me that the SS-Oberscharführer who was running the garage fire hearing had acted in the most uncouth fashion. In front of witnesses he asked the driver who is under my command whether he had heard that the Gauleiter had thanked the Jew who had saved the Maybach for him. He wished to know what form these thanks took.

Apart from the fact that this was an act of utterly outrageous tactlessness on the part of the SD Oberscharführer concerned, I also view it as an insult and a lack of respect. The Jew in question entered the burning garage and without any help brought out my valuable Maybach, which was threatened by the fire. As a result he has saved the Reich some 20,000 RM. It goes without saying that I as a decent person should thank him for this. I must add that in no way will I tolerate a police official of indirectly lower rank to me criticizing my conduct during a legal hearing. I request you to see to it that necessary steps are taken. Under no circumstances should this man be involved with hearings of the Generalkommissariat. He does not possess the maturity these hearings require.

The fact was that the Gauleiter had enthusiastically shaken the hand of the Jew who had got the car out from the garage, and had thanked him. This fact was transmitted to the official responsible for conducting the inquiry into the incident by the Generalkommissar's driver and he could not refrain from expressing his surprise over this. Whereupon the Generalkommissar believed himself to be justified in attacking the investigating official in the most unpleasant way.

Attacks of this nature against my officers and men were the order of the day.

On 1 March 1942 an action was to take place against the Russian ghetto in Minsk. The Generalkommissar received prior notification. In order to disguise the action the Council of Elders was to be informed that 5,000 Jews from the Minsk ghetto were to be resettled. These Jews were to be notified by the Council of Elders and told to get ready. Each Jew would be permitted to take along 5 kg of luggage.

As can be proved, the actual intentions of the Security Police were betrayed by the Generalkommissariat. Those Jews employed in the Generalkommissariat were not allowed into the ghetto for several days but were made to stay in the Generalkommissariat, as a result of which it became clear to the ghetto Jews that the version put out by the Security Police was not correct. In addition, further indiscretions were committed, as emerges from liaison reports. At the time it was not possible to prove these incidents. It is clear, however, that the Gauleiter used his knowledge to save his Jews.

As a result of the betrayal no Jew appeared at the appointed time. There was nothing else to do but to round the Jews up by force. The Jews put up resistance and the men taking part in the action had to use firearms. When matters were at their worst, just as the men were going all out to break down the resistance the Gauleiter appeared. I shall now quote a file note dated 5 March 1942:

At about 16.30 hours the Gauleiter, accompanied by his personal adjutant and an SS-Untersturmführer, arrived. It was already clear from a distance that the Gauleiter was unusually agitated. When I saw the Gauleiter coming towards me, I went up to him and greeted him. Immediately he began to shower me with criticism about the outrageous proceedings when the Jews had been rounded up. He reproached me with the fact that there had been repeated shooting in the ghetto, with ricochets also outside the ghetto. The Gauleiter's tone was exceptionally sharp. His rebukes could be heard by the Russian Jews standing around and by the White Russian policemen. In my capacity as specialist official responsible for the Jewish question and an SS officer I consider myself to have been grievously insulted.

The Gauleiter remained for some time in the ghetto. He reprimanded several of my men. During this time he repeatedly used expressions such as 'filthy business' and 'you haven't heard the last of this'. According to a report which cannot be substantiated 100 per cent, he is said to have distributed sweets to Jewish children on this occasion.

A file note by the then commander of the Sipo and the SD reads:

The next morning, Tuesday, 2 March 1942, at 9.00 Landrat Reuscher arrived and formally asked me for information as to where the Gauleiter's three Jewish hairdressers were. He said that the Gauleiter wanted me to give an immediate explanation, particularly since I had given instructions to exclude all German Jews from the action. I was not in a position to divulge the relevant information to Landrat Reuscher, whereupon he said he would go straight away to the German Council of Elders in the ghetto. I advised him not to do this, remarking that the several visits made by the Gauleiter yesterday to the ghetto had already had an unfavourable effect. The Landrat declared himself to be satisfied and added that he just wanted a report about the whereabouts of these Jews as soon as possible. I immediately went to Brigadeführer Zenner and informed him of this conversation. The Gauleiter had meanwhile already telephoned the Brigadeführer, who said the Gauleiter had more or less shouted him down. It was not possible to have a reasonable conversation with him. The Gauleiter held the SD responsible for the disappearance of the Jews. He demanded that the hairdressers be brought back by the evening at the latest or else he would start legal proceedings in the special court. He also said that he would no longer have anything to do with the SD. . . .

The Gauleiter apparently submitted a report to the Minister for the Eastern Territories, for on 10 March 1942 the following communication arrived:

The Reichsminister for the occupied Eastern Territories has requested a report on the last action against the Jews in Minsk. I would therefore request you to submit a report as soon as possible on the measures you carried out.

The Security Police did not respond to this communication. The Gauleiter's wish to show the Security Police in an unfavourable light is evident from the following file note dated 18 April 1942:

At 11.15 hours the Gauleiter telephoned and reported the following: the public prosecutor had informed him that a few days previously about fifteen Jewish women and men covered in blood had been led across the street. The interpreter who was accompanying them had himself fired on them in the prison thereby putting the officer on duty at considerable risk. The Gauleiter has demanded a rigorous investigation and severe punishment. The steps taken are to be reported to him immediately.

On 25 April 1942 I sent a written communication to the Gauleiter, extracts of which follow:

. . . In addition to this purely objective observation, may I, Gauleiter, make the following remarks: May I ask you to name for me the persons who have slanderously claimed that I allowed Jewish or other persons to be led through Minsk covered in blood. Time and time again I am made aware of people trying to accuse my men of degenerate sadism. My officers and men work hard every hour of every day to fulfil their difficult duty. We are faced with an enemy who does not shrink from using any means. Over the past few weeks hardly an arrest took place without my men being shot at. It should go without saying that faced with such a state of affairs we are not in a position to take a mild line. Nobody, down to the Reichsführer and the Führer, would understand it if I did not take the strongest measures to protect the lives of those officers and men who have been entrusted to me. Gentleness and time-wasting humanitarianism would have serious consequences in such a situation. I attach more worth to the life of one of my men than I do to those of a hundred Jews or partisans. Because our duties are hard and difficult I must stand up for my men and refute any slander most vehemently.

Significantly, in a communication of 28 April 1942, the Generalkommissar made no response at all to my reproaches but instead suggested that there should be a segregation of prisoners within the prison. He goes on to write:

That the Jews belong within the framework of political criminality is for me, as the bearer of a party decoration, self-evident. I would prefer it if we could send all Russian Jews as quickly and as quietly as possible to their deserved fate. In addition you will always find me only too happy to cooperate with you and your men in a friendly manner. Since my student days (1908 to 1912), as a *deutschvölkischer* student, I have been engaged in the struggle against the Jews.

Thus when Gauleiter Kube feels himself to be under attack he immediately claims to be a great opponent of the Jews. He has also taken a very strong position against the Jews in his official pronouncements when addressing officers. In addition, he has sent a number of written communications to the higher SS and Police officers for the Eastern Territories in which he unambiguously demands the solution to the Jewish question. In my view, his speeches and written communications, in which he expresses his opinion on the Jewish question, are merely a means for him to cover his tracks at a later stage. . . .

Generalkommissar Kube appears to have promised the German Jews, 5,000 of whom were delivered to the ghetto before my time, that their lives and health would be spared. There is no completely reliable evidence available to back up this claim. Nevertheless, on the basis of existing material such an inference is justified. Particularly telling is the file note dated 2 October 1942:

On the occasion of the meeting on 2 October 1942 Gauleiter Kube began to talk about the Stuttgart poet, Georg Schmückle, whom I know well personally. He praised his work, including his volume of novellas, *The Red Mask*. I pointed out that in this book of short stories the Württemberg Jewish financier, Süss Oppenheimer, had actually been glorified, to which Kube stated that we young National Socialists did not yet have the correct attitude. When it came to Jews we were always afraid of endangering our souls. As a student before the war who had a true sense of his Germanness, he had listened to Mendelssohn and Offenbach but had nevertheless not abandoned his *völkisch* ideas. He did not understand why, for example, it was unacceptable today to mention Mendelssohn or play Jewish works, such as Offenbach's *Tales of Hoffmann*. He added that he was referring solely to the Jews of the nineteenth century, who after being liberated from the ghetto had taken a colossal step forwards. It was established beyond a doubt that the Jews had culture. This stemmed from the six per cent of their blood which was Nordic, or possibly from West European and Roman influences.

Although we young National Socialists had the correct attitude from a physical or material point of view, spiritually or intellectually we were on the wrong track. He was, however, of the view that the Jewish contribution to musical history in the form of, say, a Mendelssohn could not simply be removed, without leaving a gaping hole.

The Gauleiter had learned that a German Jew had been slapped around the face by a police officer. Kube reprimanded the police officer in the presence of the Jew, demanding to know whether he too, like the Jew, had been awarded the Iron Cross. Fortunately the police officer was able to answer in the affirmative.

On 2 December 1941 the Elder of the Jews from the Altreich remarked that on the occasion of the Gauleiter's visit to the ghetto he had gained the impression that the Gauleiter wanted to treat the Jews from the Reich somewhat less harshly than the Russian Jews, who in no way could be compared to one another.

On 2 February 1942 the KdS was informed in confidence that the Jew employed as a hairdresser by the Generalkommissar in Minsk, who shaved the Gauleiter every day, had said that all those Jews working in the departments of the Generalkommissariat were under the personal protection of the Gauleiter. Each Jew had the right to lodge a complaint with the Gauleiter if they were treated in an inappropriate manner by German nationals [Reichsdeutsche]. It can be proved that this Jew's claim was not idle chatter by the fact that on several occasionas Kube reprimanded Germans for ill-treatment or verbal abuse of Jews. He could only have known about such cases from the actual Jews involved.

During a major ghetto action it was made known by informants that the German Jewish Ordnungsdienst [organization for maintenance of public order] made up predominantly of former World War I servicemen, was intending to put up armed resistance. In order to avoid bloodshed on the German side the Ordnungsdienst was made to assemble and was told that a fire had broken out in the town and they should be at the ready for fire duty. The Jews were then loaded on to trucks and *sonderbehandelt* ['given special treatment', i.e. executed]. This matter also reached the Gauleiter's ears, although how is not known. He reacted angrily to the news saying that it was brutal to eliminate these former war veterans who had fought at the front and that, besides, this type of action was outrageous.

In his letter of 28 April 1942, which I have already mentioned, Kube states that he would prefer it if all Russian Jews were sent to their deserved fate as quickly as possible. Thus it is clear that here once again he was making an exception of the German Jews.

On 30 October 1942 the Generalkommissar issued the following order:

To Hauptabteilungsleiter I, II, III
Re: Complaints to the police and SD.
Complaints concerning misdemeanours of staff members or White Russians, Jews, etc. in our employ are to be submitted to me first for approval. Hauptabteilungsleiter are requested to ensure that this order is strictly adhered to by circulating it in the departments for which they are responsible.

The Generalkommissar in Minsk
(signed) Kube

The German members of the Generalkommisariat were understandably outraged that they were named in the same sentence as Jews. For the Generalkommissar it was, however, not a question of wishing to keep German personnel or White Russians out of reach of the Security Police – his sole aim was to protect his German Jews.

An Abteilungsleiter reported on 7 November 1942 that while he had been walking through the Generalkommissariat he saw a Jew loafing around in front of a door. When asked what he was doing there, the Jew said, 'I'm waiting for the boss.' When questioned further as to whom this boss was, the Jew answered, the Gauleiter.

On not a few occasions the Gauleiter has bawled at members of the civil administration in front of Jews who happened to be standing there. The long-standing party comrade and Ortsgruppenleiter Höder was shouted at in this fashion and threatened with dismissal because he had remarked that Robert Ley would certainly be surprised if he heard that Jews were being accommodated in the Robert Ley House in Minsk. Here too the Jews in question were German.

I can say with pride that my men, however unpleasant their duties might be, are correct and upstanding in their conduct and can look anybody squarely in the eye and that back home they can be good fathers to their children. They are proud to be working for their Führer out of a sense of conviction and loyalty.

From a report written by Obersturmbannführer Dr Strauch on 10 April 1943

The Generalkommissar and his wife have donated groceries, fruit and vegetables to German Jews, in particular the hairdressers and tailors.

On numerous occasions Kube has said to me personally that Jews evacuated from the Reich could be spared without any problem since they do not understand the local language and would therefore not pose a danger in so far as their becoming involved in guerrilla activities was concerned.

I am convinced from the evidence that deep down Kube is opposed to our actions against the Jews. If he does not admit to this outwardly the only reason is his fear of the consequences. He is in agreement with actions against Russian Jews because he is able to appease his conscience by the fact that the majority of Russian Jews collaborate with the guerrillas.

I cannot conclude this report without emphasizing that almost all the information I have submitted is known in the widest circles of the civil administration and the Wehrmacht, and even to a lesser extent among the White Russians. The Wehrmacht smiles and watches the incompetence of the Gauleiter with enjoyment. Far-sighted members of the civil administration are in despair and can no longer see any way out of this bungled state of affairs. The White Russians too have lost faith in German leadership because again and again they are made to feel personally the aimlessness of the policy. In the circumstances I consider it ill-advised to retain the Generalkommissar.

(signed) Strauch
SS-Obersturmbannführer

'None of the Jews that were killed is any great loss'

Secret verdict of the SS and Police Supreme Court in Munich

1. Verdict against SS-Untersturmführer Max Täubner, 24 May 1943

Max Täubner

1. The accused is a fanatical enemy of the Jews. At the start of his service in the East he resolved to 'get rid of' 20,000 Jews if possible. Together with his work platoon [*Werkstattzug*] he was assigned to the 1./SS-Brigade in August 1942 and left Arys, East Prussia, on 8 September 1942, arriving in Zwiahel [Novograd Volynsky] on 12 September. He learned from the Ukrainian mayor that over 300 Jews were being held in a prison. The mayor asked for authorization to shoot them. The accused heard that the Wehrmacht was issuing Jewesses with certificates saying that they were not Jewish. As, in his opinion, the Wehrmacht were too sentimental he decided to carry out the execution with his platoon. Outside the village a grave was dug by the Ukrainian militia by the side of which the Jews – men, women and children – had to kneel. They were then shot at close range in the nape of the neck when the order was given.

On 17 October 1941 the accused arrived at Scholochowo [Sholokhovo] with his platoon. Here he heard that the Jews had said they intended to set fire to the 'Collective' and that two Ukrainian women had stepped on mines and had been seriously injured. On these grounds, here too the accused conducted an execution of Jews on his own initiative. While in Novograd Volynsky 319 Jews had been

> 'Kill them in a more decent way'
>
> The victims were shot by the firing-squad with carbines, mostly by shots in the back of the head, from a distance of one metre on my command. Before every salvo Täubner gave me the order – 'Get set, fire!' I just relayed Täubner's command. The way this happened was that I gave the command 'Aim! Fire!' to the members of the firing-squad, and then there was a crack of gunfire. Meanwhile Rottenführer Abraham shot the children with a pistol. There were about five of them. These were children whom I would think were aged between two and six years. The way Abraham killed the children was brutal. He got hold of some of the children by the hair, lifted them up from the ground, shot them through the back of their heads and then threw them into the grave. After a while I just could not watch this any more and I told him to stop. What I meant was he should not lift the children up by the hair, he should kill them in a more decent way.
>
> SS-Mann Ernst Göbel

executed, here it was 191. The grave was in an area overgrown with bushes, so the execution could not be observed by other people. SS-Unterscharführer Müller, who did not belong to the accused's unit, but had his permission to take part in the execution, snatched children from their mothers. Then, holding them in his left hand, he shot them and threw them into the grave. The accused took him to task about this but nevertheless did not stop him.

During the period 22 October to 12 November 1942 the accused was in a small town, Alexandri[y]a, together with his platoon. There he learned that although most Jews had been 'resettled', there were still some Jews in the area who had up to then evaded 'resettlement'. The rumour also reached his ears that the Jews intended to poison the streams. He decided therefore to clear Alexandriya of Jews, particularly since he and his platoon were unable to leave the village because of the weather and road conditions and, as a result, did not have enough work. He gave orders for all Jews to be delivered to him at his unit. Members of the Reichsarbeitsdienst declared themselves prepared to dig the grave for the execution. Four hundred and fifty-nine Jews were shot in Alexandriya.

Whereas, however, the executions in Novograd Volynsky and

Täubner on holiday showed around photos of
massacres of Jews

Sholokhovo proceeded in a more or less orderly fashion, in Alexandriya they degenerated into vicious excesses. The Jews whose job it was to saw wood in the courtyard of the quarters were beaten on the pretext that they were not working properly. They were also beaten with spades, an act in which SS-Sturmmann Ackermann particularly distinguished himself. SS-Sturmmann Wüstholz ordered the Jews to beat each other to death, promising that the survivors would not be executed. The Jews did in fact knock each other down, although they did not kill each other. The accused himself joined in with the beating and also hit Jewesses in the face with a whip. Whenever there was a break he played the song 'You are Crazy, My Child' on an accordion. Some Jews were also beaten before the execution in a cellar at the quarters. On one occasion a couple of Jews had to tear down a wooden hut. It was arranged in such a way that the hut collapsed on top of them and they were buried underneath the ruins. These Jews were injured but not killed. There were also shootings which were not always authorized. In such cases individual Jews, after they had been beaten, were simply shot dead on the spot behind the house. On one occasion a Jew was hanged because this was what the accused wanted.

198

While the members of the work platoon in Novograd Volynsky and Sholokhovo willingly took part in the executions and obeyed the accused's orders because they considered this to be necessary for political reasons, the majority, in particular the older men, did not agree with the way in which matters were conducted in Alexandriya and were forced into extremely difficult moral conflicts.

2. The accused took a number of photographs of the executions and allowed SS-Sturmmann Fritsch to take further photographs, although he knew that the photographing of such incidents was not permitted. These were for the most part pictures which showed the most deplorable excesses, many are shameless and utterly revolting. The photographs were developed in two photographic shops in southern Germany and the accused showed them to his wife and friends.

At any rate there were about ten to fifteen Jewish people, men and women, though mainly men, held in the cellar. As far as I could tell, they were not given any food at all. One evening Untersturmführer Täubner ordered me to accompany him to the cellar. We were also accompanied by Mayor Fritsch and possibly one or two other men. About ten to fifteen steps led down to the cellar, which was poorly lit, I think, possibly with candles. I must, however, add that there was normally no kind of lighting in the cellar at all. Nor was it possible for the prisoners to relieve themselves in a lavatory and, as said above, they were also not given anything to eat. As far I recall, one of Täubner's escorts had organized minimal lighting in the cellar the evening that we went down there. Upon reaching the cellar I saw that most of the some ten to fifteen Jewish people (they cannot be called prisoners for they were treated far worse than any prisoner) were cowering in the straw. Täubner was the first to go crazy in the cellar. He lashed out with a heavy wooden club at random at the Jews lying on the ground. He poked around between the legs in the genital area of an elderly Jewess. While the other people accompanying Untersturmführer Täubner also joined in the mishandling of the Jews in the same manner, I did nothing. Then Täubner ordered me to take part as well. I had no stick on me and just gave a few Jews less forceful punches or pushes with my fist.

SS-Mann Heinrich Hesse

3. Together with his platoon, the accused also stayed in Konotop for some time during the autumn of 1941. Here he was told by a Cossack captain that the commander of the Ukrainian militia, Chamrai, was in contact with Communist guerrillas. Although the accused knew that the commander of the Feldgendarmerie still needed Chamrai he ordered SS-Sturmmänner Wüstholz and Hermann to shoot him. These two men carried out the order by going to fetch Chamrai on the pretext that they were taking him to see the accused. On the way they disarmed him and shot him dead with a pistol. They then went and reported that they had carried out the orders to the accused, who dismissed them with the words, 'That's fine!' When the matter became known he ordered the two men to submit a report to the effect that Chamrai had in fact tried to attack them and had therefore had to be shot.

4. [Details about an attempt to make his wife terminate her pregnancy – Ed.]

IV

... It could not be proved that the accused executed Jews without any authority on a journey from Arys to Bialowitza in August and the beginning of September 1941. It cannot be proved false that this, as the accused himself has claimed, was mere boasting, to which activity the accused is inclined. . . .

The accused claims not to have known that he was not permitted to take photographs of executions he carried out. The accused however cannot be believed in this matter. Right from the time he served in the Luftwaffe the accused has known that photographs may not be taken of official procedures, since these are to be viewed as 'secret'. For the accused to claim he did not consider these activities to be secret is just an excuse. Witness Fritsch drew his attention to the fact that, as he understood it, the taking of such photographs was forbidden. To this the accused answered laconically, 'That's none of your business, I'll take responsibility for this.' The accused also claims not to have given the order to execute Chamrai, claiming he only gave an order for him to be fetched so that he could be shot later and that Wüstholz had misunderstood him or had pre-empted him. This is contradicted by Wüstholz's statement taken under oath, which is credible, although he initially said something else on the instigation of the accused. His statement is above all supported by the statement of ethnic German

SS-Sturmmann Hermann, who on his own decision corrected his initially false statement because he was tormented by pangs of conscience and so resolved to honour the truth. . . .

> One of the Jewish people killed by me was a Jewish woman aged between twenty and thirty, I cannot remember exactly. She was a beautiful woman. I was glad to be able to shoot her so that she did not fall into the hands of the Untersturmführer. But please don't take that to mean that I enjoyed it. I said to the Jewess when I brought her from the cellar that the Untersturmführer wanted to speak to her, or something to that effect. My only thought was that if I had to do something I should cause the person as little pain as possible. I did not want the Jewess to suffer fear of death. I then made her come out of the cellar. She went in front of me. On the way to the grave or graves, which had already been dug, I suddenly shot her from behind.
>
> SS-Mann Heinrich Hesse

V

When reaching its lawful verdict on the charges against the accused, the SS and Police Supreme Court was guided by the following considerations:

1. The accused shall not be punished because of the actions against the Jews as such. The Jews have to be exterminated and none of the Jews that were killed is any great loss. Although the accused should have recognized that the extermination of the Jews was the duty of Kommandos which have been set up especially for this purpose, he should be excused for considering himself to have the authority to take part in the extermination of Jewry himself. Real hatred of the Jews was the driving motivation for the accused. In the process he let himself be drawn into committing cruel actions in Alexandriya which are unworthy of a German man and an SS officer. These excesses cannot be justified, either, as the accused would like to, as retaliation for the pain that the Jews have caused the German people. It is not the German way to apply Bolshevik methods during the necessary

extermination of the worst enemy of our people. In so doing the conduct of the accused gives rise to considerable concern. The accused allowed his men to act with such vicious brutality that they conducted themselves under his command like a savage horde. The accused jeopardized the discipline of the men. It is hard to conceive of anything worse than this. Although the accused may have otherwise taken care of his men, by his conduct he however neglected his supervisory duty which, in the view of the SS, also means not allowing his men to become psychologically depraved. The accused is therefore to be punished under section 147 of the MStGB [Militärstrafgesetzbuch: Military Penal Code]. Since however the provisions of this punishment only provide for imprisonment or detention of up to fifteen years, it is recommended that section 5a of the Special War Punishment Statutory Order be applied, since such a deterioration of discipline requires a severe sentence.

2. By taking photographs of the incidents or having photographs taken, by having these developed in photographic shops and showing them to his wife and friends, the accused is guilty of disobedience. Such pictures could pose the gravest risks to the security of the Reich if they fell into the wrong hands. It would be extremely easy for them to be leaked out of southern Germany to Switzerland and used for enemy propaganda. The accused was also aware of this considerable danger. His disobedience is therefore to be viewed as a particularly serious case. By contrast the SS and Police Supreme Court does not consider that his conduct constitutes a deliberate undermining of Germany's military power. It is convinced that the accused never even entertained the thought that the showing of such pictures to people of weak dispositions could undermine the fighting spirit of the German people, and thus he did not take such a possibility into consideration. For this crime the accused is to be punished under section 92 of the MStGB.

3. The shooting of the commander of the Ukrainian militia is punishable under section 115 of the MStGB. The accused ordered subordinates to shoot Chamrai and should therefore be punished as the perpetrator of this crime. The SS and Police Supreme Court cannot however, in this case either, consider the accused as a murderer. In committing this act, the accused allowed himself to be led by the thought that Chamrai had connections with the Communist guerrilla bands. He knew however full well that he should not shoot Chamrai,

first because it was not his job to do so and second because he had no hard evidence that Chamrai was indeed a traitor. This crime was therefore manslaughter in the sense of section 212 of the RStGB [Reichstrafgesetzbuch: Penal Code of the Reich]. In comparison to this serious crime it is of no consequence that the accused attempted to hush up his actions. The SS and Police Supreme Court have therefore refrained from examining this cover-up attempt under criminal law.

4. Finally, the accused is guilty of incitement to an attempted abortion. Such an attempt was made by his wife. The fact that this attempt was unsuccessful because there was in fact no pregnancy is irrelevant. For this, the accused is to be punished under section 218, 48 of the RStGB.

VI

The following factors played a decisive role when determining the sentences:

It must be assumed that from the outset the accused did not act out of sadism but out of a true hatred for the Jews. He nevertheless let himself be drawn into committing acts of cruelty which are to be attributed to severe character deficiencies and a high degree of mental brutalization. In the accused's favour is the fact that he has enjoyed very little military training and as a result was not up to his role as a leader of men. For these reasons the death sentence did not seem appropriate, but the accused deserved to be punished by a severe prison sentence. The accused is fully responsible for the degenerate behaviour of the work platoon and for his personal conduct in Alexandriya. Because of his serious abuse of his leadership duties, the SS and Police Supreme Court have considered a term of imprisonment of five years under section 5a of the Military Special Penal Decree [Kriegssonderstrafrechtsverordnung] to be necessary.

In addition, the taking of tasteless and shameless pictures under circumstances where the taking of such photographs is forbidden cannot be viewed lightly. They are the expression of an inferior character. Particularly revealing in this connection is the fact that the accused evidently took particular pleasure in a photograph of a Jewish woman who was almost completely naked. As already said, this is a particularly severe case of disobedience. Fortunately, the pictures were only seen by a small circle of people. Nevertheless, the exceptional danger that arose as a result of his taking and distributing these pictures must be taken into consideration. An aggravating factor is that the accused gave a false word of honour in order to play down this misdemeanour. The SS and Police Supreme Court considers a term of imprisonment of three years the required punishment for his disobedience.

The manslaughter of the commander of the Ukrainian militia, Chamrai, too, can only be atoned for with a term of imprisonment. It is not acceptable to have a man who has put himself on the side of the Germans killed on the basis of mere suspicion. In committing this crime the accused again shows that he possesses neither moderation nor self-discipline. The SS and Police Supreme Court considers a term of imprisonment of two years to be appropriate for this crime.

I was deeply astonished that our men, as members of a workshop unit, were concerned with the killings of Jews. Indeed, I expressed my astonishment over this to Untersturmführer Täubner in Zwiahel. Täubner merely laughed at me and then said something to me which was frankly nothing short of outrageous. He said something to the effect that for him first came pigs, then nothing at all, and only then, a long way down, the Jews. . . .

I should also mention that, before the execution, Untersturmführer Täubner ordered me to take part. He literally said to me, 'Now off you go and join in!' I asked Täubner if he was ordering me to take part in the execution of Jews, to which he replied that this was not an official order. The others were going to do it voluntarily. He said to me that I was a coward. To this I answered that I had not come to Russia to shoot women and children, I myself had a wife and children at home. That's how the conversation ended.

SS-Mann Ernst Schumann

In the view of the SS, any incitement by an SS officer to abortion deserves a severe punishment. The case in question can, however, be viewed more leniently in view of the fact that the accused is a lover of children and his wife has already borne him three children. In addition, the accused was concerned that his wife would not survive a further pregnancy in her current physical condition. The SS and Police Supreme Court therefore considered a prison sentence of six months to be sufficient.

SS Judge   Field Command Post, 26 October 1942
at Reichsführer-SS
and Chief of German Police
Daily Rept No. 393/42 secr. Be/Ha.

Re: Judging the unauthorized shooting of Jews
Ref.: Communication of 26 September 1942, 1b 165 Daily Report
No. 484/42 secr., concerning the matter of punishment of Rev.-Lt
Wölfer.
Enc: 1 document

                         [Stamp]
To the   Secret Kommando matter
SS Court Head Office
Munich

I have spoken to the Reichsführer-SS about this important matter.
The Reichsführer-SS has come to the following decision:
    The most important factor to consider when deciding whether
and how to punish men for shooting Jews who have not been
ordered or authorized to do so is the motive for this action.
(1) Execution for purely political motives shall result in no punishment, unless punishment is necessary for the purpose of maintaining
order. If the latter is the case, according to the case in question the
defendant should be judged under section 92 or 142 of the MStGB,
or some other disciplinary punishment should be enforced.
(2) Men acting out of self-seeking, sadistic or sexual motives should
be punished by a court of law and, where applicable, on charges of
murder or manslaughter.
    Court personnel and courts involved in such cases are asked duly
to note these guidelines.

                     (signed) [illegible]
                     SS-Obersturmbannführer

In accordance with section 74 of the RStGB the four months the
accused has already spent in prison should be deducted when cal-
culating the overall sentence. The SS and Police Supreme Court has
sentenced the accused to a total of ten years' imprisonment. The
accused has been expelled from the SS and declared unfit for service.
The conduct of the accused is unworthy of an honourable and decent

German man. For this he has been given under section 32 of the RStGB the additional sentence of ten years' deprivation of his civil rights.

VII

In view of the fact that the accused persisted in attempting to justify his behaviour by lying in the main trial, the time he has already served in prison was not deducted from his sentence.

2. Dismissal of the case against the remaining parties, 1 June 1943

The following has been established on the basis of the main trial of SS-Untersturmführer Max Täubner, commanding officer of a supplies workshop platoon and an officer in Kommandostab RF-SS, before the SS and Police Supreme Court on 24 May 1943:

. . . The following men were party to the punishable acts committed or ordered by SS-Untersturmführer Max Täubner:

1. SS-Unterscharführer Walter Müller particularly stood out during the shootings of Jews for the brutality with which he tore small Jewish children from their mothers. He held these children out in front of him with his left hand and then, with his right hand, shot them with a pistol.

2. SS-Sturmmann Ernst Fritsch took photographs of shootings of Jews. He was aware that the taking of such photographs was forbidden. . . .

3. SS-Sturmmann Karl Ackermann particularly distinguished himself during the executions of Jews by beating Jews with a spade.

4. SS-Sturmmann Rudolf Wüstholz shot the Ukrainian captain of the militia, Chamrai. He did this on the orders of SS-Untersturmführer Max Täubner, who was acting contrary to the law, thereby making himself guilty of the crime of manslaughter.

Allowances have been made for the fact that the accused were, without exception, acting on the orders of and under the responsibility of SS-Untersturmführer Max Täubner. In this respect, their own culpability may be described as slight. . . .

The cases against these accused have therefore been dismissed.

3. The pardon

SS Judge at Reichsführer-SS   Field Command Post,
Daily Rept No. VI – 574/44secr. – Gi/Kr   16 January 1945

Re: Pardoning of Max Täubner . . .

To the
Head Office of the SS Court
Prien

In accordance with the proposal of the Head Office of the SS Court of
27 December 1941 (p. 33, Pardon dossier), the Reichsführer-SS has
issued a pardon decision.

The Reichsführer requests the Chief of the Central Office of the SS
Court to take this decision in his name as his deputy.

The RFSS grants *Täubner* 14 days' leave. This excludes travelling
time.

T. is to be informed of the following:

The Reichsführer-SS expects T. to show himself in every respect
worthy of this pardon and to conduct himself as well at the front as he
did in the prison camp.

The gist of this letter has already been transmitted by teleprinter on
14 January 1945 to the SS and Police Supreme Court.

I.A.

(signed) [illegible]
SS-Sturmbannführer

Part Two

'Delivered and Killed'

The Extermination Centres

'Their soldierly conduct is exemplary'

Kulmhof (Chełmno) extermination camp in the Wartheland Reichsgau

View of Chełmno taken from the south. Left of the church and in front of
the park running down to the River Ner, at the left edge of the picture, is
the 'castle'. Between December 1941 and March 1943 at least 145,000
people – according to criminal proceedings in the Laabs *et al.* (8 Ks 3/62)
trial in Bonn on 23 July 1965 – were murdered here in gas-vans. On 7 April
1943 the 'castle' was blown up. Between April 1944 and January 1945
several thousand more people were killed. Polish estimates put the total
number of victims as high as 300,000

1. Photographs

Kolo (Warthbrücken) railway station

Arrival of a transport from the Łódź Ghetto

Kolo Station: at first the Jews were marched through the town. After spring 1942, following protests from the local inhabitants, they were loaded into wagons and taken by narrow-gauge railway as far as the village of Powiercie, 8 km from Chełmno

During the first 'Murder Action' the victims' clothes were temporarily stored in the church. During the second 'Murder Action' the Jews were transported by narrow-gauge railway to Chełmno, where they had to spend the night before their murder in the church

Jewish men in the gas-van before their murder

Polizeioberwachtmeister Maderholz (standing in the middle) at his parents-in-law's house in Chełmno. Next to him members of the Schutzpolizei Kommando

Security policemen together with members of the Polish Arbeitkommando (work detachment). Far right, Böge, the 'Sarge' of the police Kommando. Far left (seated) the Pole, Marian, who later found himself by mistake in a gas-van with Jewish victims and was gassed with them

Unknown members of the Sonderkommando

Granary in Chełmno. During the night of 17/18 January 1945 the camp was completely cleared. The Jewish workers were murdered. Some of them – the last ones – shut themselves inside the granary. The Sonderkommando set fire to the building and the victims were killed in the blaze

2. Theodor Malzmüller on the 'plague boils of humanity'

When we arrived we had to report to the camp commandant, SS-Hauptsturmführer Bothmann. The SS-Hauptsturmführer addressed us in his living quarters, in the presence of SS-Untersturmführer Albert Plate (Bothmann's deputy). He explained that we had been detailed to the Kulmhof [Chełmno] extermination camp as guards and added that in this camp the plague boils of humanity, the Jews, were exterminated. We were to keep quiet about everything we saw or heard, otherwise we would have to reckon with our families' imprisonment and the death penalty.

We were then allocated our places in the guard unit [Wachkommando], which consisted of about fifty to sixty police officers from 1st Company Litzmannstadt Police Battalion. As I recall, there were also some officers from 2nd Company in it. The officer in charge of the guard unit was Oberleutnant Gustav Hüfing. He was from Wesel. . . .

The guardroom was situated in the village of Kulmhof. The unit members were accommodated in houses in the village. The duties of the guard unit consisted of (1) maintaining the security of the guardroom, (2) guarding the so-called 'castle' yard and (3) guarding the so-called 'camp in the wood'.

The extermination camp was made up of the so-called 'castle' and the camp in the wood. The castle was a fairly large stone building at the edge of the village of Kulmhof. It was here that the Jews who had been transported by lorry or railway were first brought. The Jews were addressed by a member of the Sonderkommando in the castle courtyard. I myself once heard one of these speeches when I was on guard duty in the castle courtyard for a day in December 1942. . . .

When a lorry had arrived the following members of the SS-Sonderkommando addressed the Jews: (1) camp commandant Bothmann, (2) SS-Untersturmführer Albert Plate from North Germany, (3) Polizei-Meister Willi Lenz from Silesia, (4) Polizei-Meister Alois Häberle from Württemberg. They explained to the Jews that they would first of all be given a bath and deloused in Kulmhof and then sent to Germany to work. The Jews then went inside the castle. There they had to get undressed. After this they were sent through a passage-way on to a ramp to the castle yard where the so-called 'gas-van' was

217

parked. The back door of the van would be open. The Jews were made to get inside the van. This job was done by three Poles, who I believe were sentenced to death. The Poles hit the Jews with whips if they did not get into the gas-van fast enough. When all the Jews were inside the door was bolted. The driver then switched on the engine, crawled under the van and connected a pipe from the exhaust to the inside of the van. The exhaust fumes now poured into the inside of the truck so that the people inside were suffocated. After about ten minutes, when there were no further signs of life from the Jews, the van set off towards the camp in the wood where the bodies were then burnt. . . .

During my visit to Kulmhof I also saw the extermination installation, with the lorry which had been set up for killing by means of motor exhaust fumes. The head of the Kommando told me that this method, however, was very unreliable, as the gas build-up was very irregular and was often insufficient for killing.

Rudolf Höss, Commandant of Auschwitz, on a visit to Chełmno on 16 September 1942

During the period that I was in the guard unit most of the time I did sentry duty in the interior of the camp in the wood. The camp was in a clearing in the woods between Kulmhof and Warthbrücken. . . . As a guard just within the camp perimeter I frequently saw mass graves, filled with the bodies of Jews who had been exterminated, being dug up by the Jewish Arbeitskommando. The bodies were then burnt in two incinerators. . . .

At the end of March 1943, shortly before the dismantling of Kulmhof extermination camp in April, Gauleiter Greiser suddenly appeared at the camp together with his staff (consisting of fifteen high-ranking SS officers). All members of the SS-Sonderkommando and the Wachkommando had to assemble in the courtyard of the castle where they were addressed by Greiser. In the presence of his staff he explained that Kulmhof extermination camp would shortly be dismantled and he wanted to thank us on behalf of the Führer for the work we had done in Kulmhof. He went on to say that everybody would be given four weeks' special leave and that we were welcome to spend it free of charge on one of his estates. He then invited all those present to a farewell party at a hotel in Warthbrücken. The farewell party was held in a big room in the hotel. After a short while everyone was drunk and fell asleep at the table. The party ended at about one or two in the morning. . . .

A few days after Greiser's farewell party all members of the SS-Sonderkommando and the police guards received four weeks' special leave. Only a few members of the SS-Sonderkommando stayed behind in Kulmhof. One of these was Polizei-Meister Lenz. Then everybody had to report to SS-Obergruppenführer Kaltenbrunner at state security headquarters in Berlin on a particular day. He addressed us all and we were once again thanked on behalf of the Führer for our work in Kulmhof.

We were then all detailed together to Yugoslavia to SS-Division Prinz Eugen, under the command of Bothmann. Here we were deployed against partisans in Yugoslavia and suffered very heavy losses. As far as I can recall, SS-Untersturmführer Plate committed suicide in Serbia after being severely wounded.

In the middle of 1944 some of those former members of the SS-Sonderkommando who were still alive were withdrawn from the SS-Division and sent back to Kulmhof to start up the extermination camp once again.

3. Gas-van driver Walter Burmeister on whether he ever thought about what he was doing

As soon as the ramp had been erected in the castle, people started arriving in Kulmhof from Litzmannstadt in lorries. . . . The people were told that they had to take a bath, that their clothes had to be disinfected and that they could hand in any valuable items before-hand to be registered. On the instructions of Kommandoführer Lange [= Bothmann's predecessor] I also had to give a similar talk in the castle to the people waiting there – how often exactly I can no longer say today. The purpose of the talk was to keep the people in the dark about what lay before them. When they had undressed they were sent to the cellar of the castle and then along a passageway on to the ramp and from there into the gas-van. In the castle there were signs marked

'To the baths'. The gas-vans were large vans about 4–5 m long, 2·20 m wide and 2 m high. The interior walls were lined with sheet metal. On the floor there was a wooden grille. The floor of the van had an opening which could be connected to the exhaust by means of a removable metal pipe. When the lorries were full of people the double doors at the back were closed and the exhaust connected to the interior of the van. . . .

The Kommando member detailed as driver would start the engine straight away so that the people inside the lorry were suffocated by the exhaust gases. Once this had taken place, the union between the exhaust and the inside of the lorry was disconnected and the van was driven to the camp in the woods where the bodies were unloaded. In the early days they were initially buried in mass graves, later incinerated. . . . I then drove the van back to the castle and parked it there. Here it would be cleaned of the excretions of the people that had died in it. Afterwards it would once again be used for gassings. . . .

I can no longer say today what I thought at the time or whether I thought of anything at all. I can also no longer say today whether I was too influenced by the propaganda of the time to have refused to have carried out the orders I had been given.

4. Kurt Möbius on the guilt of the Jews and his own lack of blame

. . . In addition Hauptsturmführer Lange said to us that the orders to exterminate the Jews had been issued by Hitler and Himmler. We had been drilled in such a way that we viewed all orders issued by the head of state as lawful and correct. We police went by the phrase, 'Whatever serves the state is right, whatever harms the state is wrong.' I would also like to say that it never even entered my head that these orders could be wrong. Although I am aware that it is the duty of the police to protect the innocent I was however at that time convinced that the Jewish people were not innocent but guilty. I believed all the propaganda that Jews were criminals and subhuman [Untermenschen] and that they were the cause of Germany's decline after the First World War. The thought that one should oppose or evade the order to take part in the extermination of the Jews never entered my head either. I followed these orders because they came from the highest leaders of the state and not because I was in any way afraid.

5. Interrogation of Adolf Eichmann

Adolf Eichmann

[Tape transcript]

E: I just know the following, that I only saw the following: a room, if I still recall correctly, perhaps five times as big as this one, or it may have been four times as big. There were Jews inside it, they had to get undressed and then a van, completely sealed, drew up to a ramp in front of the entrance. The naked Jews then had to get inside. Then the lorry was closed and it drove off.

L: How many people did the van hold?

E: I can't say exactly. I couldn't bring myself to look closely, even once. I didn't look inside the entire time. I couldn't, no, I couldn't take any more. The screaming and, and, I was too upset and so on. I also said that to [SS-Obergruppenführer] Müller when I submitted my report.

He did not get very much from my report. I then followed the van – I must have been with some of the people from there who knew the way. Then I saw the most horrifying thing I have ever seen in my entire life.

The van drove up to a long trench, the doors were opened and bodies thrown out. They still seemed alive, their limbs were so supple. They were thrown in, I can still remember a civilian pulling out teeth with some pliers and then I just got the hell out of there. I got into the car, went off and did not say anything else . . . . I'd had more than I could take. I only know that a doctor there in a white coat said to me that I should look through a peep-hole at them in the lorry. I refused to do that. I could not, I could not say anything, I had to get away.

I went to Berlin, reported to Gruppenführer Müller. I told him exactly what I've just said, there wasn't any more I could tell him. . . . Terrible . . . I'm telling you . . . the inferno, can't, that is, I can't take this, I said to him.

6. Gauleiter Greiser to Himmler, 19 March 1943

Reichsführer!

A few days ago I visited Lange's former Sonderkommando, which today is under the command of SS-Hauptsturmführer Kriminalkommissar Bothmann and stationed in Kulmhof, Kreis Warthbrücken, until the end of the month. During my visit I was so struck by the conduct of the men of the Sonderkommando that I would not like to fail to bring it to your attention. The men have not only fulfilled the difficult task that has been set for them loyally, bravely and in all respects appropriately, but also their soldierly conduct is exemplary.

For example during a social evening to which I had invited them they gave me a contribution of 15,150 RM in cash which they had that day collected spontaneously. That means that each of these eighty-five men in the Sonderkommando had contributed about 180 RM. I have given instructions for the money to be put in the fund set up for the children of murdered ethnic Germans, unless you, Reichsführer, wish it to be put to another or better use.

The men further expressed the wish that all of them, if possible, be put under the command of their Hauptsturmführer Bothmann when they are transferred to their new assignment. I promised the men that I would communicate this wish to you, Reichsführer.

I should be grateful if you would give me permission to invite some of these men to be my guests on my country estate during their leave and to give them a generous allowance to make their leave more enjoyable.

Heil Hitler
(signed) Greiser

'The Wannsee Conference decisions implemented'

The extermination camps of Belzec, Sobibor and Treblinka

Left, Franz Stangl, holding a riding-whip – a popular status symbol among the German staff (on the right, Kurt Franz)

Kurt Franz's photo album. Franz was the deputy and then the last
commandant of Treblinka. Written on one of the pages were the words
'Schöne Zeiten' ('Those were the Days'). After 1945 the word 'Schöne' was
erased. Two photos, bottom left and bottom right, were torn out. Top left,
the station; middle, Franz in about 1944 during service on the Adriatic
coast; right, with his brother. Bottom: the commandant, Franz Stangl (left)
and Franz (right) in front of the commandant's hut in Treblinka

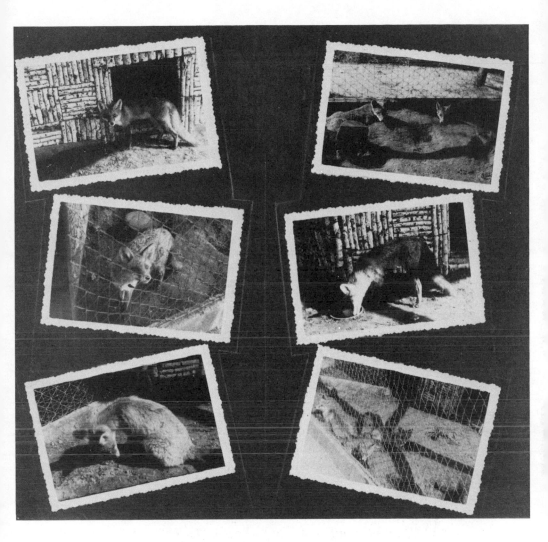

The camp zoo in Treblinka. A page from Franz's photo album

227

1. SS-Untersturmführer Josef Oberhauser on the early days at Belzec

The camp of Belzec was situated north-east of the Tomaszów to Lemberg [Lvov] Road beyond the village of Belzec. As the camp needed a siding for the arriving transports the camp was built about 400 metres away from Belzec station. The camp itself was divided into two sections: section 1 and section 2. The siding led directly from Belzec station into section 2 of the camp, in which the undressing barracks as well as the gas installations and the burial field were situated. During the time when I myself was at Belzec, the gas installation was still housed in a hut, the interior of which was lined with sheet metal and which held about a hundred people. Section 1 just contained the huts in which the Ukrainian guards were accommodated. . . .

The German camp personnel were accommodated outside the camp perimeter in two stone buildings which were situated on the right-hand side of the Lemberg road. In one of these buildings there was the office, the dining-room and the dormitories. In the second building there were only dormitories.

From Christmas 1941 I was under the command of Wirth, who at that time was the commandant of Belzec camp. At that time I was liaison officer between Wirth and Globocnik's staff in Lublin. My duties included obtaining the building materials needed to extend the camp and changing over the Ukrainian guard squads where necessary. . . . Wirth's deputy was Schwarz, who had full powers of command after Wirth.

The gassing of Jews which took place in Belzec camp up till 1 August 1942 can be divided into two phases. During the first series of experiments there were two to three transports consisting of four to six freight cars each holding twenty to forty persons. On average 150 Jews were delivered and killed per transport. At that stage the gassings were not yet part of a systematic eradication action but were carried out to test and study closely the camp's capacity and the technical problems involved in carrying out a gassing. After these first gassings, Wirth and Schwarz along with the entire German personnel left Belzec. Wirth's last official duty before his departure was to gas or shoot the fifty or so work-Jews of the camp including the Kapos

Belzec station. A foul stench and a dark cloud hung over the area even on fine summer days

[heads of working detachments]. When Wirth and his staff left I was in Lublin, where I was organizing the transport of a large amount of material. When I came back to Belzec there was no one left apart from about twenty Ukrainians guarding the place. The Ukrainian guards were under the supervision of SS-Scharführer Feix. Curiously, even SS- und Polizei-Führer Globocnik did not know anything about Wirth and his staff's departure. When he found out that Wirth had disappeared, he sent me to Belzec to find out where he had gone. I found out that he had travelled to Berlin via Lemberg and Cracow without informing Globocnik of his departure.

During the following six weeks quiet reigned at Belzec camp. At the beginning of May 1942 SS-Oberführer Brack from the Führer's Chancellery suddenly came to Lublin. With Globocnik he discussed resuming the extermination of the Jews. Globocnik said that he had too few people to carry out this programme. Brack stated that the euthanasia programme had stopped and that the people from T4 would from now on be detailed to him on a regular basis so that the decisions taken at the Wannsee conference could be implemented. As it appeared that it would not be possible for the Einsatzgruppen to clear individual areas of Jews and the people in the large ghettos of Warsaw and Lemberg by shooting them, the decision had been taken to set up two further extermination camps which would be ready by

> We were a band of 'fellow conspirators' ['*verschworener Haufen*'] in a foreign land, surrounded by Ukrainian volunteers whom we could not trust. . . . The bond between us was so strong that Frenzel, Stangl and Wagner had had a ring with SS runes made from five-mark pieces for every member of the permanent staff. These rings were distributed to the camp staff as a sign so that the 'conspirators' could be identified. In addition the tasks in the camp were shared. Each of us had at some point carried out every camp duty in Sobibor (station squad, undressing and gassing).
>
> Erich Bauer – known as the 'Gasmeister' [Gas Master] by the prisoners

1 August 1942, namely Treblinka and Sobibor. The large-scale extermination programme [Vernichtungsaktion] was due to start on 1 August 1942.

About a week after Brack had come to Globocnik, Wirth and his staff returned to Belzec. The second series of experiments went on until 1 August 1942. During this period a total of five to six transports (as far as I am aware) consisting of five to seven freight cars containing thirty to forty people came to Belzec. The Jews from two of these transports were gassed in the small chamber, but then Wirth had the gas huts pulled down and built a massive new building with a much larger capacity. It was here that Jews from the rest of the transports were gassed.

During the first experiments and the first set of transports in the second series of experiments bottled gas was still used for the gassing; however, for the last transports of the second series of experiments the Jews were killed with the exhaust gases from a tank or lorry engine which was operated by Hackenholt.

2. Erich Fuchs on his duties at Sobibor

Sometime in the spring of 1942 I received instructions from Wirth to fetch new camp staff from Lublin by lorry. One of these was Erich Bauer (also Stangl and one or two other people). . . .

On Wirth's instructions I left by lorry for Lemberg and collected a gassing engine there which I then took to Sobibor.

Upon arriving in Sobibor I discovered a piece of open ground close to the station on which there was a concrete building and several other permanent buildings. The Sonderkommando at Sobibor was led by Thomalla. Amongst the SS personnel there were Floss, Bauer, Stangl, Friedl, Schwarz, Barbel and others. We unloaded the motor. It was a heavy, Russian petrol engine (presumably a tank or tractor engine) of at least 200 HP (carburettor engine, eight-cylinder, water-cooled). We put the engine on a concrete plinth and attached a pipe to the exhaust outlet. Then we tried out the engine. At first it did not work. I repaired the ignition and the valve and suddenly the engine started. The chemist whom I already knew from Belzec went into the gas-chamber with a measuring device in order to measure the gas concentration.

After this a test gassing was carried out. I seem to remember that thirty to forty women were gassed in a gas-chamber. The Jewesses had to undress in a clearing in the wood which had been roofed over, near the gas-chamber. They were herded into the gas-chamber by the above-mentioned SS members and Ukrainian volunteers. When the women had been shut up in the gas-chamber I attended to the engine together with Bauer. The engine immediately started ticking over. We both stood next to the engine and switched it up to 'release exhaust to chamber' so that the gases were channelled into the chamber. On the instigation of the chemist I revved up the engine, which meant that no extra gas had to be added later. After about ten minutes the thirty to forty women were dead. The chemist and the SS gave the signal to turn off the engine.

I packed up my tools and saw the bodies being taken away. A small wagon on rails was used to take them away from near the gas-chamber to a stretch of ground some distance away. Sobibor was the only place where a wagon was used.

> I estimate that the number of Jews gassed at Sobibor was about 350,000. In the canteen at Sobibor I once overheard a conversation between Frenzel, Stangl and Wagner. They were discussing the number of victims in the extermination camps of Belzec, Treblinka and Sobibor and expressed their regret that Sobibor 'came last' in the competition.
>
> Erich Bauer – known as the 'Gasmeister' by the prisoners

3. The train journey to Belzec
Schutzpolizei Zugwachtmeister Jäcklein's report

Zugw. d. SchP. Josef Jäcklein
7/Pol. 24 in Lemberg   Lemberg, 14 September 1942

Report

Subject: Resettlement from Kolomea to Belzec

On 9 September 1942 I received orders to take over command of the Jewish resettlement train which was leaving Kolomea for Belzec on 10 September 1942. On 10 September at 19.30 hours in accordance with my orders, I took over command of the train together with an escort unit consisting of one officer and nine men at the railway yard in Kolomea. The resettlement train was handed over to me by Hptw. d. Schp. [Schutzpolizei Hauptwachtmeister] Zitzmann. When it was handed over to me the train was already in a highly unsatisfactory state. Hptw. Zitzmann had informed me of this fact when he handed it over to me. As the train had to depart to schedule and there was no other person who could take responsibility for loading on the Jews, there was nothing left for me to do but to take charge of the transport train in its unsatisfactory state. The condition of the train notwithstanding, the insufficient number of guards – i.e. one officer to nine men in the escort unit – would have been reason enough for me to refuse to take over command of the train. However, in accordance with my orders, I had to take over the train with the escort manpower

I had. Hptw. Zitzmann stayed at the station with his guard unit until the train departed. Both units had their hands full preventing Jews escaping from the cars, since it had meanwhile become so dark that it was not possible to see the next car properly. It was not possible to establish how many Jews escaped from the train before its departure alone, however it is probable that almost all were eliminated during their escape attempts.

At 20.50 the train departed from Kolomea on schedule. Shortly before its departure I divided up my escort squad, as had been planned beforehand, putting five men at the front and five men at the rear of the train. As the train was, however, very long – fifty-one cars with a total load of 8,200 Jews – this distribution of manpower turned out to be wrong and the next time we stopped I ordered the guards to post themselves right along the length of the train. The guards had to stay on the brake housing for the entire journey. We had only been travelling a short time when the Jews attempted to break out of the wagons on both sides and even through the roof. Some of them succeeded in doing so, with the result that five stations before Stanislau (Stanislav) I phoned the stationmaster in Stanislau and asked him to have nails and boards ready so that we could board up the damaged cars temporarily and to put some of his Bahnschutz (track guards) at my disposal to guard the train. When the train reached Stanislau the

---

Since 22 July a train carrying 5,000 Jews has been travelling daily from Warsaw to Treblinka via Malkinia. In addition there is a bi-weekly train carrying 5,000 Jews from Przemyśl to Belzec.

Dr Theodor Ganzenmüller, Staatssekretär in the Reichsverkehrs-ministerium [Ministry of Transport] on 28 July 1942 to SS-Ober-gruppenführer Karl Wolff

I should like to thank you personally and on behalf of the Reichs-führer very much indeed for your memorandum of 28 July 1942. I was particularly gratified to learn from your communication that for the past two weeks a train containing 5,000 members of the chosen people is travelling to Treblinka every day and [as a result] we are thus now in the position to carry out this population transfer at an accelerated pace.

Answer of SS-Obergruppenführer Karl Wolff, Head of Personal Staff of the RFSS, dated 13 August 1942

workers from Stanislau station as well as the Bahnschutz were at the station waiting for our train. As soon as the train stopped work began. An hour and a half later I considered it adequately repaired and ordered its departure.

However, all of this was of very little help, for only a few stations later when the train was stationary I established that a number of very large holes had been made and all the [barbed] wire on the ventilation windows had been ripped out. As the train was departing I even established that in one of the cars someone was using a hammer and pliers. When these Jews were questioned as to why they had these tools in their possession they informed me that they had been told that they might well be of use at their next place of work. I immediately took away the tools. I then had to have the train boarded up at each station at which it stopped, otherwise it would not have been possible to continue the journey at all.

As a controller I was responsible for ensuring the track was in good condition and in particular that the trains ran smoothly. During a visit to the station at Belzec the supervisor, a Secretary or Senior Secretary from Thüringen, informed me that he was having a lot of problems with the SS, who were stationed near the wood. Some time later I myself saw and had a word with a number of SS people in the waiting-room at Belzec. When I inquired, they told me that they were not members of the SS but that they had merely been given these uniforms. As they described it, most of them came from lunatic asylums or nursing homes in the Reich, where they had been involved in the killing of the mentally ill. . . .

I would like to say that one day the full significance of Belzec camp became clear to me when I saw mountains of clothes of all types behind our locomotive shed. There was also a large number of shoes there, as well as jewellery and other valuables. The SS had piled these things up there. Petrol was poured over items of clothing that were no longer wearable and they were then burnt. There were a lot of rumours that valuable items were trafficked by the camp staff in the surrounding area. So it was not surprising that women of easy virtue, in particular, were attracted to the area surrounding Belzec, where they set themselves up in business. There were apparently a lot of orgies at that time.

Senior Inspector of the Reich Railways Oskar Diegelmann, Lublin
railway directorate

At 11.15 hours the train arrived in Lemberg. As there was no replacement escort squad, my squad had to continue guarding the train until Belzec. After a short stop at Lemberg station the train went to the suburban station of Kleparow where I handed over nine wagons to SS-Obersturmführer Schulze which had been marked with an 'L' and had been designated for Lemberg compulsory labour camp. SS-Obersturmführer Schulze then loaded on about 1,000 more Jews and at about 13.30 hours the transport departed again. At Lemberg the engine was replaced and an old engine was attached which was not powerful enough for the weight of the train. The train driver never managed to reach top speed with his engine so that the train, particularly when travelling uphill, moved so slowly that the Jews could jump off without any risk of injury. I ordered the train driver on numerous occasions to drive faster but this was impossible. It was particularly unfortunate that the train frequently stopped in open country.

The escort squad had meanwhile used up all the ammunition that had been brought with us as well as an extra 200 bullets that I had obtained from some soldiers, with the result that we had to rely on stones when the train was moving and fixed bayonets when the train was stationary.

The ever-increasing panic among the Jews, caused by the intense heat, the overcrowding in the wagons . . . , the stink of the dead bodies – when the wagons were unloaded there were about 2,000 dead in the train – made the transport almost impossible.

At 18.45 the transport arrived in Belzec and I handed it over to the SS-Obersturmführer and head of the camp at 19.30 hours.

Towards 22.00 hours the transport was unloaded. I had to be present during unloading.

I was not able to establish the number of Jews that had escaped.

(signed) Jäcklein
Zugwachtm. d. Schutzpol.

Group photograph. From left to right: August Hengst (a cook in Treblinka), an unknown woman, Wachmann (camp guard) Pinnemann, Karl Pötzinger, Wachmann (camp guard) Libodenko, and an unknown person

Group photograph. From left to right (in uniform): SS-Untersturmführer Gerhardt Börner, Commandant Franz Stangl (centre), and SS-Oberscharführers Erich Bauer and Gustav Wagner, deputy commandant (all from Sobibor)

Group photograph. From right to left: SS-Rottenführer Barbel, Wachtmeister Dachsel, SS-Hauptscharführer Hackenholt, Ernst Zierke, Karl Gringers (with forage cap); second from left: Fritz Tauscher. All belonged to the permanent staff at Belzec

Christian Wirth and Gottlieb Hering, commandants at Belzec

Untersturmführer Wallerang and SS-Oberscharführer Gley (Belzec) with riding-crop, status symbol of permanent staff

4. 'The camp had clean sanitary facilities'

Professor Wilhelm Pfannenstiel, Waffen-SS hygienist, on a gassing at Belzec

During the First World War I was an air force officer and was demobilized as a first lieutenant in the reserve. In 1936 I successfully completed reserve training as a sanitation officer in the army and was promoted to Oberstabsarzt in 1939. From 1930 up to this time (1939) I held a chair in Hygiene and Bacteriology at the University of Marburg and was at the same time director of the Institute of Hygiene in Marburg. This was a normal professorship. I retained this professorship up until the end of the war.

At the end of 1939 I was called upon by the Waffen-SS to work for them as a consultant hygienist. At that time the Waffen-SS, having expanded considerably as a result of the war, needed medical experts to work for them in an advisory capacity. On a visit to Berlin at the end of 1939 I got in touch with the then Corps Doctor of Waffen-SS, Dr Dermietzel, who asked me to serve as medical adviser with a rank of SS-Sturmbannführer [a rank comparable to Oberstabsarzt – Ed.]. I already knew Dr Dermietzel from my time as SS-Oberabschnittsarzt in Oberabschnitt Fulda-Werra. In April 1940 I was then called up by

SS-Sturmbannführer Christian Wirth, extermination-camp inspector

238

the Waffen-SS and given a posting as consultant hygienist. My assignments mostly took place when there were no lectures. My work entailed inspecting, checking and improving the sanitary facilities at all the different places where the Waffen-SS was stationed and to combat epidemics. For this reason I visited the city of Lublin and the surrounding area in 1942. I had already been in Poland since 1940 in my capacity as hygienist. I was, however, always at each place for just a short time, after which I would return to the university in Marburg.

According to the available documentation, I was in the city of Lublin for the first time in August 1942. It was here that I met SS-Gruppenführer Globocnik for the first time. At the time there were plans to build a large concentration camp on the outskirts of the city of Lublin, capable of holding about 150,000 people. I visited the site to advise on the sanitary installations which were being built (provisions of drinking water and sewage drainage). I did not have any contact with the occupants of the concentration camp or the worker columns. I remained only a short time in Lublin as my assignment in connection with the concentration camp was finished. I naturally had other assignments in the area around Lublin which were also related to sanitary measures. After I had finished this work I returned to Marburg to the university. My instructions always came from Berlin, from the Sanitation Office of the Waffen-SS. I also spent some time in Berlin in order to be on call for short-term assignments. My own permanent place of residence was and always remained Marburg. . . .

When I am asked about executions of Jews I must confirm that on 19 August 1942 I witnessed an execution of Jews at Belzec extermination camp. I would like to describe how I came to be there. During my conversations with SS-Brigadeführer Globocnik, he told me about the large spinning-mills that he had set up in Belzec. He also mentioned that work at this camp would considerably outstrip German production. When I asked him where the spinning materials came from, he told me proudly that they had been taken from the Jews. At this point he also mentioned the extermination actions against the Jews, who for the most part were killed at the camp at Belzec. Around the same time Globocnik had asked a certain SS-Obersturmführer Gerstein, while he was in Lublin, how these large mills could best be disinfected. Gerstein was also a member of the Sanitation Office in Berlin. He had recommended a certain substance which could be sprayed on the individual layers of clothes. I personally had not heard of this substance. Globocnik also asked me for advice on the matter. I told him that the best thing for me to do would be to have a look at the workshop itself. I visited the camp and established that it was in an orderly condition, had clean sanitary facilities and had about 1,000 Jewish detainees.

During this first visit I was taken around by a certain Polizeihauptmann named Wirth, who also showed and explained to me the extermination installations in the camp. He told me that the following morning a new transport of about 500 Jews would be arriving at the camp who would be channelled through these extermination chambers. He asked me whether I would like to watch one of these extermination actions, to which, after a great deal of reflection, I consented. I planned to submit a report to the Reichsarzt-SS about these extermination actions. In order to write a report I had, however, first to observe an action with my own eyes. I remained in the camp, spent the night there and was witness to the following events the next morning.

A goods train travelled directly into the camp of Belzec, the freight cars were opened and Jews whom I believe were from the area of Romania or Hungary were unloaded. The cars were crammed fairly full. There were men, women and children of every age. They were ordered to get into line and then had to proceed to an assembly area and take off their shoes. I stood a little to the side of this line and watched the proceedings together with Polizeihauptmann Wirth and Obersturmführer Gerstein. The SS escorts took up guard positions outside the camp and Jewish functionaries from the camp gave the

---

Getting the detainees into the gas-chambers did not always proceed smoothly. The detainees would shout and weep and they often refused to get inside. The guards helped them on by violence. These guards were Ukrainian volunteers who were under the authority of members of the SS Kommando. Members of the SS held key positions in the camp, i.e. one SS man oversaw the unloading, a further SS man led the detainees into the reception camp, a further SS man was responsible for leading the detainees to the undressing area, a further SS man oversaw the confiscation of valuables and a further member of the Kommando had to drive the detainees into the so-called tube which led to the extermination camp. Once they were inside the so-called tube, which led from the hut to the extermination camp, there was no longer any escape.

Head of administration Hans-Heinz Schütt (Sobibor)

Lorenz Hackenholt operated the gassing installations in Belzec

arriving transports to understand that they would now be examined and instructed them to undress so that they could be deloused and take a bath. They also told them they had to inhale in a certain room to prevent them passing on any illnesses through their respiratory tracts.

I could not understand what the Jewish camp functionaries were saying but Herr Wirth explained it to me. After the Jews had removed their shoes they were separated by sex. The women went together with the children into a hut. There their hair was shorn and then they had to get undressed. . . . The men went into another hut, where they received the same treatment. I saw what happened in the women's hut with my own eyes. After they had undressed, the whole procedure went fairly quickly. They ran naked from the hut through a hedge into the actual extermination centre. The whole extermination centre looked just like a normal delousing institution. In front of the building there were pots of geraniums and a sign saying 'Hackenholt Foundation', above which there was a Star of David. The building was brightly and pleasantly painted so as not to suggest that people would be killed here. From what I saw, I do not believe that the people who had just arrived had any idea of what would happen to them.

Inside the building, the Jews had to enter chambers into which was channelled the exhaust of a [100(?)]-HP engine, located in the same building. In it there were six such extermination chambers. They were windowless, had electric lights and two doors. One door led outside so that the bodies could be removed. People were led from a corridor into the chambers through an ordinary air-tight door with bolts. There was a glass peep-hole, as I recall, next to the door in the wall. Through this window one could watch what was happening inside the room but only when it was not too full of people. After a

The people stand on each other's feet. 700–800 people in an area of twenty-five square metres, in forty-five cubic metres! The SS literally cram them together as much as possible. – The doors close. Meanwhile the others are waiting outside naked in the open air. Someone said to me: 'It's like this in winter as well!' 'Yes, but they could catch their death,' I say. 'Well, that's exactly what they're there for,' said an SS man to me. Now I finally understand why the whole institution is called the Hackenholt Foundation. Hackenholt is the driver of the diesel motor, a little mechanic who designed the installation. The diesel exhaust fumes are meant to kill these people. But the engine is not working! Hauptmann Wirth arrives. You can see that he is embarrassed that it should happen today of all days, when I'm here. So yes, there I am watching! I wait. My stopwatch has registered everything faithfully. 50 minutes 70 seconds – the engine still has not started! The people are waiting in their gas-chamber. In vain. You can hear them crying, sobbing. . . . Hauptmann Wirth hits the Ukrainian who is supposed to be helping the Unterscharführer with the engine, twelve or thirteen times in the face with his riding-crop. After two hours, forty-nine minutes – the stopwatch has registered everything – the diesel engine starts. All this time the people have been inside the four chambers, four lots of 750 people in four lots of forty-five cubic metres! A further twenty-five minutes pass. Right, many are now dead. One can see that through the tiny window as the electric light illuminates the chambers for a moment. After twenty-eight minutes only a few are still alive. Finally, after thirty-two minutes all are dead!

Report of SS-Obersturmführer Kurt Gerstein of 4 May 1945

short time the glass became steamed up. When the people had been locked up in the room the motor was switched on and then I suppose the stop-valves or vents to the chambers opened. Whether they were stop-valves or vents I would not like to say. It is possible that the pipe led directly to the chambers. Once the engine was running, the light in the chambers was switched off. This was followed by palpable disquiet in the chamber. In my view it was only then that the people sensed something else was in store for them. It seemed to me that behind the thick walls and door they were praying and shouting for help.

SS-Scharführer Karl Frenzel and SS-Oberscharführer Erich Bauer, both at Sobibor. In spring 1943 when a worker prisoner tried to take his own life and was found dying, Frenzel shouted that Jews had no right to kill themselves. Only Germans had the right to kill. Frenzel whipped the dying man and finished him off with a bullet

SS-Oberscharführer Heinrich Gley (Sobibor, Belzec) and SS-Obersturmführer Gottlieb Hering, camp commandant at Belzec

After about twelve minutes it became silent in the chambers. The Jewish personnel then opened the doors leading outside and pulled the bodies out of the chambers with long hooks. To do this they had to put these hooks in the mouths of the bodies. In front of the building they were once again thoroughly examined and the bodily orifices were searched for valuables. Gold teeth were ripped out and collected in tins. These activities were carried out by the Jewish camp personnel. The bodies were taken from the searching area directly [and thrown] into deep mass graves which were situated near the extermination institute. When the grave was fairly full, petrol – it may have been some other flammable liquid – was poured over the bodies and they were then set alight. I had barely established that the bodies were not completely burned when a layer of earth was thrown over them and then more bodies were put into the same grave. During the disposal of the bodies I also established that the whole procedure was not entirely satisfactory from the point of view of hygiene.

5. The first day at Treblinka

Kurt Franz, deputy camp commandant

It was midsummer or early autumn 1942 when I arrived at Treblinka from Belzec. I left Malkinia station on foot and it was already dark by the time I reached Treblinka. In the camp there were bodies lying everywhere. I seem to recall that they were all swollen. These bodies were dragged through the camp to the upper section by Jews. The working Jews were forced to keep moving by the [Ukrainian] guards, also by the Germans. I also saw them being beaten. What they were beaten with I can no longer say. There was tremendous confusion and a horrible din. . . .

That evening I went walking around the camp. During my walk I established that some of the guard squads were with girls and had put down their rifles. Then, as far as I could, I established order.

The next day very early in the morning I looked round the camp. I could no longer see any bodies lying around. At about 9.00 a.m., it could have been somewhat later, a transport arrived. When I got there, the men were already standing naked in the so-called reception yard.

6. 'It was my job to shoot these people'
Willi Mentz, the 'Gunman' of Treblinka

When I came to Treblinka the camp commandant was a doctor named Dr Eberl. He was very ambitious. It was said that he ordered more transports than could be 'processed' in the camp. That meant that trains had to wait outside the camp because the occupants of the previous transport had not yet all been killed. At the time it was very hot and as a result of the long wait inside the transport trains in the intense heat many people died. At that time whole mountains of bodies lay on the platform. Then Hauptsturmführer Christian Wirth came to Treblinka and kicked up a terrific row. And then one day Dr Eberl was no longer there. . . .

For about two months I worked in the upper section of the camp and then after Eberl had gone everything in the camp was reorganized. The two parts of the camp were separated by barbed-wire fences. Pine branches were used so that you could not see through the fences. The same thing was done along the route from the 'transfer' area to the gas-chambers. The work-Jews who worked in the upper part of the camp also lived there from then on. Finally, new and larger gas-chambers were built. I think that there were now five or six large gas-chambers. I cannot say exactly how many people these large gas-chambers held. If the small gas chambers could hold 80–100 people, the large ones could probably hold twice that number.

I was then transferred to the so-called hospital area. This so-called hospital was in the lower camp in a special zone which was fenced off and protected against onlookers by pine branches. In this area there was a large mass grave. This grave was dug by an excavator and must have been about seven metres deep.

Next to the mass grave there was a small wooden hut which was used by the two members of the Jewish Arbeitskommando who were on duty in the 'hospital'. These Jews wore armbands marked with a red cross. That was Küttner's idea – he was responsible for the lower camp.

Following the arrival of a transport, six to eight cars would be shunted into the camp, coming to a halt at the platform there. The commandant, his deputy Franz, Küttner and Stadie or Mätzig would be there waiting as the transport came in. Further SS members were

Excavator used for corpses at Treblinka

also present to supervise the unloading: for example, Genz and Belitz had to make absolutely sure that there was no one left in the car after the occupants had been ordered to get out.

When the Jews had got off, Stadie or Mätzig would have a short word with them. They were told something to the effect that they were a resettlement transport, that they would be given a bath and that they would receive new clothes. They were also instructed to maintain quiet and discipline. They would continue their journey the following day.

Then the transports were taken off to the so-called 'transfer' area. The women had to undress in huts and the men out in the open. The women were then led through a passageway, known as the 'tube', to the gas-chambers. On their way they had to pass a hut where they had to hand in their jewellery and valuables. The shed was manned by two work-Jews and a member of the SS. The SS member was Suchomel.

After they had undressed the men had to put their and the women's clothes in an orderly pile in a designated place. That only happened in the early days after the reorganization. Later on there were special

246

Arbeitskommandos, which would immediately sort the clothes the transport participants had taken off.

There were always some ill and frail people on the transports. Sometimes there were also wounded people amongst the arrivals because the transport escorts, SS members, police, Latvians, sometimes shot people during the journey. These ill, frail and wounded people were brought to the hospital by a special Arbeitskommando. These people would be taken to the hospital area and stood or laid down at the edge of the grave. When no more ill or wounded were expected it was my job to shoot these people. I did this by shooting them in the neck with a 9-mm pistol. They then collapsed or fell to one side and were carried down into the grave by the two hospital work-Jews. The bodies were sprinkled with chlorinated lime. Later, on Wirth's instructions, they were burnt in the grave itself.

The number of people I shot after the transport arrived varied. Sometimes it was two or three but sometimes it was as many as twenty or perhaps even more. There were men and women of all ages and there were also children.

When I am asked today how many people I killed this way, I can no longer say precisely.

7. Kurt Franz on the end of Treblinka

I cannot say how many Jews in total were gassed in Treblinka. On average each day a large train arrived, sometimes there were even two. This however was not so common.

In Treblinka I was commander of the Ukrainian guard unit as I had been in Belzec. In Treblinka as in Belzec the unit consisted of sixty to eighty men. The Ukrainians' main task was to man the guard posts around the camp perimeter. After the [prisoners'] uprising in August 1943 I ran the camp more or less single-handedly for a month; however, during that period no more gassings were undertaken.

It was during this time that the original camp was demolished. Everything was levelled off and lupins were planted. A farm was supposed to be built on the site of the camp. Against Wirth's will I put any material that was still usable at the disposal of the reserve hospital in Ostrow, 14 or 15 km away from Treblinka. The director of the hospital was an Oberstabsarzt, called Dr Friedrich Struwe. . . . I used to go and see Dr Struwe if I had any problems. . . .

The end of Treblinka. A farm is built to give future visitors the impression they are in a 'normal' area

'Barry', the dog which Franz used to set on prisoners with the words, 'Man, grab the dog!' 'Barry' tore many Jews to pieces, on numerous occasions biting off their genitals

Note:

The witnesses' statements were now read out to the accused. . . . The accused then said with considerable agitation:

'It is true that I had a dog called Barry. Or rather – to be precise – this dog was a stray from [the work and training camp of] Trawniki which had attached itself to me in the camp. . . . I never set this dog on a Jew. I never killed a person or beat any one. I would like to correct myself – the latter may have occurred once. Basically I have never done wrong to anyone nor would I ever have wished to do a wrong. I vehemently deny these attacks against me. I state that the entire thing is a sham. I believe that I am now being maligned for the sole reason that I was a member of the SS. I wore the uniform of an SS officer and for this reason alone was a familiar figure among the prisoners.'

'Food in the officers' mess excellent'

Auschwitz

Jews selected for the gas-chamber on arrival

1. 'I only took part in the murder of some three million people out of consideration for my family'

Statement of Maximilian Grabner, head of the Political Department

To kill three million people is in my view the greatest crime of all. I only took part in this crime because there was nothing I could do to change anything. The blame for this crime lay with National Socialism. I myself was never a National Socialist. Nevertheless, I still had to join the Party.

I am a Roman Catholic and today still believe in God. I believe there must be such a thing as divine justice as well as justice on earth. I only took part in the murder of some three million people out of consideration for my family. I was never an anti-Semite and would still claim today that every person has the right to life.

2. 'Grabner ordered me to pour Zyklon B into the opening'

Statement of Hans Stark, registrar of new arrivals

The Political Department (PD) of Auschwitz concentration camp was effectively independent and did not come under the authority of the camp commandant. The camp commandant was, however, the disciplinary superior of all the members of the Political Department apart from Grabner and Wosnitza. The PD took its instructions and orders either from the Gestapo regional headquarters in Kattowitz (Katowice) or directly from the RSHA. Reports and communications were sent directly to the RSHA from the PD. My job in the reception department entailed registering newly arrived prisoners and giving prisoner numbers to them. The prisoners' personal details were also taken down. The reception department would notify the relevant headquarters about the prisoners who had been delivered by them.

The reception department was involved with executions in so far as it had to take the newly arrived transports earmarked for execution to be shot instead of registering them. I was entrusted with this task.

After receiving telephoned instructions from Grabner I had to take such new arrivals to the small crematorium near by, where they were shot in a special room by Rapportführer Palitsch.

A small-calibre rifle was used for these executions that was always kept in the Blockführer's hut, which was also where we were accommodated. If there were several new arrivals to shoot I would take them all to the small crematorium. On the way I would tell them that they were going off to have a bath. In an ante-room of the execution room I would ask them to get undressed and I then went into the shooting room with the first one. Palitsch was always already there with the rifle. There were often other Blockführer or Schutzhaftlager-führer present as well. Palitsch would keep the rifle hidden behind his back so that the prisoner could not see it. Then Palitsch or I would say to the prisoner, 'Look over there!', whereupon Palitsch would take the rifle and kill the prisoner with a shot in the neck. Palitsch would hold the rifle a few centimetres from the prisoner's neck. This was how those earmarked for execution would be killed, one after the other. The bodies were then carried out of the room one after another by prisoners who would be waiting next door, in the crematorium. I do not think that the prisoners waiting in the ante-room could hear the gunfire, as there were double doors leading to the shooting room. After individual new prisoners or groups had been executed, their bodies were incinerated in the small crematorium. This was occasion-aly supervised by Unterscharführer Quakernack. . . .

After each execution a written report was submitted to the RSHA using the following formula: 'such and such a number of people have been found special lodging' ['soundsoviel Personen gesondert untergebracht worden seien']. This type of action was mainly directed against persons of the Jewish race and was called a 'Special Treat-ment' [Sonderbehandlung]. An order concerning these 'Special Treatments' had been issued by the RSHA at the beginning of the Russian campaign which had been verbally transmitted to us mem-bers of the Political Department.

As I have already mentioned, I used to receive my orders to take the newly arrived prisoners to the shooting room by telephone from Grabner. Sometimes he would come and tell me in person. I never attempted to avoid carrying out such an order. It never entered my head. I had been a member of the SS for a long time and my whole outlook was coloured by the training I had received during this period. I certainly felt that these orders were an injustice and also tried repeatedly to volunteer for service at the front; however, I was

> I commanded Auschwitz up until 1 December 1943 and estimate that at least 2½ million victims were executed or eliminated there by gassing and burning. At least a further half a million died as a result of hunger and illness, which makes a total of about 3 million. This figure represents about 70 or 80 per cent of all people who were sent as prisoners to Auschwitz. The rest were selected for slave labour in the factories and workshops in the concentration camp.
>
> Rudolf Höss, affidavit of 5 April 1945

only able to leave Auschwitz when my request to continue my studies was finally approved.

On one occasion I took an active part in an execution. This was in the autumn of 1941 in the yard of block 11. At that time some twenty to thirty Russian Commissars had been delivered by the Gestapo regional headquarters in Kattowitz (Katowice). Grabner, Palitsch and, if I remember correctly, a Blockführer from block 11 and I took them to the execution yard. The two rifles were already in block 11. The Russian Commissars were wearing Russian army uniforms — there was nothing that particularly distinguished them as Commissars. Who had established they were Commissars I do not know, but I assume that this was done by the Gestapo in Kattowitz, as many of their officials attended the execution as observers. I do not know whether or not these Commissars were sentenced to death in a regular fashion. I do not think so, for in my opinion Russian Commissars were executed by firing-squad almost without exception. The Russians were killed in pairs in the yard of the block while the others awaited their execution in the corridor of block 11. Grabner, Palitsch, the above-mentioned Blockführer and I took it in turns to shoot these twenty to thirty Commissars one after the other. Their bodies were piled up in a corner of the yard by prisoners from the bunker, if I remember correctly, and put into chests. Two bodies were put in one chest. These chests were taken to the small crematorium in a farm cart drawn by prisoners. I no longer know exactly how many of them I actually shot myself. . . .

As early as autumn 1941 gassings were carried out in a room in the small crematorium which had been prepared for this purpose. The room held about 200–250 people, had a higher-than-average ceiling, no windows and only a specially insulated door, with bolts like those of an airtight door. There were no pipes or the like which would lead the prisoners to believe that it was perhaps a shower room. In the ceiling there were two openings of about 35 cm in diameter at some distance from each other. The room had a flat roof which allowed daylight in through the openings. It was through these openings that Zyklon B in granular form would be poured. . . .

As I have already mentioned, the first gassing was carried out in the small crematorium in autumn 1941. Grabner ordered me to go to the crematorium in order to check numbers, just as I had had to do with the shootings. About 200–250 Jewish men, women and children of all ages were standing at the crematorium. There may also have been babies there. There were a great many SS members present, though I could not say what their names were, plus the camp commandant, the Schutzhaftlagerführer, several Blockführer, Grabner and also other members of the Political Department. Nothing was said to the Jews. They were merely ordered to enter the gas-chamber, the door of which was open. While the Jews were going into the room, medical orderlies prepared for the gassing. Earth had been piled up against one of the external walls of the gassing room to ceiling height so that the medical orderlies could get on to the roof of the room. After all the Jews were in the chamber the door was bolted and the medical orderlies poured Zyklon B through the openings. . . .

At another, later gassing – also in autumn 1941 – Grabner ordered me to pour Zyklon B into the opening because only one medical orderly had shown up. During a gassing Zyklon B had to be poured through both openings of the gas-chamber room at the same time. This gassing was also a transport of 200–250 Jews, once again men, women and children. As the Zyklon B – as already mentioned – was in granular form, it trickled down over the people as it was being poured in. They then started to cry out terribly for they now knew what was happening to them. I did not look through the opening because it had to be closed as soon as the Zyklon B had been poured in. After a few minutes there was silence. After some time had passed, it may have been ten to fifteen minutes, the gas-chamber was opened. The dead lay higgledy-piggledy all over the place. It was a dreadful sight.

3. 'There was Bulgarian red wine and Croatian plum brandy'

From the diary of SS-Dr Kremer

8 August 1942
From 15.8.42 up to the end of the vacation posted to SS-Hospital Prague.

Friday, 14 August 1942
Departure for Prague. Departure Münster 20.40, Osnabrück 0.57, arrival Dresden 10.12, departure Dresden 11.22, arrival Prague 15.15.

15 August 1942
From Dresden onwards weather sunny and fine. Travelled by tram from the central station to SS-Hospital Podol and taken to meet the head of the hospital, Sturmbannführer Dr Fietsch. Accommodation in a patients' room on 3rd floor, No. 344.
Doctors, etc.
Adjutant: Hstf. Koebel, pharmacist
Head of administration: Stubf. Dorn
Surgeon: Stubf. Winne from Danzig, Liek-Schüler
Internal organs: Stubf. Leppel from Cologne
Skin: Ostuf. Inden from Düsseldorf
Eyes: Oberscharf. Frederking from Langendreer
Radiology: Ostuf. Jung from Aachen
Neurology: Ostuf. Jansen

Sunday, 16 August 1942
Half-day trip round the city to see the sights with Oschf. Frederking and wife from Langendreer. Afterwards cup of mocha in a cafe (1.50 RM).

20 August 1942
Evening in officers' mess with vintage wine. Present was a doctor from HQ.

21 August 1942
Ordered an SS-Führer cap from the Schutzstaffel [SS] central uniform office in Berlin through a messenger, but he did not manage to get me one.

24 August 1942
Bought paper, spectacles and belt. . . .

27 August 1942
Brigadeführer Gentzken visited the hospital on his way to Karlsbad. Spoke about a repudiation of intellectualism especially by Goebbels, a gradual erosion of the Hochschulen and of a Ministry for Population Policy.

28 August 1942
Sent to buy caps in Berlin. On leaving informed by reception that the commanding officer wished to speak to me. He informed me that on Hstf. Koebel's orders I was not to travel to Berlin.

29 August 1942
Received orders (F.L.HSSZ 2150 28.8.42 1833 No. 1565) to report to Auschwitz concentration camp, which reportedly is one doctor short due to illness.

30 August 1942
Departure Prague 8.15 via Bohemian Trübau, Olmütz, Prerau, Oderberg. Arrival in Auschwitz CC 17.36. In camp quarantine because of numerous infectious diseases (typhus fever, malaria, diarrhoea). . . .

Receive strictly secret orders from area medical officer Hauptsturmführer Uhlenbrock and am accommodated with the Waffen-SS in a hotel room (26).

31 August 1942
Tropical climate, 38° in the shade, dust and countless flies! Food in the officers' mess excellent. This evening we had e.g. pickled duck's liver for 0.40 RM, plus stuffed tomatoes, tomato salad, etc. Water is contaminated, so we drink soda water, which is provided free of charge (Mattoni). First inoculation against typhus fever. Photographs for camp pass.

1 September 1942
Wrote off to Berlin for officers' cap, belt, braces. In afternoon attended block gassing with Zyklon B against lice.

2 September 1942
3.00 a.m. attended my first Sonderaktion. Dante's Inferno seems to

me almost a comedy compared to this. They don't call Auschwitz the extermination camp for nothing!

3 September 1942
For first time came down with the diarrhoea with vomiting and colic-type attacks of pain which have hit everyone here in the camp. It cannot be the water as I have not drunk a drop, nor can it be the bread, as those who have only eaten white bread (special diets) have also come down with it. Most probably the reason is the unhealthy continental and very dry tropical climate with its dust and masses of vermin (flies).

4 September 1942
To combat the diarrhoea: 1 day of gruel and peppermint tea, followed by a week's special diet. Charcoal and Tannalbin at intervals. Already considerably better.

Particularly unpleasant was the gassing of the emaciated women from the women's camp, who were generally known as 'Muslims'. I remember I once took part in the gassing of one of these groups of women. I cannot say how big the group was. When I got close to the bunker [I saw] them sitting on the ground. They were still clothed. As they were wearing worn-out camp clothing they were not left in the undressing hut but were made to undress in the open air. I concluded from the behaviour of these women that they had no doubt what fate awaited them, as they begged and sobbed to the SS men to spare them their lives. However, they were herded into the gas chambers and gassed. As an anatomist I have seen a lot of terrible things: I had had a lot of experience with dead bodies, and yet what I saw that day was like nothing I had ever seen before. Still completely shocked by what I had seen I wrote in my diary on 5 September 1942: 'The most dreadful of horrors. Hauptscharführer Thilo was right when he said to me today that this is the *anus mundi*', the anal orifice of the world. I used this image because I could not imagine anything more disgusting and horrific.

SS-Doctor Kremer at a hearing on 18 July 1947 in Cracow

---

5 September 1942
In the morning attended a Sonderaktion from the women's concentration camp (Muslims); the most dreadful of horrors. Hschf. Thilo – army doctor – was right when he said to me that this is the *anus mundi*. In the evening towards 8.00 attended another Sonderaktion from Holland. Because of the special rations they get of a fifth of a litre of schnapps, 5 cigarettes, 100 g salami and bread, the men all clamour to take part in such actions. Today and tomorrow (Sunday) work.

6 September 1942
Today Sunday, excellent luncheon: tomato soup, half a chicken with potatoes and red cabbage (20 g fat), dessert, and wonderful vanilla ice-cream. After the meal the new medical officer, Obersturmführer Wirths, who comes originally from Waldbröl, was welcomed. Sturmbannführer Fietsch in Prague was his former regimental doctor.

I have now been in the camp for a week but I still have not completely got rid of the fleas in my hotel room despite all countermeasures with Flit (Cuprex) etc.

I gained a refreshing impression when I made my first visit to the commandant's adjutant. Above the door to his office is the sign 'Cyclists dismount' painted on paper. Also hanging in the office of our SS local HQ was the noteworthy piece of verse:

> In life you hit the mark a thousand times
> They see it, nod and walk on by;
> But the most insignificant carper never forgets
> if you miss your target a single time.

In the evening at 8.00 went to another Sonderaktion outside.

7 September 1942
Second inoculation against typhus fever. Today rainy and cooler weather.

9 September 1942
This morning received excellent news from my lawyer in Münster, Prof. Dr Hallermann: from the first of this month I am divorced from my wife. I can now see life in all its colours again. A black curtain has risen from my life! Was later present as the doctor at corporal punishment of eight prisoners and an execution with small-bore rifle. . . .

Received soap flakes and two bars of soap. At midday a civilian came bounding up to my bike outside the sick-bay like an assassin, ran alongside me and asked me to tell him whether I was not Regierungsrat Hemm from Breslau, to whom I apparently bear a striking resemblance. He had fought together with this gentleman during WWI. How many *Doppelgänger* do I have in the world? In the evening went to a Sonderaktion (4th).

10 September 1942
In the morning attended a Sonderaktion (5th).

11 September 1942
Today Obersturmbannführer Lolling at the camp. Only when introduced to him did I find out for the first time that I am replacing Hauptscharführer Kitt, who is now convalescing in Obersalzberg.

14 September 1942
For the second time had the Auschwitz illness. Temperature of 37·8. Today had the third and last injection against typhus fever.

17 September 1942
Today ordered all-weather coat from the Kleiderkasse in Berlin, measurements: neck to waist 48, total length 133, half back/back top 22, shoulders to elbows 51, whole-arm length 81, chest 107, waist 100, seat 124. Enclosed a uniform coupon, i.e. for a weatherproof coat. Today visited women's camp, Birkenau, with [camp doctor] Dr Meyer.

20 September 1942
Today, Sunday, in the afternoon heard a concert between 3–6 o'clock in the prisoners' chapel in wonderful sunshine. The conductor was the director of the Warsaw State Opera. 80 musicians. For lunch there was roast pork, in the evening baked tench.

21 September 1942
Wrote to the Police HQ (Criminal Branch) at Cologne about Otto. In the evening duckling. Dr Meyer told me about a congenital nasal defect in his father-in-law's family.

23 September 1942
Tonight sixth and seventh Sonderaktion. In the morning Obergruppenführer Pohl and party arrived at the Waffen-SS quarters. A guard was standing outside the door and was the first to stand to attention

before me. In the evening, at 20.00 hours, dinner with Obergruppen-führer Pohl in the officers' mess, a real feast. There was baked pike, as much as you wanted, real ground coffee, excellent beer and open sandwiches.

25 September 1942
Gruppenführer Grawitz at HQ and camp. During the visit he asked me to tell him what the first thing was a doctor would recommend in infectious diseases cases. Of course I could not really give him an answer since there's no such thing as a general panacea. And what did he have in mind? When I heard, I couldn't believe it: a laxative! – As if a doctor would intervene with a laxative for every cold, throat infection, diphtheria, let alone abdominal typhus! Medicine just can't be schematized like that, quite apart from the fact that the young inexperienced doctor at the SS office just a few days earlier had killed someone with a freshly perforated stomach ulcer by prescribing castor-oil blindly.

27 September 1942
Today, Sunday evening, 4–8 o'clock, Community House social evening with supper, free beer and tobacco. Speech from Commandant Höss and musical, as well as theatrical presentations.

28 September 1942
Tonight attended eighth Sonderaktion. Hauptsturmführer Aumeier told me that Auschwitz concentration camp is 12 km long, 8 km wide and 22,000 Morgen [≈ acres] in area. Of these 12,000 acres are under the plough and 2,000 acres fish ponds.

3 October 1942
Today fixed fresh living material from human liver and spleen as well as pancreas, also fixed lice from typhus-fever patients in absolute alcohol. In Auschwitz whole streets have gone down with typhus. Today had myself administered with the first serum injection against abdominal typhus because of this. Obersturmführer Schwarz has gone down with typhus fever!

6 October 1942
Obersturmführer Entress had an accident on his motor bike. Applied dressing, Commandant Höss fell from his horse. Wirths still not back.

7 October 1942
Attended 9th Sonderaktion (foreigners and Muslim women). Wirths
back at work. Replacing Entress in men's camp (examinations, etc).

In my diary I mention in several places extracting fresh living
human material in order to conduct experiments on it. This happened in the following way: For a long time I had been interested in
changes in the human organism as a result of hunger. In Auschwitz
I talked this over with Wirths, who told me that I could extract fresh
living material for these investigations from those prisoners who had
been killed by injections of phenol. In order to select subjects I went
into the last block on the right-hand side (block 28), where the
prisoners who reported sick were examined. During the course of
these examinations the prison doctors presented the patients to the
SS doctor and described the illness the prisoner in question was
suffering from. The SS doctor then decided what the prospects were
for this patient to recover, whether he was already unfit for work,
whether he should be sent to the sick-bay or treated as an out-
patient or else whether he should be liquidated. People the SS doctor
designated for the latter category were taken away by SS personnel
on duty. Most of the prisoners who were designated to this group by
the SS doctor had been given the general diagnosis 'general bodily
weakness'. I observed the prisoners in this group carefully and
whenever one of them particularly interested me because of his
advanced stage of starvation, I ordered the medical orderly to
reserve him and to inform me when this patient would be killed by
injection.

At the appointed time the patients I had selected were led into the
same end block and taken to the room on the other side of the
corridor, opposite the room where they had originally been
examined and selected. The patient was laid down still alive on the
dissection table. I would go up to the table and ask the patient to
give me some details essential for my research. For example, for his
weight before his detention, how much weight he had lost since his
detention, whether he had taken any medication recently, etc. After
I had been given this information a medical orderly would come and
kill the patient with an injection in the heart area. To my knowledge
all these patients were killed with phenol injections. The patient
died immediately after being given such an injection. I myself never
administered fatal injections.

Dr Kremer at a hearing on 30 July 1947 in Cracow

9th October 1942
Sent off a parcel with 9 pounds of soft soap worth 200 RM to Münster. Weather: raining.

10 October 1942
Extracted and fixed fresh live material from liver, spleen and pancreas. Got prisoners to make me a signature stamp. For first time heated the room. More cases of typhus fever and *Typhus abdominalis*. Camp quarantine continues.

11 October 1942
Today, Sunday, there was roast hare for lunch – a real fat leg – with dumplings and red cabbage for 1.25 RM.

12 October 1942
Second inoculation against typhus, later on in evening severe generalized reaction (fever). Despite this in the night attended a further Sonderaktion from Holland (1,600 persons). Ghastly scenes in front of the last bunker! (Hössler!) That was the 10th Sonderaktion.

13 October 1942
Untersturmführer Vetter arrived. Sturmbannführer Cäsar also gone down with typhus after his wife died of it only a few days ago. Attended the sentencing and subsequent execution of seven Polish civilians.

14 October 1942
Received all-weather coat (size 52) from Berlin. Price 50 RM. On the suggestion of the Santitätsamt inquired about the start of the winter semester with the vice-chancellor's office.

15 October 1942
Tonight the first hoar-frost has appeared outside. In the afternoon it was sunny and warm again. Extracted fresh live liver, spleen and pancreas material from an ictus [jaundice] case.

16 October 1942
Soap, soap flakes, sewing material. This morning sent off the second packet worth 300 RM to Frau Wizemann. In the camp had a Jew with syndactyly [= webbed hands or feet] photographed (father and uncle same condition).

17 October 1942
Attended trial and eleven executions. Extracted fresh live material from liver, spleen and pancreas after injection of pilocarpin. Went to Nikolai with Wirths. Before we went he informed me that I would have to stay longer.

18 October 1942
Attended 11th Sonderaktion (Dutch) in cold wet weather this morning, Sunday. Horrible scenes with three naked women who begged us for their lives.

19 October 1942
Went to Kattowitz with Obersturmführer Wirths and Frau Höss to buy epaulettes for the weatherproof coat. Came back via Nikolai.

24 October 1942
Six women from the Budyer revolt killed by injection (Klehr).

25 October 1942
Today, Sunday, wonderful autumn weather, went on bike tour to Budy via Roisko. Wilhelmy back from his trip to Croatia (plum brandy).

31 October 1942
Wonderful autumn weather for about two weeks, hence day in, day out sun-bathing in the garden of the Waffen-SS house. Even the clear nights are relatively mild. Because Thilo and Meyer on home leave I am acting troops doctor. Have to visit my HQ so applied for five-day leave to visit SS-Hospital Prague.

1 November 1942
Today, Sunday, after duty at the medical centre, mainly taking blood samples from venules, left Auschwitz on the fast train for Prague at 13.01. Raining during the journey, train was completely packed. In the evening at about 22.30 arrived in Prague where I took several trams in complete darkness until I finally reached the SS hospital and was then packed off upstairs by a sister, whom I knew already. Was put up for the night on an ottoman in Dr Schreiber's office.

2 November 1942

Was dragged from my dreams and from the primitive horse-blanket bed by Dr Schreiber. After breakfast in the kitchen of the officers' house handed over the three parcels with boots and apple compote for Münster, worth 300 RM. Then went to see Chef Sturmbannführer Fietsch and then usual lunch at 'German House'. Later collected my parade boots (32 RM) in Gerstengasse and returned to first-class stew at 17.30 in the officers' house with plenty of meat. . . .

3 November 1942

After breakfast took the 17 to market where I managed to find press studs and a swish potato grater. From there back to the centre where I ordered myself some glasses for lecturing for 14.50 RM and went back to the 'German House' for lunch. At 3 o'clock I then visited the Viktoria cinema to watch *Andreas Schlüter*. I was positively surprised by the extremely stylish and tasteful décor of the place and must say that I don't think I have ever been to such an elegantly appointed cinema before. The film was made on an enormous budget. Heinrich George was outstanding. He portrayed once again how in this life a person with creative leanings does not find the appreciation he deserves from his fellow men and finally perishes amid intrigues and hostilities. The final message made a deep impression on me after my own experiences: 'Life does not go on for ever but the work remains eternal.'

4 November 1942

This morning first thing tried to take some photographs of Prague Castle from the Oberlandrat building and the Mauerbrücke. The light was very capricious. Then shopping in the old city, where I managed to buy a fountain pen for 7.50 RM near the Altstätter-Ring and a lady's handbag. Then back for a stew in the hospital at 12.30. Here I was told that I had to vacate my room as an Obersturmbann-führer wanted to take it over. I then took my cases into the room belonging to a patient from IIb, in the accident ward. After lunch he however then had the foresight to throw a cursory glance into my room and immediately thought better of the swap, so I was then able to move back upstairs with my suitcases. The person in question was Obersturmbannführer Deutsch, who told me that Sturmbannführer Fietsch had been his regimental doctor. It turned out he also knew Obersturmführer Wirths well and he asked me to send him his best regards. He is, as he told me, somewhat weak-willed and has all kinds of problems with his wife and children.

Some time after lunch I went back into town, photographed Wenceslas Square from the Landesmuseum as well as the Thein-kirche. Then I picked up my spectacles and went to the Willy Forst film, *Operette*, which had been described as a massive success and was already playing in its second week at the Astra in Wenceslas Square. Maria Holst was excellent in the female lead role. I was completely enchanted when I left yet another first-rate and elegantly appointed picture-house: One can only manage one thing at a time – either love or work – both at the same time are not possible. If success is there then it happens as to a mountain climber who has reached the summit. The striving is over, one is lonely and isolated. At any rate the film with its Makart scene, its Straussian operettas and its refined and magnificent song-and-dance numbers is quite disturbingly enchanting.

5 November 1942
In the morning sent off fourth parcel, value 300 RM, to Frau Wizemann. Contents: lady's handbag with fountain pen, spectacles, etc., parade boots, writing paper, brown shirts, potato grater, etc. Then a little shopping in town and lunch at the 'German House'. Gloomy, rainy weather. In the evening packed for tomorrow's departure at 8.00 and evening in the mess where I put away a whole litre of a wonderful-tasting Bulgarian red wine which really put me in a good mood. Didn't get to bed until 12.00.

6 November 1942
Woken early at 6.00 by the sister and was already at the station (trams 21 and 7) not long afterwards, where I boarded the fast train to Mährisch-Ostrau at 8.10. In Prerau I boarded the fast Vienna–Cracow train and had just entered a second-class compartment when a Generalmayor [brigadier] started up a conversation with me. I was alone with him for almost the whole journey, and he told me about his experiences at the front and shook me by the hand when he had to get off. Journey time from Prague to Auschwitz over nine hours. On arrival I immediately went to the officers' mess, where once again I ate until I was really full.

8 November 1942
Tonight took part in two Sonderaktionen, in rainy and gloomy autumn weather (12th and 13th). In the morning Hauptscharführer Kitt, a pupil of mine from Essen, came and paid his respects to me at the sick-bay. In the afternoon another Sonderaktion, the 14th I have participated in up to now. In the evening cosy evening company in the Führerheim as guests of Hauptsturmführer Wirths. There was Bulgarian red wine and Croatian plum brandy.

10 November 1942
Today first light snowfall. Frost during the night.

13 November 1942
Extracted fresh live material (liver, spleen and pancreas) from a previously photographed, severely atrophied Jewish prisoner aged eighteen. Fixed as always, liver and spleen in Carnoy [fixing solution] and pancreas in Zenker [fixing solution] (Prisoner No. 68,030).

14 November 1942
Today, Saturday, variety show in the communal house (really big!). Particularly popular were the dancing dogs and the two bantams which crowed to order, the wrapped-up person and the cycling group.

15 November 1942
Morning attended a trial.

16 November 1942
Sent off a packet of soft soap (about 12 pounds) worth 300 RM to Mia and Gretchen.

17 November 1942
Sent small crate to Frau Wizemann (5th parcel) worth 300 RM. Contents: (14 kg!) 2 bottles of brandy, vitamin and strengthening preparations, razor blades, washing and shaving soap, thermometer, nail clippers, bottle of iodine, preparation in 90% alcohol, X-ray plates, cod-liver oil, writing materials, envelopes, perfumes, cotton wool, needles, tooth powder, etc, etc. In the evening snow flurry which has transformed the streets into slush and mire. Got ready for tomorrow's departure for Prague.

At the medical centre: Jambor, Brauner, Biedermann, Wilks and in the sick-bay Klehr and Scherpe, all old 'barbed-wire' warriors and concentration-camp 'old hands'. Stabsscharführer Ontl talked me into giving him a coupon for riding breeches. The pharmacist, Hauptsturmführer Kroemer, proved himself very comradely over the supplies of the necessary reagents. Sauther, the dentist, has now been transferred to Minsk.

18 November 1942
This afternoon left at 13.20 via Oderberg. Changed trains at Mährisch-Ostrau. Via Prerau and Olmütz for Prague. Arrived at 22.11 and had good connection to the hospital. The night sister, Anna, made sure that I could have the same room I had had before.

19 November 1942
After reporting to the chief doctor and breakfast fetched suitcase from station and then lunch in the 'German House'. After lunch handed in the pieces of uniform that had been lent to me and packed my case.

20 November 1942
Breakfast, said goodbye to Deputy Medical Officer Himstedt from Hameln, Sturmbannführer Matz from Stettin, Sturmbannführer Küttner, Hauptscharführer Dreddling, Untersturmführer Fasching, Hauptsturmführer Koerber and, amongst others, Untersturmführer Jung, the radiologist, who has promised me some nice X-rays for my lecture. After my ticket was issued, my luggage was brought to Hibermor station. Departure 16.13 via Dresden, Leipzig, Hanover, Osnabrück. Arrival in Münster 6.38.

24 November 1942
For first time in new Anatomy building on Westring.

4. 'The highest number of gassings in a day was 10,000'

Statement by Rudolf Höss

. . . I was ordered to report to Himmler, in Berlin . . . where he told me roughly the following: The Führer has ordered the solution to the Jewish question in Europe. There are already several so-called extermination camps in the General-Gouvernement. . . . The efficiency of these camps is, however, poor and they cannot be expanded. I myself visited the Treblinka camp in 1942 . . . in order to find out more about the conditions there. The exterminations were carried out by the following method: There were chambers the size of a small room which were supplied with gas from car engines by connecting pipes. This process was unreliable, as the engines had been taken from old vehicles and tanks which had been taken as booty and would often not start. As a result, the transports could not be processed efficiently enough for the action programme to be adhered to closely. The action involved was the clearing of the Warsaw ghetto. . . . For all the reasons described above, explained Himmler, the only possibility of extending these installations so that they corresponded to the overall plans lay in Auschwitz: first because it was situated at a junction of four lines, and second because the area was sparsely populated and the camp could be completely isolated. For these reasons he had decided to move the mass extermination programme to Auschwitz and I had to set to work to carry this out immediately. He told me I had four weeks to prepare precise building plans which corresponded to these guidelines. He also told me that this assignment was so difficult and of such importance that he could not entrust simply anyone with it. He already intended to entrust another high-ranking SS officer with the assignment but did not consider it expedient at this stage in the plans for two officers to be in command side by side. I thus received clear instructions to carry out the extermination of the transports delivered by the RSHA.

I had to liaise with SS-Obersturmbannführer Eichmann from Amt 4 (unit under the command of Gruppenführer Müller) about the order in which the transports would arrive. At the same time [1941 – Ed.], there were also transports of Russian prisoners of war coming in from the areas under the control of the Gestapo regional HQ of

Breslau, Troppau and Kattowitz, which on Himmler's orders [and on] the written instructions of the Gestapo chief in Auschwitz had to be exterminated. As the new crematorium installations were not ready until 1942, the prisoners had to be gassed in temporary gas-chambers and then incinerated in graves dug in the ground. I shall describe the way the gassings proceeded:

Two old farmhouses which were situated in an isolated spot in Birkenau had been made airtight and were fitted with heavy wooden doors. The transports themselves were unloaded on a siding in Birkenau. Those prisoners fit for work were selected and taken to the camps. All luggage was removed and later taken to the stores. The others, those who were to be gassed, were marched over to the gassing installations, which were about one kilometre away. The sick and disabled were taken there by lorry. When transports arrived during the night they were all taken over by lorry. They all had to undress behind walls made out of brushwood outside the farmhouses. On the doors was the sign 'Disinfection Room'. The Unterführer on duty had to tell the people through an interpreter to make sure they knew where they had left their things so that they could find them straight away after they had been deloused. In this way any uneasiness was prevented right from the start. The people, now undressed, then went into the rooms. Each had a capacity of 200–300 people. The doors were bolted and two cans of Zyklon B were sprinkled through the hatches into each room. The Zyklon B was a crystalline mass of prussic acid. It took between three and ten minutes to take effect, depending on the weather conditions. After half an hour the doors were opened and the bodies were taken out by a Kommando of prisoners, who worked there permanently. They were then burned in trenches. Before incineration gold teeth and rings were removed. Firewood was piled up among the bodies and when there was a pile of about one hundred bodies in the grave, the wood was lit with rags drenched in paraffin. When the fire had caught, the rest of the bodies were thrown on. The fat which was collecting on the bottom of the trenches was poured back on to the fire with buckets. This helped to accelerate the burning process, in wet weather particularly. The incineration took six to seven hours. The stench of the burnt bodies reached the camp itself when the wind was blowing from the west. After the trenches had been cleared the charred remains were crushed. This was done on a cement slab with wooden pounders. These remains were then taken to a remote part of the Vistula by lorry and poured into the river.

After the new large incineration plants had been set up the following process was used: In 1942, once the first two large crematoria were ready (the other two were ready six months later), the mass transports from France, Belgium, Holland and Greece began. During that period the following procedure was adopted: The trains would run on to a specially built three-track ramp exactly midway between the crematoria, the effects store and the Birkenau camp. The selection of those fit for work took place directly on the ramp. This was also where luggage was deposited. Those who were fit for work were taken to the various camps and those that were to be exterminated into one of the new crematoria. Once there the latter went into a large underground room to undress. This room was fitted out with benches and facilities for hanging up clothes. Here too it was explained to people through interpreters that they were going to be taken to be bathed and deloused and that they should make sure they knew where they had left their clothes. Then, still underground, they went into the next-door room, which was equipped with water pipes and shower attachments, creating the impression that it was a shower-room. Right up to the end, two Unterführer had to stay in the room to prevent people from getting worried.

Sometimes prisoners did realize what was happening. This was particularly true for the transports from Belsen, as most of them were originally from the East and knew that when the trains reached Upper Silesia they were almost certainly being led to their death. With transports from Belsen, security measures were stepped up and to prevent mayhem breaking out the transport was divided into smaller groups to be sent to the individual crematoria. SS men would form a dense human chain and push anyone who resisted into the gas-chambers by force. However, this happened very seldom as the procedure was made easier by the measures that had been taken to calm down the transport.

I particularly remember one example: a transport from Belsen had arrived and after about two-thirds [were in the gas-chamber] – they were mostly men – a revolt broke out among the last third who were still in the undressing room. Three or four SS-Unterführer came into the room with their weapons in order to get them to hurry up and undress. . . . As they came in the lighting cables were torn out and they were attacked, one was stabbed to death and all their weapons were seized from them. It was now completely dark in the room and there was a wild shoot-out between the guards posted at the entrance and the prisoners inside. When I reached the scene I ordered the

271

doors to be shut and the gassing of the first two-thirds [*sic!*] to be completed and then I went into the [undressing] room with some guards and some hand torches and forced the prisoners into a corner. They were then led out one by one and shot on my orders with a small-calibre weapon in a room next door to the crematorium.

Very often women would hide their small children in their under-clothes and their clothing and leave them in the undressing room when they went into the gas-chambers. The prisoner detachment which carried out the incineration and was in the command of the SS would have to search the clothes and if they found any such children send them later into the gas-chamber. After half an hour the electric ventilation was started up and the bodies were taken by hoist into the incinerators situated above the gas-chambers.

The incineration of about 2,000 people in five ovens took about twelve hours. In Auschwitz there were two installations each with five double ovens and two each with four fairly large ovens. In addition there was also the temporary installation as described above. The second temporary installation was destroyed. All clothing and per-sonal effects were sorted in the effects store by a prisoner detachment which worked there permanently and was also accommodated there. The valuables were sent to the Reichsbank in Berlin every month. The clothing was first cleaned and then taken to armaments factories for the workers from the East and the resettlers working there. Gold taken from teeth was melted down and taken once a month to the Sanitätsamt of the Waffen-SS.

. . . The highest number of gassings in one day was 10,000. That was the most that could be carried out in a day with the available facilities. . . .

5. 'So that in the future it would be impossible to establish how many people had been burnt'

Rudolf Höss on the elimination of the mass graves

On the occasion of his visit in the summer of 1942 the Reichsführer-SS watched the entire extermination process carefully from the unloading [of the transport] to the clearing of Bunker II. At that time the bodies were not burnt. He did not have any complaints, nor did he talk about anything he had seen either. Gauleiter Bracht and Obergruppen-führer Schmauser were also present. Shortly after the Reichsführer's visit, Standartenführer Blobel from Eichmann's office arrived and transmitted to us an order from the RFSS that all the mass graves were to be dug up and the bodies were to be incinerated.

The ashes were to be dispersed so that in the future it would be impossible to establish how many people had been burnt. Blobel was already experimenting with different incineration methods in Kulmhof. He had been ordered by Eichmann to show me the installa-tion and so together with [SS-Hauptsturmführer] Hössler I went to

In January 1942 I was dismissed from my position as commanding officer of Sonderkommando 4 and by way of punishment was trans-ferred to Berlin. I stayed there for a time without work, under the command of former Gruppenführer Müller at Amt IV. In the autumn of 1942 I was appointed as Müller's representative and had to travel to the Eastern Territories to eliminate traces of the mass graves which had resulted from the executions carried out by the Einsatzgruppen. I was engaged in this work until the summer of 1944.

SS-Standartenführer Paul Blobel

Kulmhof to inspect them. Blobel had had a number of different temporary ovens built and was using wood and petrol residues as fuel. He had also tried destroying the bodies by blowing them up with explosives but this had not been very successful. The ashes were first ground to dust in a bone mill and then scattered in a large expanse of wooded land. Standartenführer Blobel was given the job of pinpointing all the mass graves throughout the Eastern Territories and of eliminating them. His staff was code-named '1005'. The work itself was carried out by Judenkommandos [units of Jews] who were shot after work in a particular area had finished. The concentration camp of Auschwitz provided a constant supply of Jews for Kommando '1005'. . . . Standartenführer Blobel had a fairly clear idea of the numbers of mass graves in the Eastern Territories, but was duty-bound to strict silence.

Glossary and Abbreviations

1a The operations officer in a military HQ or formation.

1a Abteilung The section of the former Berlin police headquarters responsible for the collection of political-police intelligence. Its functions were taken over by the new Gestapo in 1933–4.

1c The intelligence officer in a military HQ or formation.

1c-Dienst Intelligence Service. The title of the SS organization set up under Heydrich, precursor of the **SD**.

1. Generalstabsoffizier First General Staff Officer.

2. Staatsanwalt Assessor Second public prosecutor having passed through the stage of 'Referendar' and the second state examination.

Abteilung (1) A staff branch, section or subdivision of a main department or office (amt, Hauptamt, or Amtsgruppe).
(2) A military unit or detachment up to battalion strength or equivalent level of command.

Abwehr (lit. defence) The espionage, counter-espionage and sabotage service of the German High Command – Amt Ausland/Abwehr.

Abwehr Offizier (AO) Counter-intelligence officer.

Aktion T4 Extermination of so-called 'incurables' (mentally and physically handicapped people) (T4: after address of central office in Berlin, Tiergartenstrasse 4).

Altreich Germany before annexation of Austria.

Amt A main office, branch or directorate of a ministry; or an independent ministry, e.g. Auswärtiges Amt.

Amtsgruppe A branch of a Hauptamt (*see* **Amt**).

Anhaltelager A temporary detention camp.

Anschluss Annexation of Austria in March 1938.

AOK *see* **Armee-Oberkommando**.

Arbeitseinsatz (lit. 'mobilization of labour') Nazi term for the deployment of labour, occasionally used as a euphemism for deportation and extermination.

Armee-Oberkommando An Army HQ.

Aussendienststelle Outstation or outpost of the **Sipo** and **SD** (alternative form of Aussenstelle).

Aussenstelle *see* **Aussendienststelle**.

Bahnsschutz   Railway protection (Bahnschutzpolizei: with status of auxiliary police).

BdS   Befehlshaber der Sicherheitspolizei und des Sicherheitsdienstes. Commander of the Security Police and Security Service in occupied territories, subordinate to the **HSSPF** for particular tasks but under direct **RHSA** control. Latterly the title of the Inspekteur der Sicherheitspolizei (IdS) in certain areas of the Reich.

Befehlshaber   A senior military commander.

Befehlshaber der Ordnungspolizei   Commander of the uniformed police at regional and Wehrkreis level and in occupied territories, subordinate to the HSSPF (previously entitled Inspekteur der Ordnungspolizei).

Dienststelle   A headquarters, administrative office, station or depot.

Einsatzgruppe   Special Force: mobile SS and police unit for special missions in occupied territories (the mass murder of Jews, Communists and partisans in Eastern Europe).

Einsatzgruppenchef   Head of an **Einsatzgruppe**.

Einsatzkommando   Special Unit. An individual detachment of an **Einsatzgruppe**.

F.d.R [d.A.]   Für die Richtigkeit (der Abschrift); testifying to the correctness of a document.

Feldgendarmerie/Feldgendarm   Military police.

Feldkommandant   Commanding officer of a **Feldkommandantur**.

Feldkommandantur   Sub-area HQ (local garrison command), sub-area of Oberfeldkommandantur = military administrative area headquarters.

Gau   Regional party district.

Gauleiter   Regional party leader.

geh.   Geheim = secret.

Gendarmerie   The rural police, including motorized units for traffic control.

Gendarmeriepostenführer   Head of military police unit.

General-Gouvernement   General Government: main part of German-occupied Poland.

General-Gouverneur   Governor-General.

Generalkommando   An army corps HQ.

Generaloberst (lit. 'Colonel-General')   No equivalent in either British or US armies.

Generalstab   General Staff (army).

Gestapo   Geheime Staatspolizei (Secret State Police).

GPU (Russian abbrev.)   State Political Administration.

Grenzpolizei Kommissariat   A regional frontier HQ of the Grenzpolizei-controlled Grenzposten (outposts).

Hilfspolizei   Auxiliary Police, recruited largely from Nazi Party formations, who assisted the regular police in various functions (e.g. the Bahnschutzpolizei) but were not an integral part of the Ordnungspolizei (Orpo).

Höherer SS- und Polizeiführer   Senior SS and Police Commander: Himmler's personal representative in each Wehrkreis and liaison officer with the military district commander and other senior regional authorities. Also established in occupied territories. Nominally the commander of all SS and police units in his area.

HSSPF *see* **Höherer SS- und Polizeiführer**.

Inspekteur der Ordnungspolizei   Original title of the **Befehlshaber der Ordnungspolizei**.

KdS   Kommandeur der Sicherheitspolizei und des SD.

Kommandostab   HQ Staff.

Kreis   An administrative district; also the principal subdivision of a Gau.

Kriminalangestellte   Employee of the Criminal Police.

Kriminalassistent   Lowest rank in lowest grade of Criminal Police.

Kriminalkommissar   The lowest rank in the upper officer class of the Criminal Police (= Obersturmführer). Promotion to Kriminalrat (= Hauptsturmführer).

Kriminalpolizei   The Criminal Police, which, together with the Gestapo, formed the Security Police (Sipo).

Kriminalrat *see* **Kriminalkommissar**.

Kriminalsekretär   Next rank up from *Kriminalassistent*.

Landesgericht   A county or district court of the first instance, dealing with more important civil and criminal cases than an Amtsgericht.

Landrat   Head of administration of Landkreis, i.e. district administrator.

Leiter   Chief, leader or commander of an office, station or authority.

NSDAP   Nationalsozialistische Deutsche Arbeiterpartei – National Socialist German Workers' Party (Nazi Party).

Oberabschnitt   The main territorial division of the SS in Greater Germany, approximately equal to a Wehrkreis.

Oberarzt   Medical officer: equivalent Wehrmacht rank = Oberleutnant.

Oberpräsident   Senior administrative official in a Prussian province.

Oberstabsarzt   Medical officer: equivalent Wehrmacht rank = Major.

O.1   1. Ordonnanzoffizier = deputy to 1a officer, i.e. deputy operations officer.

OKH   Oberkommando des Heeres (Army High Command).

OKW   Oberkommando der Wehrmacht (Armed Forces High Command).

Ordonnanzoffizier   Operations officer.

Organisation Todt A semi-military government agency established in 1933. Its main function was the construction of strategic highways and military installations.

Ortskommandant Commanding officer of **Ortskommandantur**.

Ortskommandantur Town HQ, Major's command in a small town (army administration).

O.U. (= Ortsunterkunft) Billets, quarters.

Polizeirat Senior police official.

Protektorat The Protectorate. Became a military district under the name Wehrkreis Böhmen Mähren late in 1942 (Bohemia Moravia).

Rayon Smallest subdivision of an administrative area.

Referat A subsection or 'desk' within a Gruppe.

Referent The official in charge of a **Referat**, an expert.

Regierungsbezirk Subdivision of a Prussian province, also a Bavarian administrative district.

Regierungsrat A government councillor, the lowest rank in the Higher Civil Service.

Reichsarbeitsdienst The National Labour Service, compulsory for youth of both sexes.

Reichskommissariat (für das Ostland) German civil administration in occupied Soviet territories, except in the Ukraine for which a separate RK was formed. It was divided into General Kommissariate with subordinate Gebiets (district) and Stadt (city) Kommissariate.

Reichsleiter The highest-ranking Party official, most of whom also held ministerial and administrative posts.

Reichsstatthalter The Reich Governor of a Land or a Reichsgau. Frequently identical with the Party Gauleiter.

Reichstag German parliament.

RSHA Reichssicherheitsauptamt (Reich Security Head Office), formed in 1939 under Reinhard Heydrich. Its departments included the **Gestapo**, the Criminal Police and the SD.

SA Sturmabteiling (storm troopers).

Schirrmeister Supply Technician.

Schutzhaftlager A camp for prisoners in protective custody, i.e. concentration camp.

Schutzmannschaft Auxiliary police recruited in the eastern occupied territories from the local population.

Schwurgericht Court of full-time judges and lay judges for particularly serious crimes.

SD Sicherheitsdienst (Security Service) of the SS.

Selbstschutz Militia.

Sipo Sicherheitspolizei (Security Police) of the SS.

Sonderbehandlung (lit. 'special treatment') SS term for immediate execution of prisoners.

SS Schutzstaffel (lit. 'defence echelon'). Police and security organization run by Heinrich Himmler.

Staatspolizeistelle Regional HQ of the Gestapo in a Wehrkreis or capital of a Prussian province or a Land or Reichsgau and controlling Stapo-Aussendienstellen.

Stapostelle *see* **Staatspolizeistelle**.

Verwaltungsgerichtsrat Senior official in the administrative court.

völkisch Racial-nationalist.

Volksdeutsch Ethnic Germans.

Volksgemeinschaft National Folk Community: Nazi slogan for the allegedly classless German society.

Wehrmacht Armed forces (army, air force and navy).

Wehrmachtsführungsstab Operation staff of the Armed Forces High Command.

Zollbefehlstelle Customs command post.

This glossary is adapted from one that appeared in Helmut Krausnick and Martin Broszat, *Anatomy of the SS State*, and is reprinted by kind permission of HarperCollins Publishers.

Table of equivalent ranks

Equivalences in some cases are approximate; ranks in the SA equated almos

Army	Police	Auxiliary police and technical corps
Gemeiner, Landser		
Grenadier	...............................Anwärter..........................	
Obergrenadier		
Gefreiter	......................Unterwachtmeister....................	
Obergefreiter	......................Rottwachtmeister....................	
Stabsgefreiter	......	......
Unteroffizier	...........................Wachtmeister....................	
Unterfeldwebel	.... Oberwachtmeister....................	
Feldwebel	.... Zugwachtmeister....................	
Oberfeldwebel	.... Hauptwachtmeister..............	
Stabsfeldwebel		Bereitschaftswacht-meister
......	.... Meister.........................	
	.... Obermeister	
..................Leutnant..................		Zugführer
...............Oberleutnant		Oberzugführer
...............Hauptmann		Bereitschaftsführer
..................Major.....................		Abteilungsführer
............Oberstleutnant.............		Oberabteilungsführer
....................Oberst		Landesführer
......	......	......
...............Generalmajor..............		......
..............Generalleutnant		Chef der Technische Nothilfe
.... General		
...............Generaloberst..............		
Generalfeldmarschall		

exactly to Waffen-SS ranks

Party officials (selected ranks)	Waffen-SS	British equivalents
	SS-Schütze	(Junior) Private
	SS-Oberschütze	(Senior) Private
Helfer	SS-Sturmmann	Lance-Corporal
Oberhelfer		
Arbeitsleiter	SS-Rottenführer	Corporal
Oberarbeitsleiter	SS-Unterscharführer	Senior Corporal
Hauptarbeitsleiter		
	SS-Scharführer	Sergeant
	SS-Oberscharführer	Colour-Sergeant
Bereitschaftsleiter		
Oberbereitschaftsleiter	SS-Hauptscharführer	Sergeant-Major
	Hauptbereitschaftsleiter	
	SS-Sturmscharführer	Warrant Officer
Einsatzleiter	SS-Unterstumführer	2nd Lieutenant
Obereinsatzleiter	SS-Obersturmführer	1st Lieutenant
Haupteinsatzleiter	SS-Hauptsturmführer	Captain
Gemeinschaftsleiter	SS-Sturmbannführer	Major
Hauptgemeinschaftsleiter	SS-Obersturmbannführer	Lieutenant-Colonel
Hauptabschnittsführer	SS-Standartenführer	Colonel
Hauptbereichsleiter	SS-Oberführer	Brigadier-General
Hauptdienstleiter	SS-Brigadeführer	Major-General
Hauptbefehlsleiter	SS-Gruppenführer	Lieutenant-General
Gauleiter	SS-Obergruppenführer	General
Reichsleiter	SS-Oberstgruppenführer	'Colonel-General'
	Reichsführer-SS (Heinrich Himmler)	Field Marshal

Einsatzgruppen

Mobile execution units in Eastern Europe

Einsatzgruppe A (Baltic countries)
Einsatzkommandos 2, 3
Sonderkommandos 1a, 1b

Einsatzgruppe B (White Russia)
Einsatzkommandos 8, 9
Sonderkommandos 7a, 7b
'Vorkommando Moskau' (November 1941)
  ('Advance Party Moscow')

Einsatzgruppe C (Northern and Middle Ukraine)
Einsatzkommandos 5, 6
Sonderkommandos 10a, 10b

Einsatzgruppe D (Bessarabia, Caucasia, Southern Ukraine)
Einsatzkommandos 11a, 11b, 12
Sonderkommandos 10a, 10b

Document sources

All file references and details refer to the Zentrale Stelle der Landes-justizverwaltungen in Ludwigsburg, unless otherwise indicated. The *Ereignismeldungen UdSSR* [Reports on Events USSR] of heads of the Sicherheitspolizei and SD and the *Tätigkeits- und Lageberichte der Einsatzgruppen der Sicherheitspolizei und des SD in der UdSSR* [Action and Situation Reports of the Einsatzgruppen of the Sicherheitspolizei and the SD in the USSR] have been quoted from copies held in Ludwigsburg. The same applies for the *Nürnberger Dokumente* [Nuremberg Documents], i.e. for all documents which were submitted as evidence in the Nuremberg trials by the Allies.

PART ONE

[I] **Blaskowitz:** 'Vortragsnotizen für einen Vortrag beim Oberbefehlshaber des Heeres am 15.2. in Spala': ZSt. USA Film 7, Frame 550 ff. The document is also called 'Denkschrift Blaskowitz'. *Olkusz:* Picture captions based on files 205 AR-Z 308/67, *Auswärtiger Einsatz:* ZSt., CSSR 1, file 147, frame 97/1 ff.

[II] **Kovno:** 'Einsatzgruppe A, Gesamtbericht bis zum 15. Oktober 1941', of Franz Walter Stahlecker, Head of Einsatzgruppe A. Nbg Dok. 180-L. Report of Oberst a.D. von Bischoffshausen of 19.4.59 at ZSt: 207 AR-Z 14/58, p. 297 ff. Statement of photographer Gunsilius of 11.11.58: 207 AR-Z 14/58, p. 133 ff. Statement of a Gefreiter [lance-corporal] from Bakers' Coy Röder 8.7.59: 2 AR-Z 21/58, p. 3647 ff. Statement of sergent of Bakers' Coy Lesch of 8.7.59: 2 AR-Z 21/58, p. 3657 ff. Statement of further member of Bakers' Coy (Schmcink) of 2.8.60: 204 AR-Z 21/58, p. 116. Statement of medical orderly Hippler of 11.11.58: 207 AR-Z 14/58, p. 125 ff. *Paneriai:* Statement of Pflüger 18.6.59: 207 AR-Z 14/58, p. 1683 ff. Statement of Hamann 5.6.59: ibid. p. 1263. Statement of Schroff: ibid., p. 1247 ff. *Jäger-Bericht:* 'Gesamtaufstellung der im Bereich des EK.3 bis zum 1. Dez. 1941 durchgeführten Exekutionen': ZSt. File No. 108, Frame No. 27–38. Statement of Jäger 15.6.59: 207 AR-Z 14/58, p. 1923.

[III] **'Pushed to their psychological limits'/Einsatzgruppen:** Ohlendorf's affidavit of 5.11.45: Nbg Doc. 2620 PS. Statement of Fix 7.1.60: II 204 AR-Z 15/60, vol. 3, p. 10. Statement of Tögel 26.1.65: 213 AR 1898/66, vol. xi, p. 2516 ff. Tätigkeits- und Lagebericht vom 31.7.41: Nbg Dok. NO-2651. Statement of Kiebach 1.11.63: 204 AR-Z 269/60, p. 1431 f.

Statement of Trill 26.5.64: 204 AR-Z 269/60, vol. xi, p. 2282. *Babi Yar:* Statement of Höfer 27.8.59: 2 AR-Z 21/58, vol. vi, p. 4035 ff. Statement of Werner 28.5.64: 204 AR-Z 269/60, vol. xi, p. 2306 ff. Statement of Heidborn 1.11.63: ibid., vol. vii, p. 1423. *Gas-vans:* Statement of Becker 26.3.60: 9 AR-Z 220/59, vol. i, p. 194 ff. Statement of Rauff 28.6.72 in the embassy of the Federal Republic of Germany in Santiago (Chile): II 415 AR 1310/63 – E32, p. 545. Becker 5.6.42 to Rauff: ZSt. USA Film 1, Frame 9. Becker 16.5.42 to Rauff: Nbg Dok. PS-501. Statement of Findeisen 29.9.67: 208 AR-Z 269/60, vol. 31, p. 12 ff. *Gas-vans in Stalino and Rostov:* Statement of Friedrich Zopp 28, 29.6.62: II 204 AR-Z 15/60, p. 81 f. (Stalino) and 87 f. (Rostov). Statement of Lauer 4.6.64: 204 AR-Z 269/60, vol. xi, p. 2390.

[IV] **Forced to obey orders (*Befehlsnotstand*):** Statement of Kripo official at Grenzkomm. Neu-Sandez, Bornholt, 10.9.63: ZSt. 1. Befehlsnotstand – B59 (April 1964), p. 7. Statement of auxiliary policeman Müller 28.6.65: loc. cit., B77 (June 1966), p. 2. Statement of member of Polizei-Reiter-Abt. III, Plappert, 20.5.64: loc. cit., B66 (Oct. 64), p. 16. Statement of member of 3rd Police Battn 307, Adamec, 9.2.66: loc. cit., B80 (June 66), p. 5. Statement of Police Reservist Wolberg 12.11.64: loc. cit., B79 (June 66), p. 4. Statement of Polizeioberwachtmeister Schröder 20.7.67: loc. cit., B89 (June 69), p. 18. Statement of Kriminalassistent in Kolomea, Schwenker, 20.4.64: 2 AR-Z 277/60, vol. vi., p. 2919 f. Statement of police reservist from 3rd Police Battn. 91, Hermann, 7.2.63: 205 AR 512/63, vol. 3, p. 248 ff. Statement of Kriminalsekretär in Riga, Krüger, 18.7.68: loc. cit., B93 (June 69), p. 23. Statement of Kripo official in Jaslo, Salzer, 28.4.66: loc. cit., B82 (June 66), p. 10 f. Statement of member of EGr A, Munich, 11.12.63: 207 AR-Z 7/59, vol. 42, p. 7052 ff. Statement of Ehlers 17.4.59: loc. cit., B2 (July 61), p. 60. Statement of Six 24.5.61: ibid., p. 53 f. Statement of Hartl of 16.1.57: loc. cit., B9 (July 61), p. 65 ff. Statement of Schulz 1.8.58: 202 AR-Z 52/59, p. 516 ff.

[V] **Landau:** Introduction and biographical sketch based on verdict of Stuttgart LG 16.3.62 (Ks 9/61). Diary: ZSt. File. various, 301 Cj, vol. 169, p. 278 ff. and File No. 301 AAK misc., vol. 118, p. 511 ff. Katzmann in a report of 30.6.43: Nbg Dok. L-18.

[VI] **'Execution as popular entertainment':** *Zhitomir:* 637 Propaganda Company photographed the hanging of Kieper. Statement of Selle 9.10.65: Js 4/65 GStA Fr/a/M. Ref: rejected witnesses N-Z. Statement of lorry-driver of 6th Technical Battalion, Awater, 27.2.64: 4 AR-Z 11/61, vol. iv, p. 782 ff. Statement of Häfner of 16.6.65: 204 AR-Z 269/60, vol. xiii, p. 3087 ff. Statement of Huhn of 16.3.66: Js 4/65 GStA Fr/a/M. Ref: Interrogations of Accused, p. 23 f. of interrogation. Statement of Army Judge to Oberkommando of 6th Army, Dr Neumann, 8.10.65: Js 4/65 GStA Fr/a/M. Ref: rejected witnesses. Order of Rundstedt of 24.9.41 (to armies belonging to the army group and to the Oberkommando of rear army area, distribution list not printed): Nbg Dok. NOKW-541. *Rösler:* About 2,000 Jews were killed in the murder action described by Rösler, 2–3 km outside Zhitomir. According to information (final report of 30.12.64: the SK 4a of Einsatzgruppe C and units working with this Kommando, p. 195, 114 AR-Z 269/60) at ZSt. the massacre did not take place in July but August 1941. The Rösler report is on p. 195 ff. Statement of Heidborn 1.11.63: 204 AR-Z 269/60, vol. VII, p. 1417 f. *Vinnitsa:* Report of customs official Tappe 2.10.62: II 204 AR-Z 15/60, vol. III, p. 51 ff. *Bobruisk:* Statement of Wirtschaftsführer Grabow 24.4.59: 202 AR-Z 52/59, vol. IV, p. 368 f. *'Twelve Toppers':* Statement of former Truppenbetreuer Thoma 1.6.62: 4 AR-Z 287/59, p. 232 ff. *Libau:* the picture captions based on contents of verdict of Hannover LG of 14.10.71 (2 Ks 3/68), p. 171 ff. It was not revealed who had taken the photographs. – Statement of interpreter Fahrbach 16.4.64: 7 AR-Z 18/58, vol. IX, p. 1828. Statement of Vandrey, Bootführer beim Hafenkapitän, 17.7.59: ibid., vol. I, p. 116 f. Statement of Führer of 2nd Coy, Police Battn 13, Rosenstock, statement of 7.1.64: ibid., vol. VIII, p. 1629 f. Statement of war reporter Hartmann 13.7.65: ibid., vol. X, p. 2104 f. Statement of Oberbootsmaat Schulz 10.9.63: ibid., vol. VII, p. 1332 ff. Statement of Adjutant from Marine-Anti-Aircraft Division 707 Lucan 15.7.59: ibid., vol. I, p. 85 f. Letter of Kügler 31.12.41: ZSt. USSR 245 Ac, p. 89. Letter of SS- und Polizeistandortführer (Dr Dietrich) of 3.1.42: ibid., p. 64a. – The figure of at least 2,700 victims was mentioned in the verdict of Hannover LG (loc. cit.).

[VII] **Byelaya Tserkov:** Introduction based on verdict of Darmstadt LG of 29.11.68 against Callsen *et al.*, p. 374 ff. (Ks 1/67 GStA Fr/a/M), and the statements of the accused. – Statement of Offiziersanwärter Liebe 14.6.65: Js 4/65 GStA Fr/a/M, Special Volumes: Interrogations [Sonderbände Vernehmungen], vol. VII, p. 1272 ff. Report of Dr Reuss 20.8.41: ZSt. Various. File 301 AAu, vol. 121, p. 490 ff. and Ks 1/67 GStA Fr/a/M, vol. XXXVIII, p. 7780 ff. Report of Kornmann 21.8.41: ibid., p. 495. Report of Groscurth 21.8.41: ibid., p. 485 ff. Statement of Wilczek 15.1.68 in the main trial against Callsen *et al.* at Darmstadt LG: Ks 1/67 GStA Fr/a/M, minutes of court proceedings, vol. IV, p. 987 f. Report of Tewes/Wilczek 22.8.41, ZSt. Various, loc. cit., p. 494. Statement of Reichenau 26.8.41: ibid., p. 493. Statement of Häfner 31.5.65, p. 15 ff. of hearing (Js 4/65 GStA Ffm., file on interrogation of accused).

[VIII] **'Practical work':** *Jacob:* Letter of 24.4.41: ZSt. Various, vol. 99, p. 321 f. Letter of 29.10.41: ibid., p. 335. Letter of 5.5.42: ibid., p. 327 ff. Letter of 21.6.42: ZSt. File No. 26, Frame 611 f. *Photos:* Seven photos, of which only five were kept, were confiscated by a 1946 Czechoslovak Government commission from the flat of a company lawyer at the textile firm Kunert (Warndorf). According to the company lawyer they were obtained from a doorman at the firm, the former Bezirks-Oberwachtmeister der Gendarmerie, Hille. According to information of the ZSt. (II 204 AR 1218/70) this was a mass shooting on 14.10.42 in former Gebietskommissariat Sdolbunov, south of Rovno/Ukraine. Very probably these were executions in connection with the liquidation of the Misocz ghetto, which is compatible with statement of Gendarmerie-Gebietsführer Josef Paur of 28.4.61 (204 AR-Z 48/58, vol. 35, p. 6750 ff.) and 26.6.61 (ibid., p. 6759 ff.). One of the photos is sometimes referred to as the 'gassing photo' in Treblinka. This is clearly incorrect. *Kretschmer:* 204 AR-Z 82/59, p. 7 ff. The italics are not Kretschmer's but underlining in the letters made by Karlsruhe Police Directorate in 1945.

[IX] **White Russia:** *Slutsk:* Nbg Dok. PS-1104. *Slonim* (Gerhard Erren) Situation Report 25.1.42: ZSt. Various, vol. 25, p. 126 ff. Statement of Metzner 18.9.47: ZSt. Poland 91, Frame 8. *Kube* to Lohse 31.7.42: Nbg Dok. PS-3428. *Strauch* on Kube: ZSt. USA Film 1, Frame 164 ff. Both quotes from Strauch's report (*Referat des Sicherheitsdienstes in Minsk*) of 10.4.43: ZSt. USSR 107, pp. 291, 292.

[X] **SS secret verdict:** The verdict of SS and Police Supreme Court in Munich on 24.5.43 is in Az. St.L. 29/42. Judge: SS-Standartenführer Dr Reinecke (president) and SS-Obersturmbannführer Dr Brause. Other judges: SS-Stubaf. Sukkau, SS-Ustuf. Gamperl, SS-Ustuf. Tarnow. Counsel for the prosecution: SS-Sturmbannführer Meurin (ZSt. misc., vol. VIII, p. 119 ff.). The statement of opinion of 1.6.43 (St.L. 29/42) is signed: 'Breithaupt, SS-Gruppenführer and Generalleutnant der Waffen-SS, on behalf of the Gerichtsherr' and 'Meurin, SS-Sturmbannführer and SS-Judge', ibid. p. 131 f. Decision to pardon of 16.1.45; loc. cit., p. 145. – On 3.11.43 the sixty-nine photos were burnt on Himmler's orders and the SS court was instructed to destroy the negatives. Report of SS judge to Reichsführer-SS of 26.10.42: File: 'Documents' in Verf. Ks 1/67 GStA Fr/a/M. (Leutnant of Schutzpolizei Wölfer and other Schutzpolizisten had 'eliminated' the Jew Mandelmann in February 1942 in Radom because he had allegedly acted as an informer for the Sipo and was a nuisance to the Schutzpolizisten.) Statements: Göbel of 25.3.76: 204 AR 132/61, p. 1344; Hesse of 10.12.74: ibid., pp. 1268, 1273; Schumann of 4.11.75: ibid., p. 665 ff.

PART TWO

[I] **Chełmno:** Statement of Malzmüller 27.6.60: 203 AR-Z 69/59, vol. 3, p. 412 ff. Affidavit of Höss, Nbg Dok. NO-4498 B. According to the report on the mission the visit took place on 17.9.42 (Nbg Dok. NO-4467). Statement of Burmeister 24.1.61: loc. cit., vol. 4, p. 629 f. Statement of Möbius 8.11.61: loc. cit., vol. 5, p. 877. Eichmann: ZSt., vol. 1, p. 175 f. of the proceedings and police interrogation of Eichmann. Greiser's letter to the Reichsführer-SS marked 'Der Reichsstatthalter in Reichsgau Wartheland, Posen, den 19. März 1943, A.Z.: P.562/43' (ZSt. USA Film 1, Frame 92 f.). Himmler informed Greiser on 27.3.43 that he approved all proposals (ibid., Frame 89).

[II] **Extermination camps:** Statement of Oberhauser 14.12.62: 208 AR-Z 252/59, vol. 9, p. 1681 ff. Statement (SS-runes) of Bauer 20.11.62: 208 AR-Z 251/59, vol. 8, p. 1593 f. Statement of Fuchs 8.4.63: 208 AR-Z 251/59, vol. 9, p. 1784 f. Statement of Bauer on number of victims: loc. cit., p. 1595. Jäcklein's report: ZSt. USSR, File No. 410, Frame 520 f. Ganzenmüller/Wolff correspondence: ZSt. USA Film 1, Frame 255 f. Statement of Diegelmann 12.12.61: 8 AR-Z 80/61, vol. II, p. 274 ff. Statement of Pfannenstiel 25.4.60: 413 AR-Z 220/69, vol. IV, p. 583 ff. Statement of Schütt 7.6.61: 208 AR-Z 251/59, vol. 4, p. 665. Gerstein's Report of 4.5.45: 110 AR 2027/65. Statement of Franz 2.12.60: 208 AR-Z 230/59, vol. 8, p. 1493 f. Statement of Mentz 19.7.60: 203 AR-Z 230/59, vol. 6, Frame 1130 ff. Statement of Franz 4.12.49: 203 AR-Z 230/59, vol. 3, p. 505 f.

[III] **Auschwitz:** Statement of Grabner 18.9.45 to Police HQ Vienna, Staatspolizei Ref. I/e. Statement of Stark 23.4.59: AR-Z 37/58 SB 6, p. 937. Affidavit of Höss 5.4.46: Nbg Dok. PS-3868. Kremer's diary (copy): AR-Z 37/58, Sonderband (special vol.) Kremer. Münster LG, which was handling Kremer's case, had only a copy at its disposal (6 Ks 2/60). It is held today in the Staatsarchiv Münster (Staatsanwaltschaft Münster, no. 157). For the trial the copy was compared with the original from Auschwitz. Kremer had, however, already identified the copy as his. Excerpts from the Polish trials: CC Auschwitz through the eyes of the SS, Katowice 1981 (Ed. Dr Jadwiga Bezwinska), p. 213 (18.7.47) and 218 f. (30.7.47). The editors used the certified translation from the Polish rendered by the court interpreter. The version of Kremer's statement published in Katowice in 1981 is, however, linguistically more precise. This is clearly Kremer's statement, which was taken down in German. The version submitted to Münster LG had been taken from the Polish translation and translated back into German. Höss's statement of 14.3.46: Nbg Dok. NO-1210. Statement of Hofmann 27.4.61: AR-Z 37/58, special vol. 49, p. 8720 f. Statement of Höss on elimination of mass graves (Kommando 1005): Nbg Dok. NO-4498B. Affidavit of Blobel 6.6.47: Nbg Dok. NO-3824.

Biographical details

Barbel, Heinrich. SS-Rottenführer. Served in 'euthanasia' Institutes of Grafeneck and Hartheim, later Sobibor and Belzec.

Bauer, Erich. Tram conductor. Served in SA. Lorry-driver for 'euthanasia' Organization. Held rank of SS-Oberscharführer in Sobibor. Known as the 'Gasmeister' (gas master) or 'Bäder' (bath attendant) by prisoners. Detailed by Erich Fuchs to operate engines for gassings with which at least 3,000 Jews were killed (verdict of Landgericht *Hagen* v. *Fuchs*). In 1950 sentenced to life imprisonment by Schwurgericht Berlin-Moabit.

Becker, August, Ph.D. Chemist. NSDAP 1930, SS 1931. From 1938 worked in Amt II of RSHA. From January 1940 to October 1941 worked as gassing expert in T4. Until autumn of 1942 responsible for inspection of gas-vans, after which worked for Zentralhandelsgesellschaft Ost [Central Trading Company of the Eastern Territories] and foreign-intelligence service at RSHA. In November 1942 was promoted to SS-Obersturmführer. After 1945 worked among other things as sales representative. In 1960 declared unfit for imprisonment or trial.

Blaskowitz, Johannes. Led Eighth Army in the war against Poland and was made Oberbefehlshaber Ost [Commander-in-Chief of the Eastern Territories] in October 1939. Wrote two memoranda on atrocities of SS and police in Poland. From October 1940 in France. On several occasions removed from his posts. As a result refrained from voicing criticism. In May 1944 Commander-in-Chief of Army Group G in Holland. Capitulated to the English there on 5 May 1945. After the Allies began criminal proceedings against him, for relatively minor war crimes, committed suicide on 5 February 1948 in prison in Nuremberg by jumping out of a window.

Blobel, Paul. SS-Standartenführer. Commander of Sonderkommando 4a of Einsatzgruppe C. At least 60,000 – mostly Jewish – people fell victim to Blobel's activities. In 1948 sentenced to death in Nuremberg. Executed in 1951 in Landsberg.

Börner, Gerhardt. Head of Finance Department in Sonnenstein Gassing Institute. SS-Untersturmführer in Sobibor.

Bothmann, Hans. Kriminalkommissar and SS-Hauptsturmführer. Commandant at Chełmno. Committed suicide in 1946 after imprisonment by British.

Brack, Viktor. SS-Oberführer. Head of Hauptamt II at Führer's Chancellery. Organized the 'Euthanasia Aktion'. Played a significant part in extending extermination camps in 'Aktion Reinhard'. Sentenced to death in Nuremberg Doctors' Trial and executed in Landsberg.

Burmeister, Walter. SS-Unterscharführer. Lange's driver at Posen (Poznań) Stapo [Staatspolizei] regional headquarters. In late autumn 1941 transferred to Chełmno to work as gas-van driver. Sentenced to thirteen years' imprisonment as accessory to the murder of more than 150,000 people.

Callsen, Kuno. Persönl. Referent in Amt III of RSHA under Ohlendorf. SS-Hauptsturmführer (later Sturmbannführer). Teilkommandoführer and for a time Blobel's (see above) deputy. In 1973 sentenced to seven years' imprisonment by Schwurgericht Darmstadt.

Carl, Heinrich. Before the war NSDAP Kreisgeschäftsführer in Rendsburg. From 1941 Gebietskommissar in Slutsk. After 1945 senior clerk in law firm. Died 1959.

Dachsel, Arthur. Incinerated bodies in Sonnenstein Euthanasia Institute, member of permanent staff at Sobibor and Belzec. Wachtmeister in Reserve Schutzpolizei. Promoted by Himmler to Oberwachtmeister for his service in 'Aktion Reinhard'.

Dietrich, Fritz, Ph.D. SS- und Polizeistandortführer of Libau from September 1941 to November 1943. SS-Obersturmbannführer. Executed in 1948 in Landsberg.

Eberl, Irmfried. Medical doctor, SS-Untersturmführer, director of Brandenburg and Bernburg Gassing Institutes. Afterwards camp commandant at Treblinka. Relieved shortly afterwards and sent back to Bernburg. Hanged himself in February 1948 in pre-trial detention.

Ehlers, Ernst, Dr. SS-Obersturmbannführer, Einsatzgruppe B. At start of 1944 commander of Sicherheitspolizei and SD in Brussels. After 1945 Verwaltungsgerichtsrat in Schleswig-Holstein. Shortly before trial at Schwurgericht Flensburg for murder (during activities as Sipo and SD commander in Brussels) committed suicide on 4 October 1980.

Eichmann, Adolf. SS-Obersturmbannführer, director of 'Judenreferat' [Jewish Desk] at RSHA. Organized ('from his desk') deportation of Jews to extermination camps. In 1946 escaped from detention by Americans, travelled to Argentina with help of Church and disappeared there. After his abduction by Israeli secret agents was brought to trial in 1961. Death sentence carried out on 1 June 1962.

Erren, Gerhard. Sports teacher. National Socialist since 1931, could not become Party member at first (official admission 1.5.1933) because he belonged to the Grenzschutzfreikorps 'Oberschlesische Landesschützen' which came under authority of Reichswehr. In 1933/4 at Gau Sport School in Upper Silesia. From 1934 full-time political Leiter of NSDAP. From 1937 until beginning of war Kameradschaftsführer at Ordensburg Krössinsee. From August 1941 to July 1944 Gebietskommissar and NSDAP political leader in Slonim (Byelorussia). On 2 March 1944 was accepted by the SS and made Sturmbannführer. In February 1945 in charge of ideological training (in 'final resistance') of Waffen-SS. From 1950 employed as teacher in Hamburg. In 1960 suspended from teaching. Between 1961 and 1971 teacher in private schools. In 1974 sentenced to life imprisonment by Hamburg Landesgericht. In the trial summing up he was referred to as a member of the 'master race', one who went through Slonim with dog and whip openly beating up Jews.

Findeisen, Wilhelm. SS-Oberscharführer. Heydrich's driver. Afterwards gas-van driver with Sonderkommando 4. Convicted as accessory.

Franz, Kurt. Cook. Not a member of NSDAP or affiliated organizations. In 1937 joined Waffen-SS (3rd SS-Totenkopfstandarte Thuringia), among other things doing guard duty at Buchenwald concentration camp. End of 1939 summoned to Führer's Chancellery and detailed for service in 'euthanasia' institutes at Grafeneck, Brandenburg, Hartheim and Sonnenstein. From spring 1942 in Belzec. From midsummer 1942 in Treblinka. Took over Ukrainian guard squads and rose to be deputy camp commandant. Because of his well-groomed appearance known as Lalka ('the Doll') by the prisoners. Afterwards in Trieste and northern Italy (persecution of partisans and Jews). After 1945 worked as labourer on bridges, from 1949 to arrest in December 1959 worked as cook. In so-called 'Treblinka trial' (1965) sentenced to life imprisonment by Düsseldorf Landesgericht. The verdict stated: 'He ill-treated, punched, beat and killed when it gave him pleasure and when he felt like it. It did not bother him in the least when his dog Barry leapt at helpless Jews at his bidding . . . and wounded and tore them to pieces in his presence . . . A large part of the streams of blood and tears that flowed in Treblinka can be attributed to him alone.' Franz used to set his dog on the prisoners with the words 'Man, grab the dog!' to the

291

prisoners. The verdict states, to prevent any misunderstanding: 'By the word "man" he meant Barry; the word "dog" referred to the prisoner.'

Frenzel, Karl. Craftsman. Incinerated bodies in several 'euthanasia' centres. In 1942–3 Sobibor. Head of work Kommando who herded victims brutally into the gas chambers.

Fritsch, Ernst. SS-Sturmmann in 1st Workshop Platoon [1. Werkstattzug] in Kommandostab RFSS-Nachschubführer. In 1939 mayor and deputy Ortsgruppenleiter of the National Socialist Party in Altenheim near Kehl. Known as 'Bürgermeister' for this reason. After 1945 re-elected mayor of Altenheim.

Fuchs, Erich. Skilled motor mechanic. In May 1933 NSDAP and SA. In 1940 drafted to T4. Worked as Director Dr Eberl's driver in gassing centres Brandenburg and Bernburg. In February 1942 transferred to Belzec for six weeks, where he installed gassing systems. In April in Sobibor for at least four weeks (operating engines for gassing). Afterwards (as SS-Scharführer) in Treblinka, which at time was under command of Dr Eberl. Towards end of 1942 returned to Bernburg. December 1942 to February 1943 at Wiesloch psychiatric institution ('euthanasia research'). March 1943 removed from T4. After 1945 lorry-driver, motor mechanic and car salesman. The Schwurgericht at Landesgericht Hagen sentenced him to four years' imprisonment in 1966 for being an accessory to the murder of at least 79,000 people.

Ganzenmüller, Albert. Dr Ing. (doctorate in engineering). Staatssekretär in Ministry of Transport [Reichsverkehrsministerium] and deputy chairman of German Railways [Deutsche Reichsbahn]. In 1959 the Dortmund public prosecutor gave him immunity from criminal prosecution. In 1973 the Landesgericht at Düsseldorf started legal proceedings against him for a few days. Trial halted in 1977 owing to his inability to stand trial.

Gerstein, Kurt. Engineering graduate. Studied medicine. In May 1933 NSDAP (expelled October 1936 for hostile – religious – activity). In 1938 imprisoned in Welzheim concentration camp for short time. After murder of a sister-in-law in Hadamar gassing centre ('euthanasia') wanted, according to his own account, to look at 'these ovens and chambers'. In March 1941 joined Waffen-SS (SS-Führungsamt, Amtsgruppe D, Santitätswesen [Sanitation Matters] der Waffen-SS, Hygiene Department). 'In January 1942 I was made head of the Health Technology [Gesundheitstechnik] Department. At the same time I was recruited by the Reichsarzt-SS und Polizei to perform the same function.' SS-Obersturmführer Gerstein, according to his own account a 'specialist in prussic acid' (Zyklon B), in June 1942 was instructed to have 100 kg transported to Poland. On 17 August met SS-Obergruppenführer Globocnik in Lublin and witnessed mass extermination in Belzec and Treblinka. Afterwards Gerstein informed, among others, the Swedish legation. He was not admitted to the nunciature in Berlin. In May 1945 he was taken prisoner by the French as an SS member. On 25 July 1945 he was found hanging in the cell of a military prison in Paris. It is not known whether he killed himself (official version) or whether he was killed by other SS members he was imprisoned with. Gerstein wrote a number of reports on his experiences. These have been put in question by certain inaccuracies, but appear to be correct on all substantial points.

Gley, Heinrich. Male nurse. In Grafeneck and Sonnenstein 'euthanasia' institutes. From August 1942 to August 1943 in Belzec (worked on 'ramp duty', supervised undressing hut, execution of sick in so-called military hospital). SS-Oberscharführer.

Globocnik, Odilo. Master builder. In 1931 joined the then prohibited NSDAP in Austria. Convicted on a number of occasions for illegal activities for the party. After the annexation of Austria was Gauleiter in Vienna. For among other things financial irregularities was removed and transferred to personal staff of the Reichsführer. In November 1939 made SS- und Polizeiführer in Lublin district. Himmler transferred him in 1942 to 'Aktion Reinhard' (cover name for the 'final solution' in the General-Gouvernement of Poland). In September 1943 Höherer SS- und Polizeiführer in the Adriatic coastal region operational zone. On 21 May 1945, after capture by British troops, killed himself in Kärnten.

Göbel, Ernst. Joined SS in 1930 or 1931, latterly Scharführer; in 1939 joined Ninth SS-Infanterie-Totenkopfstandarte. In 1941 transferred as member of Waffen-SS to 1. Werkstattzug in Kommandostab RFSS-Nachschubführer.

Grabner, Maximilian. Woodcutter, building worker. In 1930 joined Austrian Bundesgendarmerie, in 1935 detective at Austrian police headquarters in Vienna. Until December 1943 head of Political Department in Auschwitz. Latterly SS-Untersturmführer. In 1947 sentenced to death by war tribunal in Cracow and executed.

Greiser, Arthur. Reichsstatthalter of Wartheland Gau. SS-Obergruppenführer. NSDAP 1928. In 1945 arrested by the Americans and handed over to the Poles. On 14 July 1946 hanged outside his former residence in Posen.

Gringers, Karl. Posted to Hadamar, Hartheim and Belzec. Killed in Italy in 1944.

Hackenholt, Lorenz. SS-Hauptscharführer. Driver for Brack, the 'Euthanasia' functionary. Delivered bottled gas to gassing centres. Disappeared after 1945.

Häfner, August. Joined NSDAP 1932, SS 1933. Kriminalkommissar, SS-Obersturmführer and Teilkommandoführer in Sonderkommando 4a. In 1973 was sentenced to eight years' imprisonment by Darmstadt Landesgericht.

Hans, Kurt. SS-Obersturmführer and Teilkommandoführer in Sonderkommando 4a. Sentenced to eleven years' imprisonment as accessory to murder in 1968.

Hartl, Albert. Catholic priest. SS-Obersturmbannführer. Involved with spying on Catholic Church for RSHA (Gestapo). In 1941 attached to Einsatzgruppe C. After 1945: writer.

Heidborn, Erich. Police Reserve Battalion 9, with 3rd Company/3rd Platoon attached to Sonderkommando 4a in 1941.

Hengst, August. Cook in Brandenburg, Bernburg and Treblinka.

Hering, Gottlieb. Kriminalkommissar in administration of gassing centres Sonnenstein and Bernburg. From August 1942 camp commandant of Belzec. 1943 promoted to SS-Hauptsturmführer. On 9 October 1945 died in Stetten/Remstal.

Hesse, Heinrich. SS-Sturmmann in 1. Werkstattzug in Kommandostab RFSS-Nachschubführer. Final rank SS-Standarten- Oberjunker.

Höfer, Fritz. Among other things driver in Sonderkommando 4a and from spring 1942 to spring 1944 driver for commander of Sicherheitspolizei and the SD in Kiev.

Hofmann, Franz. Joined NSDAP and SS in 1932. Auxiliary policeman. From 1933 until end 1942 in Dachau (last post deputy Schutzhaftlagerführer). In Auschwitz among other duties Schutzhaftlagerführer of gypsy camp at Birkenau and senior Schutzhaftlagerführer in main camp. Last promotion in 1944 to SS-Hauptsturmführer. Sentenced to life imprisonment in 1961 for murder in two cases (Dachau) by Munich Schwurgericht II. Because of his activities in Auschwitz he was sentenced a second time to life imprisonment by the Schwurgericht at the Frankfurt am Main Landesgericht.

Höss, Rudolf. Classical *Gymnasium* education until sixth year. Trained in agriculture. In 1922 joined NSDAP (No. 3240). In 1923 involved in a vehmic murder (sentenced to ten years' imprisonment, amnestied in 1928). In 1934 joined SS. In November 1934, Dachau (Block- and Rapportführer), 1938 adjutant to camp commandant in Sachsenhausen. In November 1939 Schutzheftlagerführer, rank SS-Hauptsturmführer. Transferred to Auschwitz in May 1940. From December 1943 led Amtsgruppe D (concentration camps) in the Wirtschafts- und Verwaltungshauptamt [economic and administrative office] of the SS. In May 1944 returned to Auschwitz, in order to organize the murder of 400,000 Hungarian Jews. In May 1945 went underground bearing military passbook under the name of 'Franz Lang, Bootsmaat der Marine' [coxswain]. In March 1946 was arrested by British military police and handed over to Poland in June. On 2 April 1947 sentenced to death in Warsaw and hanged on 16 April in Auschwitz.

Hössler, Franz. SS-Untersturmführer, Schutzhaftlagerführer in Auschwitz-Birkenau. At end of war was at Bergen-Belsen. In 1945 sentenced to death by a British court and executed.

Huhn, Heinrich. SS-Sturmscharführer. Member of Sonderkommando 4a ('Sarge').

Jacob, Fritz. Gendarmeriepostenführer; 1939–42 trainer and teacher (sport and criminal law) at Ebersbach Gendarmerieschule. In May 1942 with fifty Gendarmerie Reservists 'given marching orders to the East' (Jacob). According to own account, had job of cordoning off the area during executions (Jews and gypsies) and during a 'punishment action' against fifty arbitrarily selected villagers (men, women and children) because a Ukrainian guard had been killed. He claims not to have done any shooting himself. Last post: Gendarmerie-Gebietsführer. In 1926/7 he met Rudolf **Querner** in Zittau (Gendarmerie Inspector): 'At the time I was a respected sports teacher and ski instructor. Frau Querner took skiing lessons from me as did Querner himself' (Statement of 4 October 1960, II 204 AR-Z 233/59 vol. I, p. 235). About himelf: 'In principle, I was not opposed to the Jews' (ibid.).

Jäger, Karl. Businessman. NSDAP 1923, SS 1932. Commander of Einsatzkommando 3 of Einsatzgruppe A at the beginning of the campaign against the USSR. End of 1941 until September 1943 also commander of Sicherheitspolizei and SD for Generalbezirk Lithuania, which had its HQ in Kaunas. At end of 1943 chief of police in Reichenberg/Sudetenland. After 1945 an agricultural worker near Heidelberg. Arrested in April 1959. Hanged himself in custody on 22 June 1959.

Janssen, Adolf. SS-Obersturmführer (later Hauptsturmführer) and

Teilkommandoführer in Sonderkommando 4a. In 1968 sentenced to eleven years' imprisonment.

Kremer, Johannes Paul. In 1914 received Ph.D. (for a histological study on the tissue structure of insects) and in 1919 M.D. In 1927 head of Anatomical Institute of University of Münster. In 1929 qualified as university lecturer in anatomy; 1936–45, senior lecturer, giving lectures on heredity, sports medicine, radiology and anatomy. Joined NSDAP 1932, from 1934 member of 8. SS-Reiterstandart (Sturmarzt). In June 1941 with rank of SS-Hauptscharführer joined Reserve Waffen-SS and in November 1941 promoted to Untersturmführer. Only sent for temporary service during university vacations (once in SS Hospital in Dachau). In July 1942 assessor in Gau Disciplinary Court of North Westphalia to NSD-Doctors' Federation. On 8 August 1942 sent to SS Hospital in Prague during university vacation. On 29 August sent from Prague to Auschwitz (till 18 November). After this returned to the Anatomical Institute in Münster. In December 1942 president of the Gau disciplinary court of Gau-North Westphalia for the NSD-Doctors' Federation. In February 1943 promoted to SS-Obersturmführer in the Reserve Waffen-SS. In August 1945 detained by the British occupation forces for membership of SS. During the hearings his activities in Auschwitz became known and his diary was confiscated from his apartment. Extradited to Poland at the end of 1946. In December 1947 sentenced to death by Polish People's Supreme Tribunal in Cracow following a trial against forty defendants for crimes committed in Auschwitz. Sentence commuted to life imprisonment in January 1948. Released in January 1958 for good behaviour and in view of his age (seventy-four). In August 1958 briefly taken into detention in Münster/Westphalia. In 1960 sentenced to ten years' imprisonment by Münster Landesgericht as an accessory to murder. Kremer left the court a free man as his sentence was considered to have been served by the time spent in imprisonment in Poland.

Kretschmer, Karl. Pharmacist. Member of Schutzpolizei 1928–38. From mid-1938 member of Stapo. Joined NSDAP in 1949. Was not accepted by SS following failure to satisfy requirements during a course on ideology. In August 1942 sent for service in Russia as Obersturmführer. September to end November 1942 officer in charge of administration (Verwaltungsführer) in a Teilkommando of Sonderkommando 4a in Kursk. Then posted to Kommandeur of Sicherheitspolizei and SD (KdS) in Zhitomir, KdS Stuhlweissenburg in Hungary and to Sonderkommando Ost, which supervised the staff of the Vlasov Army. After 1945 application to return to police force turned down.

Kube, Wilhelm. Son of a Prussian sergeant, born in Glogau on 13 November 1887. Studied history, political science and some theology. Worked as journalist. Member of number of *völkisch* anti-Semitic groups. In 1924 member of Reichstag for 'National Socialist Freedom Movement' (Nationalsozialistischen Freiheitsbewegung). In 1928 head of NSDAP group in Prussian regional parliament. In 1932 founded the 'German Christians' (Deutsche Christen). In 1933 Gauleiter of Austria and Oberpräsident of Brandenburg. In 1936 dismissed after sending Reichsleiter Buch an anonymous letter, signed 'some Berlin Jews', on 26 April 1936 making false allegations: 'You are the most senior judge in the Party which is fighting against every decent Jew. As one of our kin, you ought not to be doing such a thing. Do you know that your wife has got Jewish blood?' Kube was nevertheless made Generalkommissar of the Byelorussia Generalbezirk. He was killed on 22 September 1943 by a Russian partisan smuggled in as a serving girl.

Kügler, Wolfgang. Detective. SS-Untersturmführer and Teilkommandoführer of Einsatzkommando 2, then head of Libau (Liepaja) regional headquarters of the KdS Latvia.

Landau, Felix. Born 1910. In 1911 his mother married Landau, a Jew, who gave his name to the child. Following his stepfather's death (1919), Landau attended a boarding-school run by a Catholic lay order. Was expelled from apprentice boarding-school for active recruitment activities for the NS Youth (joined National Socialist Worker Youth in 1925). Apprenticeship as skilled furniture-maker. In 1930 joined Austrian Bundesheer (2. Dragonerschwadron). Joined NSDAP March 1931. May 1931 political leader of a NS-Heeressprengels (army district). June 1933 expulsion from Bundesheer for NS activities. Member of SA from June 1933 to April 1934, after that in SS. Participated in Dollfuss affair 1934. Imprisoned until 1937. Renewed propaganda activities. Because of threat of arrest fled to Germany, where he became a naturalized citizen. Found employment as a police official (Kriminalassistent). In 1938 posted to Vienna Gestapo regional headquarters and married first wife. In 1940 transferred to KdS/SD in Radom (General-Gouvernement) where he met shorthand-typist Gertrude. Reported to an Einsatzkommando in June 1941. From July 1941 in Drohobycz, Lvov district (30,000 inhabitants, half of whom were Jews), where the Einsatzkommando was reorganized into an outpost of the Sicherheitspolizei and SD.

Until May 1943 Landau was in charge of organizing Jewish labour. At the end of 1941 he lived with his mistress in an aristocratic villa. After his divorce from his wife in 1942 (his wife was judged the guilty party) married Gertrude in 1943 (divorced 1946). Last rank SS-Hauptscharführer. In 1946 recognized in Linz by a former 'worker Jew' and arrested by the Americans. In August 1947 escaped from Glasenbach prison camp. Lived under the name Rudolf Jaschke, ('design, planning, consultancy, interior decoration, refrigeration equipment') in the Nördlingen district. Was sentenced to life imprisonment by Stuttgart Landesgericht in 1963.

Lange, Herbert. Kriminalkommissar and SS-Sturmbannführer. In 1940 head of a Sonderkommando which murdered the mentally ill, Poles and Jews (partly with gas-vans). Then first commandant of Chełmno extermination camp. In 1942 Kriminalrat in RSHA (concerned among other things with investigating assassination attempt of 20 July 1944). Died in Berlin on 20 April 1945.

Lohse, Hinrich. Joined NSDAP 1923, 1925 Gauleiter and 1933 Oberpräsident in Schleswig-Holstein (1933 member of Reichstag). In 1937 SA-Obergruppenführer, 1939 Reichsverteidigungskommissar and 1941 Reichskommissar for the Ostland (Baltic). Sentenced to ten years' imprisonment in 1948. Released in 1951 'for health reasons'. Died in 1964.

Malzmüller, Theodor. Police Guard Battalion XXI Łódź. Served in Chełmno.

Mentz, Willi. SS-Unterscharführer. Unskilled worker in sawmill. Passed master milkman's examination. In 1932 joins NSDAP. In 1940 took care of cows and pigs in Grafeneck gassing centre and from 1941 to early summer 1942 worked in the gardens of Hadamar gassing centre. June–July 1942 to November 1943 posted to Treblinka where he was in command of the agricultural labour squad. His main activities were at the so-called military hospital, a place where the sick and frail were executed. These people were killed with a shot in the back of the neck and fell into the hospital grave where they were incinerated. As nobody checked to see whether the victims were really dead, many prisoners are said to have been burned alive. In December 1943 spent a short time in Sobibor, after which served in Italy taking part in 'Aktion Reinhard' (persecution of Jews and partisans). After 1945 worked again as a master milkman. In the so-called 'Treblinka Trial' was sentenced to life imprisonment. The verdict stated: '. . . because shooting was the activity he was normally engaged in, the Jews simply called him the "Gunman"'. How many people Mentz killed in the military hospital in the method described could never be clearly established. The only thing that is certain is that the number of Jews from the transports he killed single-handedly runs into thousands and that over and above these he liquidated some hundreds of worker-Jews.'

Metzner, Alfred. Administrative officer, driver and interpreter for Gebietskommissar in Slonim. Took part in barbarically cruel executions as marksman. Executed in August 1950 in Poland.

Möbius, Kurt. In 1941 Schutzpolizist, in 1942 Police Battalion Litzmannstadt (Łódź) and Chełmno. In 1965 sentenced to eight years' imprisonment as accessory to murder of at least 100,000 people.

Oberhauser, Josef. SS-Obersturmführer. In 1935 SS (Totenkopfstandarte 'Brandenburg') and NSDAP. At outbreak of war with 'Leibstandarte Adolf Hitler'. From 1940 worked in Grafeneck, Brandenburg and Bernburg gassing centres burning corpses. In November 1941 assigned to the SS- and Police HQ staff in Lublin district ('Aktion Reinhard'). According to his own account from end 1941 to July–August 1942 in Belzec. From August 1942 assigned to Christian Wirth, inspector of the extermination camps. On Himmler's instructions promoted to Untersturmführer in June 1943. In 1948 sentenced to fifteen years' imprisonment by Magdeburg Landesgericht (for participation in 'euthanasia' crimes and membership of SS). Amnestied in April 1956. Then casual worker and barman in Munich. In 1965 tried by jury in Landesgericht I at Munich and sentenced to a total of four years and six months' imprisonment 'for the crime of acting as an accessory in the common murder of 300,000 people and for his role in the common murder of 150 people'.

Ohlendorf, Otto. SS-Gruppenführer. Chief of Sicherheitspolizei (Head of Department III at the RSHA) 1939 to 1945. June 1941 to June 1942 head of Einsatzgruppe D. Sentenced to death in Nuremberg in 1948 (Einsatzgruppen Trial) and executed in Landsberg in 1951.

Pfannenstiel, Wilhelm. Prof. Dr med., from 1931 to 1945 Professor Ordinarius of Hygiene and Director of Institute for Hygiene at the University of Marburg/Lahn. SS-Standartenführer and consultant hygienist to SS. Preliminary proceedings abandoned.

Plate, Albert. SS-Hauptscharführer. Bothmann's deputy at Chełmno.

Pötzinger, Karl. At outbreak of war SA-Scharführer. Posted to Brandenburg and Bernburg 'euthanasia' centres (incinerated bodies) and Treblinka and Sobibor. Killed in 1944.

Pradel, Friedrich. Polizeikommissar and Major in Schutzpolizei, director of motor vehicles department of Sicherheitspolizei at RSHA (II D 3a). Participated in development and application of gas-vans. After 1945 went back into police force. In 1966 sentenced to seven years' imprisonment by Hanover Landesgericht.

Querner, Rudolf. Senior SS- and Polizeiführer. In 1943 SS-Obergruppenführer. Committed suicide on 27 May 1945 after capture.

Rauff, Walter. SS-Standartenführer. In 1941 in RSHA head of Amtsgruppe II D (Technik) and there among other duties responsible for supplying the Einsatzgruppen with gas-vans. After 1945 fled to South America and died in Chile on 14 May 1984.

Reuss, Josef Maria, Doctor of theology. Military chaplain to 295th Infantry Division (Army Group South). From 1946 Professor of Pastoral Theology and director of priests' seminary in Mainz. In 1954 made titular bishop and suffragan bishop in Mainz.

Rösler, Karl. Major, commander of 528th Infantry Regiment. Submitted report on 3 January 1942 on mass shootings which took place in July 1941 in Zhitomir from which Armed Forces High Command (OKW) withdrew its participation.

Schniewindt, Rudolf. General of the Infantry, commander in Wehrkreis IX.

Schulz, Erwin. Brigadeführer. In 1941 director of Berlin-Charlottenburg Police Academy and at same time head of Group 1B (training and education) in RSHA. Head of Einsatzkommando 5 when sent to USSR. Sentenced to twenty years' imprisonment in Nuremberg and released early.

Schumann, Ernst. Driver with 1. Werkstattkompanie in Kommandostab RFSS-Nachschubführer. Last rank: SS-Rottenführer in Waffen-SS.

Schütt, Hans-Heinz. Head of administration in Grafeneck, Hadamar and from April to August 1942 in Sobibor. From October 1942 member of Waffen-SS.

Schwarz, Gottfried. SS-Hauptscharführer. Worked in crematorium in Grafeneck and Bernburg and deputy camp commandant in Belzec. Killed in 1944 in Istria (final operation of 'Aktion Reinhard').

Six, Franz. Prof. Dr, SS-Oberführer. RSHA (Department VII), Head of Vorkommando Moscow (Einsatzgruppe B). Sentenced to twenty years' imprisonment in Nuremberg Einsatzgruppen Trial and released early in 1952. Afterwards advertising consultant.

Stahlecker, Walter. NSDAP February 1932, according to own account since 1921. SS-Brigadeführer and Generalmajor of the police. Head of Einsatzgruppe A (before which KdS/SD in protectorate of

Bohemia, Moravia and KdS/SD in Norway). Killed on 23 March 1942.

Stangl, Franz. Detective. SS-Obersturmführer. Deputy head of office in Hartheim and Bernburg gassing centres. Commandant in Sobibor and Treblinka. Sentenced to life imprisonment by Schwurgericht Düsseldorf. Died in detention on 28 June 1971.

Stark, Hans. Born 1921. At age of sixteen joined SS-Totenkopfstandarte 'Brandenburg'. Stationed at Sachsenhausen, Buchenwald and Dachau concentration camps. December 1940 Blockführer in Auschwitz (political department from June 1941). Stark was granted leave from December 1941 to March 1942 in order to finish his school education. From November 1942 to March 1943 study leave (law). Last promotion: SS-Untersturmführer. After war studied agriculture. From 1953 to 1955 taught at the agricultural school in Gross-Gerau (Hessen). Later, economic adviser to agricultural chamber in Frankfurt am Main. From 1957 until his arrest in April 1959 teacher in agricultural school of Lovenich/Weiden. In 1965 Stark was sentenced to ten years' detention in a juvenile prison, following trial by jury at Frankfurt Landesgericht, as he had been under twenty-one at the time of the crime. The verdict states: 'At further gassings of Jewish people in May 1942 Stark often took some Jewish women to one side before the gassing. When the other Jewish people were in the gas-chambers he lined the women against the wall of the yard of the small crematorium. Then he would shoot one or two women in the chest and feet. When the other women were trembling, falling on their knees and begging the accused Stark to let them live, he would shout at them, "Sarah, Sarah, come on, stand still!" Then he would shoot them all, one after the other.'

Strauch, Eduard. Dr jur. Studied theology in Erlangen and Münster, afterwards law. In 1931 joined NSDAP and SA and in same year moved to SS. SS-Obersturmbannführer; 1941 heads of Einsatzkommando in Latvia, 1942 KdS White Russia. 1944 KdS Wallonia (Lüttich). Sentenced to death in Nuremberg Einsatzgruppen Trial, extradited to Belgium and there given a further death sentence. Death sentence not carried out because of mental illness. Died September 1955.

Täubner, Max. Aircraft engineer. Joined NSDAP 1932 (expelled for unpunctual payment of membership dues and readmitted in 1937), joined SS January 1933. SS-Untersturmführer in 1. Werkstattzug in Kommandostab RFSS-Nachschubführer. Attempt to bring Täubner to trial after the war failed in 1960. Memmingen Landesgericht and the Munich Oberlandesgericht (Provincial High Court) refused to open the main trial on the grounds that the existence of a prior verdict by the SS court prohibited the carrying out of new criminal proceedings (although Täubner had neither been accused or judged for the murder of the Jews). The Bundesgerichthof (Federal Court) upheld this decision on 24 May 1972 (2 ARs 80/72).

Tauscher, Fritz. Polizeioberleutnant in the administration of Sonnenstein gassing centre (under cover of being a register office). According to own account, from October 1942 to March 1943 in Belzec concerned with exhuming bodies and dismantling of camp. Committed suicide in custody in 1965.

Tewes, Ernst. Catholic chaplain at 4/607 Military Hospital. After 1945 called to cathedral chapter Munich. From 1968 to 1984 suffragan bishop and at same time bishop for Munich region.

Tögel, Richard. Schutzpolizist. 1941 Police Battalion 9, Member of Einsatzkommando 10a (Einsatzgruppe D).

Trill, Viktor. Auxiliary policeman and later driver in Gestapo in Brühn. SS-Oberscharführer. Member of Sonderkommando 4a.

Wagner, Gustav. Worked in office of Hartheim gassing centre. Deputy camp commandant of Sobibor. SS-Oberscharführer. Known as 'Welfel' (Yiddish = wolf) by the prisoners on account of his brutality. After 1945 went to Brazil. Extradition order from the Federal Republic of Germany was turned down by Supreme Court of Brazil in 1979. In October 1980 Wagner took his own life at his home.

Wallerang, Bernhard. SS-Untersturmführer with Lublin SS- and Polizeiführer.

Werner, Kurt. Driver for Gestapo at Hildesheim and 3rd Motorized Coy in Pretzsch. Afterwards Police Reserve Battalion 9 and Sonderkommando 4a. Took part in executions in Lutsk, Zhitomir, Babi Yar.

Wilczek, Gerhard. Protestant chaplain (military chaplain) at Military Hospital 4/607. After 1945 parish priest.

Wirth, Christian. Detective. NSDAP 1931. SS-Sturmbannführer (1943). Among other posts office manager in so-called euthanasia programme in Brandenburg, Hadamar and Hartheim. First commandant of Belzec, from August 1942 inspector of extermination camps. Shot dead in 1944 in Istria.

Wolff, Karl. Representative of publishing company. SS-Obergruppenführer and Waffen-SS general. In 1931 joined NSDAP and SS. In July 1933 became personal aide to Himmler. From November 1936 to September 1943 chief of personal staff of Reichsführer SS. Afterwards

senior SS and Polizeiführer in Italy. Sentenced to fifteen years'
imprisonment in 1964 in Munich for the deportation of Jews to
Treblinka.

Zierke, Ernst. 'Male nurse' in Grafeneck and Hadamar gassing
centres. From June 1942 in Belzec (working on ramp and supervision
during undressing), autumn 1943 posted to Sobibor.

Zopp, Friedrich. Member of Sonderkommando 6.

Chronology

1933

30 January	Hindenburg appoints Hitler Chancellor. National Socialists take over power.
27 February	Burning of Reichstag building.
28 February	Reichstagsbrandverordnung (Reichstag Burning Decree) issued to protect people and state. Important fundamental laws of Weimar Constitution annulled. The quasi legal persecution of opponents to the regime begins.
23 March	Enabling Act: grants government powers to introduce, without consulting parliament, legislation which deviates from Constitution. Together with Reichstagsbrandverordnung forms legal foundation for National Socialist dictatorship.
February/March	First concentration camps set up. SA and SS members are deployed as auxiliary policemen to guard prisoners.
1 April	Jewish boycott. Action against Jewish businesses ('Don't buy from Jews'), lawyers and doctors centrally organized by NSDAP.
7 April	Law on career civil service [Berufsbcamtengesetz]. 'Elimination' of Jews from public service by 'Aryan paragraphs' (Aryan paragraphs also exclude Jews from membership of societies, associations, etc.).
April	Professional restrictions (*Berufbeschränkung*) imposed on Jewish doctors and pharmacists.
22 September	Reichskulturkammergesetz (Reich Chamber of Culture Law). Jews are excluded from cultural life.

1934

30 June/1 July	Röhm coup put down. SA loses power.
20 July	SS strengthened and takes over control of most concentration camps formerly under SA control.

1935

21 May	Army Law: 'Aryan descent' is a prerequisite for active service in German army.
16 September	Nuremberg Laws. 'Reich Citizenship' law removes citizenship and all political rights (active and passive right to vote, to hold public office, etc.) from Jews and so-called Jewish '*Mischlingen*' (people of partly Jewish descent). 'Law for the Protection of German Blood and Honour' makes marriages and extra-marital sexual relations between Jews and Aryans an offence punishable by imprisonment.

1936

1 to 16 August	Summer Olympic Games in Berlin. For propaganda reasons anti-Jewish measures are avoided for duration of the games and slogans removed from streets.

1937

5 November	Secret discussions in Reich Chancellery: Hitler reveals his war plans.

1938

13 March	Annexation of Austria (Anschluss).
26 April	Registration of all Jews with assets exceeding 5,000 RM.
14 June	Registration of Jewish enterprises. Beginning of so-called Aryanization. Pressure to sell to certain people or firms (IG-Farben, the Flick group, major banks, etc.) Payment of

	sales proceeds, far below market value, into blocked accounts.
6 July	Law prohibits numerous Jewish business activities.
August	'Zentralstelle für jüdische Auswanderung' (Office for Jewish Emigration) established in Vienna (within eighteen months 150,000 Austrian Jews induced to emigrate).
July to October	Further laws limiting professional activities of Jewish doctors and lawyers.
9–10 November	'Reichskristallnacht' ('night of broken glass'). Pogrom organized by the NSDAP. Official pretext was the murder of a German legation secretary in Paris by a young Jew. Numerous synagogues and Jewish businesses destroyed. More than ninety Jewish citizens are murdered.
12 November	'Atonement payments' by German Jewry of 1,000 million RM for the damages caused during 'Reichskristallnacht'. Insurance awards, amounting to more than 10 million RM, are paid to the German Reich.
15 November	Jewish children are excluded from German schools.
28 November	Regierungspräsidenten ('presidents of regional councils') are empowered to impose curfews on Jews (the 'Judenbann').
3 December	Decree provides for compulsory disposal of Jewish stores, businesses, etc.

1939

24 January	Establishment of Reichszentrale für jüdische Auswanderung (Reich Central Office for Jewish Emigration) in order to organize and accelerate the emigration of the Jews (almost 80,000 Jews left Germany in 1939).
15 March	German troops invade Czechoslovakia. Bohemia and Moravia become German protectorates.
1 September	German army invades Poland: beginning of Second World War.

September	Ill-treatment and murder of thousands of Jews begins. Establishment of first concentration camps and ghettos in Poland. SS and police arbitrarily shoot Jews and Poles in towns and villages (exciting the protests of Oberbefehlshaber Ost Johannes Blaskowitz).

1940

January	Beginning of 'euthanasia' programme, Aktion T4, in extermination institutes within German Reich (killing of mentally ill with carbon monoxide).
July	Murder of German Jewish mentally sick in Brandenburg extermination institute.

1941

22 June	German invasion of Soviet Union and subsequent annexation of the Baltic states to Reichskommissariat Ostland.
June–August	SS organizes pogroms against Jews in the Baltic states and the Ukraine using local populations (according to the report of Einsatzgruppe A, by 29 June about 2,300 Jews were 'rendered harmless' in Kaunas).
From July	Beginning of mass shootings of Jews by Security Police and SD Einsatzgruppen and Einsatzkommandos (see 'Jäger-Bericht') and police units (e.g. Police Battalion 322 and Polizeiregiment Mitte). Wehrmacht also takes part in mass shootings of Jews.
31 July	Göring orders Heydrich to make preparations for the 'Endlösung der Judenfrage' ('Final Solution of the Jewish Question', i.e. elimination of Jewry).
August	Execution of Jewish children in Byelaya Tserkov (Ukraine).
24 August	'Euthanasia' programme discontinued. Killings continued by other means (poison, starvation, etc.).
3 September	First experimental gassing with Zyklon B in

	Auschwitz concentration camp. Zyklon B established as murder method.
29–30 September	Mass shooting of 33,771 Jews from Kiev in Babi Yar ravine by members of Sonderkommando 4a from Einsatzgruppe C and members of Polizeiregiment Süd.
Mid-October	Beginning of deportation transports on Deutsche Reichsbahn (German Railways). Goods or cattle wagons mostly used for transporting Jews. Many do not survive the transports, owing to poor hygiene and inadequate supplies of food and water.
Autumn	Beginning of dispute between Generalkommissar for White Russia, Gauleiter Kube, with the SS over the way in which Jews are exterminated, lasting until 1943. SS members lodge complaints about Kube.
October–November	Extermination camp of Chełmno (Kulmhof) set up in Warthegau.
Late autumn	The RSHA puts gas-vans at disposal of Security Police and SD Einsatzgruppen.
5 December	First transport of Jews to Chełmno extermination camp. The victims are killed in gas-vans with exhaust gases.
Beginning to mid-December	So-called 'Dezember-Aktion' ('December Action') – mass shootings – in Libau (Liepaja) watched by a great number of spectators. Further mass executions in the Baltic states.
Autumn/winter	Unauthorized massacres of Jews by Täubner's Werkstattzug in Russia.

1942

20 January	Berlin/Wannsee conference: participating departments receive reports on completed extermination actions and organizational matters for the 'Final Solution of the Jewish Question' discussed.
Spring	Locally stationed Security Police and SD units take over job of exterminating the Jews in the USSR.

308

Early March	Belzec extermination camp completed as part of 'Aktion Reinhard' ('final solution of Jewish question' in General-Gouvernement). The two further extermination camps envisaged by 'Aktion Reinhard' are Sobibor and Treblinka. The Jewish victims are killed in the camps in gas-chambers with engine-exhaust fumes (carbon monoxide). The manpower deployed for 'Aktion Reinhard' consists for the most part of 'experienced' personnel who had worked on Aktion T4.
17 March	Beginning of 'Aktion Reinhard' extermination programme. Jews from Lublin are deported to Belzec concentration camp.
Early May	Mass extermination in Sobibor extermination camp starts.
End May/Early July	Construction work on Treblinka extermination camp commences.
22 July	Deportations from Warsaw ghetto to Belzec and Treblinka.
23 July	Mass gassing begins in Treblinka extermination camp.

1943

18 January	First resistance against the deportations in the Warsaw ghetto.
Spring	Sonderkommando '1005' starts its activities in the East. The bodies of murdered Jews are dug up and burned. The mass graves are filled in and levelled off.
7 April	Chełmno extermination camp discontinues activities. The traces of the extermination are eliminated.
April/May	Uprising in the Warsaw ghetto and subsequent extermination of inhabitants of the ghetto.
2 August	Uprising of prisoners in Treblinka extermination camp.

14 October	Uprising of prisoners in Sobibor extermination camp.
19 October	Lublin SS- und Polizeiführer, Globocnik, announces the end of 'Aktion Reinhard' and dissolution of the camps. Most SS personnel involved in 'Aktion Reinhard' are transferred to the Adriatic coastal operation zone to fight the partisans and select and deport the Jews in that area.

1944

16 May	'Hungarian Action' starts in Auschwitz concentration camp (by 8 July 1944 476,000 Hungarian Jews have been deported).
June–August	Chełmno concentration camp resumes activities (more than 7,000 Jewish victims).
7 October	Uprising of Jewish prisoners belonging to a Sonderkommando in crematorium IV in Auschwitz–Birkenau. The prisoners blow up the crematorium. The uprising is suppressed.

1945

18 January	Evacuation of Auschwitz concentration camp begins.
27 January	Auschwitz is liberated by Soviet troops.
From January	Evacuation of most concentration camps to the 'interior of the Reich'. Innumerable exhausted prisoners die during transports or in the grossly overcrowded reception centres or are shot at the roadside by SS guards if they cannot march fast enough.
2 April	Hitler prophesies world's eternal gratefulness for having instigated the stamping out of the Jews.
7 May	Unconditional capitulation of Germany. End of war in Europe.

Index of selected persons and places

312